English Girls' Boarding Schools

Mallory Wober

Allen Lane The Penguin Press

Copyright © Mallory Wober, 1971
First published in 1971

Allen Lane The Penguin Press
Vigo Street, London W1

ISBN 0 7139 0239 6

Printed in Great Britain by
Latimer Trend & Co. Ltd, Plymouth
Set in Monotype Times

Contents

Acknowledgements

My thanks go to Mr Iredale and Mr Wilfred Childerley who welcomed me back to work at King's; to Andrew Lewis and Tony Porter who did a great deal of data analysis; to Mrs A. Pullen and Mrs A. Burniston for invaluably 'holding the fort' on many occasions; to Maurice Punch for his friendship and Roger Bullock for his music; and to all those who set up and worked for the overall project on boarding schools research, of which it was a pleasure and an education to be a part. Finally, I thank the staff of schools, and particularly the girls, in whose company there was never a dull moment.

Preview

What is life like in girls' boarding schools? Can one discover generalizations about the schools themselves, as entities; or about the feelings and the experiences of the girls who live and learn in them? Very few men have had any detailed experience of the inner workings of girls' boarding-school life; there are almost certainly not more than a few hundred male staff in all these schools. Yet it was my job to try to discover and describe some of the facts that might answer the above questions. Over the period of a year I lived for about twenty weeks either in, or as a daily visitor to, a succession of twenty-three schools in all. I spent as much of this time as I could in talking with people and collecting the written information which forms the substance of this book.

Many atlases start with maps covering a broad area without much elaboration. They then go on to show in greater magnification much more detail. This is what I will do here. This introduction will survey the general outlines of what I have found; the next ten chapters try to deal with the complexities of human life as it is lived in relatively unusual circumstances; finally, in the Overview, I shall try to set out what we have seen in a wider context of the history, possible present and future functions of education.

I am very aware of some of the problems that arise when a man tries to study life in a women's world. These problems add to those which attend all researches in social science. Researchers should be as open as possible in discussing the relevance of these matters to 'the truth' of what is reported as having been found. Readers, too, should not take what they read for granted. An appendix discusses these matters and I believe is a necessary 'guidebook to the guidebook' on life in girls' boarding schools.

Some people may assume that there is an identity between the terms 'girls' boarding schools' and 'girls' public schools'. These two entities are not in fact the same thing, though they do overlap. There is no hard and fast definition of what a public school is. Tyrrell Burgess in his book *A Guide to English Schools** points out that the

* *A Guide to English Schools* (Harmondsworth, 1964).

Association of Governing Bodies of Girls' Public Schools includes members from independent, direct grant and even 'other' schools. There is probably a core of about 140 secondary schools that most people would agree to call 'public schools'. Most of these are independent (that is, they have autonomy over raising and spending their revenue) though a few are direct grant.* However, the number of secondary schools for girls with boarding rises to 360 if we include other independent schools, and even this number excludes over 100 'private' schools or independent bodies which have not been 'recognized as efficient', by the (then) Ministry of Education.

So, although it may not be a straightforward task to define a public school, it is simpler to say what is meant by boarding. This is where pupils live in a school in which the adults are not their parents or relatives; the children experience a regime which differs from that which they find at home with their families. There is some point in attempting to be precise about what is meant by boarding, for we shall be trying to generalize about the nature and functions of such a phenomenon. We should then need to know whether, or in what ways, these conclusions might apply to communities such as children's homes, summer camps or children of school staff who attend the same school on a 'day basis'. These are all examples where one might have a problem in deciding if the children are 'boarders' and whether generalizations derived from a study of boarding communities might or might not apply in their case.

What are the things I studied about life in the schools, and how were they chosen? The guidelines were determined by the fact that I was entrusted with this research project by Dr Royston Lambert, who had set up a Boarding Schools Research Unit at King's College, Cambridge. By 1966, when I started looking at girls' schools, Dr Lambert and his team had already devised a framework of sociological ideas and questions which set out the kinds of questions they were asking in their studies of boys' and co-educational boarding schools. To try and make these investigations comparable my questions (though changed in some details to make them relevant for girls) closely followed the format of the boys' research.

Each school was seen as an organization, or an entity with a social structure. Elements of the structure include individuals' roles within it, patterns of status and authority, the provisions for privilege, reward and punishment, the goals, aspirations and attitudes held by

* These statements refer to the situation during 1966–7.

various sub-groups or individuals. All these elements can be studied, as well as what happens when there are structural changes – for example, alterations of routine, of status, of goals, and so on. In this way we can try to understand the functioning and inter-effects of the numerous elements of the structure. In this respect, the study is sociological. But there was a second focus of equal importance, and that is the individual girl. By means of statistics examining girls' attitudes, and their answers to other questions, we can learn about the careers of girls in their schools. This constitutes a different social-psychological perspective in the enquiry.

Every girl who filled in a questionnaire was asked how happy she was as a pupil in the community. This gives a measure of satisfaction which is then compared with a wide range of other matters. Pupils were also asked about their previous education, their family relationships and sometimes about their friends and activities in the holidays. Staff were not asked directly to estimate their job satisfaction; they showed how their activities were divided between different types of duties; they then showed which of these they found most and least rewarding. Girls were given a questionnaire, based on the ideas of the American sociologist Robert Merton, about the adjustment of individuals within organizations; this form followed very closely the form devised by Royston Lambert for use in boys' schools. The principle is that six situations are imagined (for example: 'you have been chosen to play for the school') and the pupil is asked how he or she would choose to behave from a number of alternatives set down (for example: 'play as hard as I can', or 'try to get off it . . .'); the choice reflects whether the person approves or not of the organization's goals and methods.

Two very short tests were given. In fact, in the state of modern theory these are thought of as assessing facets or styles of personality as much as 'intelligence'. The first test involves finding the correct solution to an anagram type of problem. This involves an effort of imagination, some analytic thinking about the problem, and a 'convergence' or decision about the answer. It was hoped that this test might indicate intellectual or 'analytic' ability, and perhaps be associated with certain attitudes, age perhaps, or other matters. Social-psychological theory also expects more analytic-minded people to be socially more independent rather than involved in 'affiliation', or being preoccupied with social relationships. It was not known if this test would accord with this theoretic picture, nor even what exactly it would measure. To find out more is in fact one of the purposes of research.

The second test derives from work developed in America by J. P. Guilford, and followed in this country by Liam Hudson, whose book *Contrary Imaginations* is well known. This work distinguishes between people whose style of ability is 'convergent' (and who presumably would be those who are good at the first type of test), and those whose style of ability is 'divergent'. Liam Hudson has shown among boys, an arts–science split in interests between 'divergers' and 'convergers'. This association of interests with types of ability joins the field of intellectual assessment with that of social adjustment. Here divergent-ability was measured by counting how many different meanings girls could think of for a given number of ambiguous words such as 'post' and 'form'. This second test is sometimes wrongly thought of as measuring 'creativity', assuming this to be merely a kind of pyrotechnic fluency. Creativity should perhaps be better measured by a high score on both tests, indicating an ability to range over a wide field of ideas, and also to focus on a product. It was hoped the tests would be of some use in integrating the study of ability and personality factors with that of the predicament of individuals in communities.

Royston Lambert, with his colleagues, developed a scale for assessing 'institutional control', which is the intensity of the rules, physical limits on privacy etc., whereby an individual is prevented from having complete freedom of movement and action. This scale for boys' schools has been adapted for the girls' schools. Scores on one scale are not comparable with those on the other. Further, the scale is not of 'equal intervals' like a thermometer where a difference of 85 over 80 is thought of as being the same as a difference of 65 over 60 degrees. The scale does enable us to *rank* schools, to say which exerts more control than another, and which has less control. Even here, there is a problem of assessing the equivalence of different parts of the scale; let us say one school has a relaxed routine, but very limited physical amenities, while a second has a severe routine but lavish amenities. They may get 'equivalent' total scores for 'institutional control', but we must be careful what we mean by this equivalence. The scale is nevertheless useful in making comparisons.

These then are some of the ways in which the research set about asking its questions. The first answers begin to emerge from the point at which one selects schools to visit; the nature of these answers takes twists and turns, however, as more emerges from further questions, so one should be careful about accepting or presenting things as simple when they are not.

An example of this concerns the issue of whether or not the boarding schools are 'divisive'. Divisiveness during times when there are pervasive forces aiming at achieving economic and cultural homogeneity in a society is taken as anti-social. By definition, as boarding is a circumstance shared by around one per cent of the overall girls' population in all schools, it is an experience which divides boarders from day girls. However, we see that only eighteen per cent of the schools considered in Chapter One are for boarders only. Four-fifths of the schools combine day girls with boarders, so the two 'kinds' of girls are not all totally cut off from each other. There are only 4,500 girls in local authority-maintained boarding places* (apart from special schools for the physically handicapped, or ESN) compared with probably over 40,000 girls boarding in all kinds of schools; this means that something like ninety per cent of boarders are fee-payers, which certainly is a socially divisive factor separating their experience from that of others. In some schools fees run at over £600 p.a. (in 1967), though there are others where the nominal cost is nearer £300. There are state-maintained boarding schools where parents pay as little as £20 p.a., and at least one well-endowed establishment where girls sharing a certain predicament are educated totally free.

The complexity of using economic criteria to establish a case for divisiveness is further illustrated by reference to those, possibly few, families who are 'upwardly socially mobile'. They may pay to send children to board, when it is no easy matter for them to afford it. One girl went to boarding school for two years only, sent by her parents at considerable financial sacrifice because they thought she would enjoy it and benefit from it. She seemed to be moved by her experience, as much by her parents' gesture as by the quality of life she encountered. Girls in other schools where the quality of life fell below what they considered dignified, on the other hand, partly

* Figures given in Chapter V of *The Girls' Schools* by Kathleen Ollerenshaw (London, 1967).

despised their parents for making financial sacrifices. One girl, however, thought strongly that sacrifices could be made, and were worth making. She wrote:

And don't tell me its unfair because the average tenant of a council estate can't afford to send his children to a Public School!! Of course he can if he is prepared to make sacrifices and if he wants to. . . . Let's take an example:

A Council house tenant with a wife and 3 children – lets suppose he sends the 2 eldest away to Public School (∴ they are at home for 16 weeks of the year)

Average wage per week of a road labourer = £35 = £1,850

Amount spent on food (£2 per head per wk) =

    = £6 × 52 = £312 (mother, father & 1 child)

    = £4 × 16 = £64   (2 children)

       Total = £374

Amount spent on rents; rates; taxes etc (Approx £5 per week. Council house remember)

       Total = £260

Amount spent on clothing & Luxuries etc (this is where the sacrifice comes in – NB)

£100 each per parent; £100 for children.

       Total = £300

     Cost of living = £934 per yr

     Total wage = £1,850 (regardless of private incomes)

     Amount which could be spent on education

       = £886

That is certainly enough to send at least 2 children to Public Schools – especially to one of the cheaper Public Schools.   (17)

These remarks were provided with what read as an angry essay written by one sixth-former to whose class I had appealed for observations. The force of her words gains from the knowledge that her own family background was one of financial difficulty and not of wealth. As a person of exceptional energy and talent she pointed out that socio-economic divisiveness is partly at least a product of attitudes and abilities which accept situations rather than setting out to battle against them. Some families, who might not otherwise afford to send their children to boarding schools, become involved in work with companies overseas, which often pay for children's boarding 'at home'. In at least some cases this is done as a means of affording a boarding education. Half the schools I visited had less than fifteen per cent of their girls who came from families abroad, but the one with most expatriates had forty per cent of its girls from overseas.

Most of the schools I visited, however, did not attempt to excuse or in any way rebut the notion that they may be socially divisive. In several ways they did the opposite, pointing out in lists of governors and staff where people had titles, distinctions, or Oxbridge degrees. The heads of the schools I visited were largely Oxbridge graduates. But though many schools point out exalted social status where they can, their staffs have a wider range of 'ordinary' experience. While it is said that in boys' boarding schools a sizeable proportion of staff were themselves boarding-school-educated, and that this tends to preserve and transmit a boarding ethos, only a fifth of the girls' school staffs may themselves have been boarders. Even among housemistresses, who might be particularly important in creating an ethos, there were relatively few who had been boarders themselves. Staff's previous experience included one-third who had taught only in day schools prior to their present jobs; only fifteen per cent had worked only in boarding schools before.

Judging from figures on staff, girls' boarding schools are not as élitist as lists of governors or heads might suggest; nor are they highly inbred with staff only circulating within member schools of the system. The schools visited mostly acknowledged that they corresponded to 'grammar' schools, though some did say they were 'comprehensive'. The latter did so on a basis of having numbers of pupils whose results on Common Entrance examinations were used as an 'allocation' criterion within, rather than as an admissions criterion into, schools. I did not come across any ESN or remedial classes, and it is virtually certain that the distribution of abilities in the schools I visited was in general academically superior to that which would be found in maintained schools overall. This excludes the range of independent schools not recognized as efficient, among which there may be several which cater principally for 'well-off ESN' pupils and others of limited ability, of which I did not visit any examples. In terms of academic intentions, the boarding schools are divisive because they have aspirations for their pupils other than those which apply in the maintained schools.

Among the girls, thirty-five per cent had fathers who had not been boarders and forty-five per cent had mothers who had not been boarders in their day. In the pupils' own generation, only one-fifth of the brothers were not boarders, and a quarter of the sisters. Three-quarters of the girls had themselves been to fee-paying (though not necessarily boarding) preparatory schools. So while we are looking at a generation that is largely itself involved in a particular type of education, it does stem in considerable part from a previous generation who were not boarders. This is evidence of 'educational mobility' into the system. Of the day girls met in boarding schools, thirty-five per cent had fathers who had boarded and one-quarter had mothers who had boarded. As these daughters were now day girls, this is some evidence of educational mobility away from the system. These girls are still, however, in independent schools for the most part, and it may be that independence as much as boarding is what parents pay for.

Some people wonder what effect single-sex boarding has on a girl's social life and sexual preferences. The boarders mostly (sixty per cent of them) say that their holiday friends come from 'outside of schools like this one'; three-quarters say their holiday friends include both sexes (instead of friends being 'mainly girls' or 'mainly boys'). In fact it is the day girls who keep somewhat more to holiday friends within the same school and who are more inclined to have 'mostly girl' friends out of term. I do not see any evidence that (on their own word) boarding drives any large number of girls 'boy mad', nor that it promotes homosexual tendencies. One might even infer to some extent that girls are more likely as they grow older to find friends from outside the boarding-school background; certainly they think in these terms.

All these points have been made in relation to the question about divisiveness. It shows that the question ceases to be: are boarding schools divisive, or not? It becomes: in what ways are boarding schools divisive, and in what ways are they not? They are in that they set out to foster and communicate what we may call middle-class culture. They are cohesive in one way since they draw pupils from wide catchment areas including overseas, while day schools will tend to be divisive in regional terms. As regards ethos, the girls' schools may be less divisively staffed and organized than are the boys' schools. Signs are that many boarders will send their own daughters in time as day girls to independent schools (thus just staying 'within the system'), and also that many will transfer daughters to maintained schools (especially as these improve) thus going 'out of the system'.

The rising expense of boarding is likely to lead to a contraction in numbers of schools. Yet educational mobility into the system still exists; while several bursars looked nervously to the future, at least one confidently welcomed the idea of Britain joining the European Common Market. Over several decades he foresaw greater prosperity and a greater demand and ability to pay for boarding.

What are the schools trying to do? I think we can chiefly deal with this question in terms of what the various members of the schools think they are trying to do. Prospectuses are written by heads and other senior 'members' of the communities, and talk about promoting individual fulfilment and equally much about instilling a sense, and the practice of social responsibility. One clear difference in schools' intentions at this level concerns religion. Some schools are run by convents, and others belong to the Woodard group of Church of England schools; other schools term themselves non- or multi-denominational, and one has a house for girls of different religion.

The institutional control index already mentioned enables us to distinguish further between schools. We can arrange them in a rank order of severity of control and imply differences in educational approaches, and trace out patterns of concomitants associated with each of these approaches.

We know what girls think about goals being pursued in schools; and a less adequate sample suggests staffs' views. While staffs' views of what schools should do and what they actually strive to do are fairly well in step, among girls there are substantial differences on the two questions. The difference between the two groups concerns their ideals, for they agree fairly well about what actually happens. Girls think schools should give priority to working towards good jobs and careers; their own aspirations similarly concern the desire to do well at work and exams above all.

If goals are arranged into three groups, which concern the individual's benefit and development, the (school) community's benefit, and mixed benefit, girls see most effort being spent on the community, with individual benefit coming third. Staff agree that relatively least effort is devoted to goals linking individual and community. Girls in particular think that not much is being done (overall, a few schools are exceptions) about preparing them to deal with the roles of wife and mother, or to help them in their relationships with boys. The last point is very noticeable to a visitor and most girls bring up the matter sooner rather than later. They are excited about boys; everything they read, see or hear seems to remind them about this, and they want access. Some schools make social arrangements with 'brother schools' for meetings of societies and joint activities such as choirs and dances. In one case the girls seem to reject the nominated 'brother school' (perhaps because the idea evokes incest-taboos as they are not interested in brothers but in boy-friends) and favour an alternative which one might call a 'cousin-school'. Elsewhere, the girls' school says 'there is no boys' school nearby with whom we can make a convenient arrangement; so-and-so are too far away'. What this appears to mean is that no independent boys' school is near enough; the nearby maintained schools are not so eligible as sources of formal dance partners. This is an aspect in which many girls' schools are certainly divisive.

After expressing their ideals, and their observations on what schools are trying to achieve, what do people think the schools succeed in attaining? Both staff and girls agree that goals serving the community are most efficiently achieved; and that goals benefiting the individual are least effectively attained. In some schools one hears variations of what one might call the 'perverse goal doctrine' advanced to justify this situation. This says that it is precisely by learning to accommodate to goals designed to serve the community, to acknowledge the common good, that the individual is strengthened. There is indeed some force in this argument. However, this avenue to individual betterment is more likely to be followed if the leadership is trusted and 'charismatic'. It needs to be able to demonstrate convincingly that the community-goals being pursued really are to the benefit of individuals in the community, and are not 'for the school' in an abstract sort of way. An example is the case of the goal of promoting an understanding of Christian principles. This was the item on which the greatest difference in ideal showed up between the girls and staff. Girls seemed to see this item as purely an organizational matter, irritating to many of them; if they had thought of this goal as being concerned with the benefit of individuals, they might well have favoured it more. The goal of 'learning to live with other people happily' was highly regarded by the girls. We must conclude that, on the question of goals, girls think schools fall substantially behind their ideal of what should be happening. Even staffs' opinions lie in the same direction, though not so strongly.

These views on goals were collected from sixth-formers. They may give a discouraging evaluation of events. A majority of girls – and this question applied to all ages – are, however, happy in school. Schools vary greatly in this respect. The least happy school had what we might call a forty per cent level of satisfaction. However, the best school had eighty per cent of its girls happy. Happiness seems to reach a minimum at age 15. This is parallel with several other low points of individual adjustment which also occur at that age. Happiness for boarders is not related to their type of previous educational experience, their tested ability or their type of personal aspirations. Happier girls are to some extent those who are better thought of by their heads. On the whole, day girls are happier than boarders in school, which is notable since the day girl and boarder samples presented similar cross-sections of ages and abilities, and the boarders even came in greater proportion from the more lenient schools. Also, day girls were mostly experiencing school communities not supposed to be designed for them but for boarders. Lest we think that day girls are therefore quite simply better off than boarders, one must say that further information on the state of family relationships shows that the position is more complex. It will be returned to later.

It is not easy to say which girls will be happy on an individual level. But at the level of schools, we can see that several factors coincide with happier schools. Happier schools are those I visited in summer rather than winter terms; they are the more lenient schools; in happier schools there is a greater desire to excel at the arts (and less enthusiasm for work). This last piece of evidence appears in spite of the finding that the majority of girls want schools to contribute to their academic progress, and their own private aspirations are most often firstly to do well at work or exams and only secondly to do well at arts. The happier schools have slightly more girls who want to become prefects – to take on official responsibilities – and their girls show a higher rating of success for their schools on attaining the five most favoured goals.

Not surprisingly, schools with a high preference among the girls for artistic success were the most lenient schools; in them there was also a better level of pastoral care and readiness to communicate; this latter was also a feature of the happier schools. Now because many of the characteristics I am mentioning are each connected to one central quality, it does not mean that all those characteristics naturally occur together. Thus lenient schools are somewhat happier in summer; and happier schools are more lenient. But this does not mean that schools become more lenient in summer, or by accident that I visited the most lenient schools in summer. Lenience and season have no mutual connection; but they are both related to happiness.

The happier schools are those with smaller boarding communities (with one or two notable exceptions – as there are, indeed, to all these generalizations), and in them the pupils have had a greater extent of private preparatory school background. They have not had more or less boarding prep schooling than the girls in the unhappier schools. This illustrates two distinctions: adjustment measured by happiness among boarders is not associated with a 'training' in boarding prep school; but it is associated with experience of independent schooling. This suggests that the independence distinction from other schools may be more important than the boarding–non-boarding distinction. The second point is that these are not findings that we could discern on the level of the individual girl; but they do apply for schools. Thus we see schools as organizing or focusing systems, which tend to concentrate attitudes within particular schools and make them more contrastable with attitudes and patterns elsewhere.

Happier schools also contain girls who say that boarding has a beneficial effect on family relationships; but happier schools do not necessarily contain more girls from happy or from unhappy families. So a girl from an uneasy home background may go to an unhappy school, in which case she may tend to say that boarding is having a poor effect on her family relationships. If she goes to a happy school she may more likely say it is having a good effect on her home life. Now here I shall invoke the distinction I have just made about effects noticeable at the level of individuals and those discernible among schools. Regardless of schools, girls who are happier at home will tend to be happier in school. The importance of the effects of parental attitude can be deduced from noting that, in schools where a large proportion of parents had themselves been boarders, their daughters tended to say boarding had a good effect on family relationships.

Some of the things the girls wrote suggest that a distinction can be made between a separation that is geographical and social, and one that is psychological. It appears that, for some, boarding does not constitute a psychological separation. From what we see above, this may more likely apply when girls are properly prepared for the experience, and if the school itself does not disappoint too greatly. Three-quarters of the boarders consider that their experience benefits family relationships. This is more in fact than say they are happy at school. It is also the boarders who say they have better family relationships than day girls indicate. This may be a case where 'absence makes the heart grow fonder'. Remembering that it was the day girls who said they were happier in school, we see that though happiness in school and at home are closely associated, they do not always march together.

In my view it cannot be said that the evidence is for the case that boarding in general harms family relationships. Boarders say they are better off at home than day girls (though they are not quite so happy in school), and that, overall, boarding is benefiting their family life. For some, this may be a fantasy that is being developed, an escape from family reality. Yet for many it can be said that their separation adds perspective, heightens the reality of home life and increases its value. Certainly there are many exceptions, and many girls who have been unhappy in school (and some staff even) will not recognize what I am writing about. Nevertheless, I am describing what a majority have said.

Apart from girls' own happiness, I used two other criteria to evaluate what is happening to girls in boarding. These were both ratings made by headmistresses – only one rater for each girl. This showed that day girls were not seen as making any better or worse use of the academic facilities than boarders. Proponents of boarding might say that boarders were considered to have more facilities and time overall, so boarding would be more useful for them. Certainly heads were asked to rate the girl's approach, rather than her net gain; so there may be reason to support the above view. This makes it more dramatic to note that heads rated more day girls than boarders as being outstanding contributors to the community; if we widen our comparison to include all those who were generally public-spirited compared with those who were not, boarders and day girls were judged equal. But day girls were certainly in excess among the best on this rating scale.

A composite score indicating social conformity (the questionnaire referred to as derived from the work of Merton) showed that half the girls have a conformist attitude in school, and nearly half the remainder are 'ritualistic' – that is, they accept the letter of the law if not the spirit. There was quite a lack of innovative attitudes, which may be related to the apparent dearth of 'underlife' – or the cult of mischief and of disillusion with the formal society which appears to be common in boys' boarding schools. Among girls, choice of rebellious attitude items was rare, even on the topic of religious observance for which they showed they were not very keen. On some issues, the boarders were less conformist than day girls – for example, on the attitude towards the possibility of being made prefect. This reflects what we saw with the heads' ratings, that day girls were thought to be contributing better socially.

As with happiness in school, conformity reaches a minimum at the age of 15. There is some evidence that the rebels may include more able girls, especially on the test of divergent ability; but this is restricted to an examination of those at the extremes of a small group of most dissident girls. Over the whole range of types of conformity, schools with more conformist societies were not more or less divergent in ability; but the more able the girls were on a test of convergent ability (problem-solving) the less conformist and more rebellious the schools were as groups. We must distinguish here between institutional control – which is the strictness of the school's formal regime – and conformity which is the girl's response.

It might be thought that girls would be more rebellious in the more severe schools; but this was not so. There was no correlation between institutional control and levels of conformity. This reinforces a 'psychological' interpretation that, although social structures are obviously important, yet structure does not always define people's reactions, to explain which we must also look at how structures are run. That is to say, a certain kind of headmistress in a lenient school may not help to produce 'creative conformity'; but even in a very strict school, a remarkable head and staff can avoid rebellion and produce a healthy community. In fact, they would also be likely to change the social structure, unless its limitations were mainly imposed by physical or financial bounds. These variations of staff and structure may not occur frequently, but obviously do so often enough to obliterate an expected correlation between severity of structure and individuals' conformity.

Royston Lambert has suggested that, in boys' schools, experience of preparatory boarding schooling will accustom boys to the culture of the system, and one could infer that girls with similar pre-schooling might be better adjusted to the system and consequently happier as boarders in secondary school. There is no link found, however, between boarding pre-schooling and the level of conformity in the secondary schools. On the other hand, there is some suggestion that schools where many of the pupils' parents had themselves known boarding, or where the girls themselves had had private pre-schooling, would tend to be among the more conformist societies. This may be because the parents know which schools to choose to produce the educational results they want.

Conformity to the school is not noticeably linked with happiness; the detailed evidence is that at the four schools in which there was nearest to a 50–50 proportion of girls with private and with non-private pre-schooling, there was a relatively higher proportion of rebels. Psychological theory suggests that if there are two ways (in conflict) of appraising things, then this is a 'dissonant' situation, and it may be resolved by a decision being made in favour of one side. The dilemma in a school with equal proportions of girls from two different cultural backgrounds is: which way will the situation go? It is possible that it may remain in discomfort, as one can observe in several schools, with the influence of school and parents pulling one way (in an effort to produce a relatively subdued person – the Lady, to develop one kind of design of 'super-ego'), and the influence of youth culture, liberal mass media and educational reformers pulling in the other direction (to encourage freedom in self-expression, the free modern woman, the mobile person).

I have tried to describe some of the ways in which conformity is encouraged among the new girls. They are expected to do what 'the school' says – conform to the formal system; and they must in general avoid becoming social outcasts among the other girls – that is, they must conform with the intra-formal system. One supposes that there will be this need to conform more especially among the younger girls, simply because it is the rare girl who has the inner resources to stand on her own in the midst of a fairly uniform community. A very few girls have developed an inner life which enables them to get along apart; this would not mean, however, that they would not mind it if they became unpopular, as they would then have to busy themselves with fending off hostile behaviour. So people are drawn into the life of the group, even if only to go along quietly with its outer forms. Occasionally a girl may have a reference group outside the school; this may be true for foreigners, or members of another religion. Then they may take a back seat in social life, referring their perceptions of events to a system of evaluation rooted outside rather than inside the school.

Among a few girls I have got the impression that a private world is created within the self; a fantasy world can be less or more creative, and may hinge around animals, or soft toys among younger girls, or the arts among the older ones. Perhaps poetry is a particular sign in practice of an individual at odds with the community; for music and painting are non-verbal, and their message or expression can be ambiguous, or taken as emanating from the composer as much as from the performer. But poetry is spelled out in words, and offers a form in which much more complex and penetrating and precise statements can be made, or socially critical feelings expressed. It is an art which is acceptable in formal terms and strained feelings can be contained and offered up therein – unless they are too thinly veiled.

I must separate what I am saying about poetry, written by a minority of special individuals, from the more widespread wish to do well at the arts. A question on aspirations included sections on the arts, and this was a popular choice compared to the possibility of preferring other 'aspirations'. Schools with girls who were keener to excel at arts were those with happier pupils; these were schools where parents had more boarding experience, and where girls had had more boarding pre-schooling. Thus a general preference for arts (within which the individualist poets are likely to be few) seems to occur in what one might call 'healthy, lenient, traditionally patronized' schools. This, incidentally, is different from the picture involving those who aspire to do well at work. Schools with parents who have had more boarding experience themselves, where the girls have been to private prep schools, or have had boarding pre-schooling, tend to be schools where there is less keenness to excel at work. Less keenness to excel at work is also found in the more lenient schools, and those where girls say that boarding is having a good effect on their family relationships. The overall picture is one where girls from boarding-experienced families tend to go to lenient schools and to say that they are happier and that boarding is helping their family relationships; schools with such populations contain a higher proportion wanting to do well at arts. On the other hand, we find the picture where families with less boarding experience have their daughters in schools where there is a generally greater ambition to do well at work, which is also associated with stricter formal control and the feeling that boarding has a poor effect on family relationships (though these two last factors are mutually independent).

Returning to the question of conformity, in some kinds of school the pattern includes certain population and organizational characteristics, and attitudes such as the desire to excel at work; in other kinds of school another pattern leads to preferences to excel at arts (or less commonly to do well at games, or domestic science). Formal control is likely to be implied in the selection process by which parents apply to certain schools, and schools try to select applicants who will suit them – unless financial pressure leads them to take almost anyone who will pay. This yielding to financial pressure will, of course, mean that a school may have to reduce its levels of success on some criteria, which will involve changes in ethos, social control mechanisms and probably staffing too. Elements of the control system which can be changed are items like the ways in which time and space are used as commodities which have reward value; also there are regulations which affect how and what people may see (books, papers, magazines, films, boys, television), what they can hear, smell (perfumes), taste and feel or touch (for example, hot water is available more easily to certain privileged girls in some schools). External relations such as visits, letters and telephone calls are all subject to control. Variations on these themes give rise to stricter or more lenient patterns of control, each of which has its own distinctive atmosphere.

One feature of formal control is the use of privilege and punishment systems to encourage certain sorts of behaviour. It is possible for reward and punishment systems to be independent; thus technically it would be possible for senior girls to be punishable in ways that would not interfere with their privileges. But my impression is that it is one of the characteristics of the system that reward and punishment systems overlap. Thus in one school consistently responsible behaviour is rewarded by allowing certain facilities to visit the nearby town; conversely, the withdrawal of such rewards, or their postponement, is felt as a punishment. Some girls do not like this, perhaps because it is effective in producing conformist behaviour. However, it seems to operate in most schools with the effect of getting the girl to see that she can make her own contract with society by which she can increase her gains in return for developing certain attitudes and behaviour.

The schools try to give greater rewards for taking active organizational responsibility (e.g. becoming a prefect) than for merely conforming. The prefect in fact takes on duties, thereby losing an amount of personal freedom. To counterbalance this, symbolic rewards are often given to prefects; they are called on platforms, praised, awarded sashes and given badges. But it seems that these symbolic rewards are nowadays of limited appeal. There is also perhaps less respect in general for those who exercise authority. I do not know whether the younger girls do not draw any feelings of security from living in a society for which other people provide the mainstays and supports. I suspect that they do find security in the social order; but also that they tend not to identify with it and respect it as might have been the case in previous years.

Although, therefore, there are parts of the system which do not easily attract support, the punishment and reward arrangements help to keep it going without it necessarily being impervious to change; often one finds that important issues of the time in a school are changes being made or mooted in the machinery of reward and punishment. It might be more correct to say that the overlap and interdependence of reward and punishment mechanisms is not merely a characteristic, but a cornerstone of the system.

Within the formal control mechanism the girls develop social rules of their own. Among the younger girls it might well have been the case that had I devised a suitable measuring index we would have found a more stringent and pervasive level of intra-formal control; while among the older girls a greater individuality may more commonly be allowed, and less strong requirements of the pupil culture would apply. This means that the pupil culture among the younger girls may be very different from that of the older ones, in respect of the ways and the extent to which it exerts control over the members, and with regard to the attitudes and views girls may be expected to show, or conceal.

The turning point between these two cultures comes at the age of 15, when there seems to be a relatively great degree of social ambiguity as to how girls should express themselves both with regard to one another, and to the formal system. Should they be fun-loving? Or intellectual? Should they make expectations about what other people may do? Should they be mischievous and disregard the rules? Should they see themselves as likely exam-passers and get on the academic treadmill, or develop other interests? All these and other questions focus as a multiple dilemma for the 15-year-olds, and at this stage their own sub-culture would appear to be least firm with its answers. So it may not be surprising that we find happiness and social conformity reaching a minimum at this age which is a half-way stage in many boarders' careers.

Pastoral care responsiveness among boarders is also at a minimum at age 15 (though day girls show they are at their readiest to discuss personal problems in school at that age). On the whole, there is little evidence to suggest that pastoral care is flourishing in most schools. Three times as many people may want to consult friends as will consult staff (they say) about personal problems. This illustrates an area of strength of the pupil culture, and a facet of it which marks a cleavage from that of the staff and the formal structure. This is not an absolute division, and boarders are quite ready to consult staff about problems concerning their work. Also there is an amount of individual reticence regarding the pupil culture, and one-third of the boarders after the first year say they would not want to consult anybody in school about personal problems – not even friends. They may in the event unbottle problems, but they say they do not want to.

Pastoral readiness differs from school to school, and is greatest in lenient schools, and in schools where girls are happy. Girls who do well on the divergence test tend to be more communicative about personal problems, though this does not mean they will be more ready to talk with staff; those who have better convergent ability are more likely to consult with staff on personal problems; this also applies to those who hope to become prefects.

A most important goal in the girls' view is that schools should teach people to live together happily; another is that schools should develop an inner morality that will sustain any girl. This leads to the vexed question of whether morality is immutable in some respects, or subject to fashion – which latter possibility is expressed usually in dignified terms by use of the word 'values' to replace the idea of 'principles'. One area of moral question concerns the subject of sexual behaviour and the significance of virginity. This latter topic is enshrined to a greater or less extent in the forms of expression manifest in Christianity. There may be links then between attitudes to staff who propound Christianity in certain ways, and attitudes towards sexual experience and boys.

The majority of schools I visited were Anglican, and there was little open sign of a cult of the Virgin, with any implications this might have for ordinary personal behaviour; however, an element of reverence for virginity exists even in Protestant faiths and this among other things is evoked by the enactment of formal ritual in church. At one school there were prominently exhibited pre-Raphaelitic pictures of girls at their confirmation suggesting an image of purity which implies sexual virtue; though elsewhere these links are probably sensed at a more submerged level of conscious awareness. I therefore think, as a very personal interpretation, that some of girls' objections to Christian worship may be connected with their drive to gratify their sexual curiosity, which schools are generally controlling; and with the fact that schools' moral position is importantly represented in their institution of communal worship. One might note that cathedral concerts and performance of Masses are popular, and I think might remain so even if repeated weekly or even daily – as organ recitals. But it seems to be the element of formal worship, with its possible anti-sexual connotations, that alienates so many souls.

Girls' views of staff may also affect their attitudes towards Christian sexual morality. It seems that if they see spinster staff as advocating personal purity, and the staff are older and show no sign that they had chosen spinsterhood from some idealistic point of view, then girls may reject what such staff advocate. Girls may see the existence of such staff as an implied threat of sexual or marital failure for themselves, and shy away from respecting the kind of purity and virginity which they may feel is implied in formal religion. On the other hand, spinster staff could put forward a justification for sexual purity couched in a romantic presentation of popular themes. Thus it might be possible to devise a female counterpart to a Galahad figure, one who openly and nobly aims for higher things than common human sexuality. This could earn a response in religious fervour among girls. It could be said that, for some, the Virgin Mary is made a real model for admiration by certain nuns, who themselves can inspire respect for their own religious life, even without demanding that others join it so unequivocally. Another variant of this idea was sensitively explored (even if in a masculine way which women's liberationists would now decry) in *The Prime of Miss Jean Brodie*. In most schools I visited, however, I got the impression that girls often showed a distaste for the spinster's predicament, a perception that gave pain and hurt to many staff who were otherwise trying to contribute as best they could, but which prompted some of them to withdraw socially to some extent. Thus the distance of some staff in pastoral care may be related to the girls' attitudes towards Christianity and sexual morality.

There may be another reason why so many girls are averse to divine worship. This is bound up with the direction of individual development encouraged by schooling. My case is that among younger girls suitable conditions of personality exist which would enable fervent group worship to be organized. At this age girls are not so individualized, and they are more inclined to pool their feelings in the activities and expressions of a group. If at that age they are brought to accept the complex of stories and beliefs that underlie Christianity, they could vigorously express this in occasions of communal worship. Now while the school is with one hand trying to inculcate acceptance and belief in the Christian epic, with the other it is also encouraging an intellectually inquiring attitude and the feeling that there is still a great deal to be learned – about everything. This undercuts the chances of instilling Christian belief. The result is a limited chance of response to group worship. An interesting school where formal worship was accepted, perhaps even popular, taught Christianity with some emphasis on its content of mystery. This, together with the clear example of respected staff standing in awe at the mysteries of existence, must have contributed to the success of Christianity there.

Among the older girls in most schools then, a greater individuality has been brought about by maturing in the world, and by formal education dispersing interests into various specialist directions. Among such people successful group worship is also possible, but depends on achieving something nearer the highly select circumstances which apply as when those of similar belief and attitude are gathered together in convents. In fact the psychological state of older girls is one where greater privacy of expression is being developed; the community of beliefs and attitudes is probably much less than exists among younger girls, and is certainly not as agreed upon basic religious matters as is the case among convent members. The conditions are therefore unfavourable for successful and sincere group worship, and one should probably consider it remarkable if this in fact sometimes occurs.

The difference in individual psychological development between younger and older girls can be paralleled by a more hypothetical line of spiritual development. In this scheme one starts with the 'immediate' person, being one who is preoccupied with her own needs and their satisfaction. Later, there develops the 'intermediate' person; she is concerned with the needs of others and with achieving – if it is possible – a rational explanation of the world's phenomena confronting her. In fact this can apparently be achieved by removing from one's ken a range of phenomena which preoccupy other people. Thus a whole range of occult, 'supernatural' or para-psychological phenomena are dismissed by the rationalist person as nonsense. She would even probably include in this latter category the person whom I shall now try to describe.

It is interesting that the English language offers us no suitable word readily to complete a triad with the two '-mediate' types described above. The third type (perhaps a-mediate) is one whose awareness looks beyond the sense-data which mediate most of our experience; she may structure her thoughts according to formal religious beliefs, or try to leave them partly unstructured. She is not necessarily a mystic, with all the social isolation that that state connotes. A person of this sort can be quite connected socially, yet maintain through the medium of formal religion, or even through that of an art like music or poetry, an area where her sensitivity is still striving to become further aware. A distinguishing characteristic of religious belief is, however, that there is something in this mysterious area which will respond to human devotion, attention or worship. If this analysis is at all true then older girls will require different forms of worship if they include a greater proportion who grow into being this third type of person and if they are not to be alienated from religion, or from a religious point of view remain retarded in the stage of intermediate beings.

Lest one get the impression that religion among boarders is manifest only as unsuccessful attempts at group worship, I must point out that this is not so. For some girls the lack of spatial privacy means that they sometimes develop techniques of inner wandering and exploration, of fantasy and religious openness. In some schools there are opportunities to be alone in beautiful countryside; this is not always spent looking for boys in barns (which does occur), but affords the chance to connect with much of the inspiration that is conveyed in English literature. For others there are opportunities to contact a few of the public through schemes of social work, though by the nature of seclusion in boarding these occasions are relatively scant. In all, however, there are various ways in which schools allow opportunities for different kinds of religious sensitivity to develop, and these can be expressed in participation in the schools' formal worship.

Finally, when we look at how girls in mainly-boarding schools rank their schools on achieving goals of inculcating moral sense, neighbourliness and Christian principles, we see that these are more highly ranked, on average, than is indicated by boarders in mainly-day schools. So though this study has not dealt with true day schools, there is some sign that boarding is trying to do something much more complex, perhaps with slightly greater success, than is tackled in this area by day schools.

I have summarized my own views and given my own analysis of what the material contained in the following chapters amounts to. It is necessary for a better understanding to read these chapters in full, even though they themselves represent only a selection of the information gathered. Moreover, the information was gathered in response to selected questions. These selective stages undoubtedly pattern the material to some extent according to my own ways of thinking. This machinery of bias cannot be avoided – merely pointed out. The one thing that is reported accurately is the body of quotations from what the girls wrote. These are shown just as they wrote them, abbreviated to highlight the point being made. The number by each extract shows the girl's age when she wrote down her remarks.

One: The System

This book sets out to describe girls' boarding schools. In treating this subject, one implies that girls' boarding schools are an entity, of which each member shares important characteristics, and that these commonly shared characteristics mark off the girls' boarding schools from other educational enterprises. In a way, this is defining the girls' boarding schools as a system, rather than letting their characteristics, when examined in comparison with those of other schools, fall together by similarity and interdependence.

We should first consider what is meant by 'system'. This is a resilient idea, on which sociologists can write until their books break the shelves they stand on (a sociological breakthrough). I understand by 'system', a set of things, people, ideas or phenomena which are connected together by causes, effects, characteristics and relationships; this set of things is also less connected with those things whose relative independence, or exclusion, helps to define the boundaries of the system.

In practice, the definition of what is a system depends partly on the perspective of the viewer. An English sociologist may make out large differences between English independent and maintained schools, and a Chinese social democrat may agree with his analysis. However, a Chinese Red Guard or an English Maoist may view distinctions of ownership in English schools as irrelevant. Thus some observers may see in English girls' boarding schools similarities in their aims, their atmosphere, their clientele, their staffs. Others may not accept such a view. Catholics may see schools as divided between Catholic schools and the rest; differences due to religion might outweigh similarities as to boarding or day education in such a view. This chapter therefore sets out to describe how the schools were selected to be visited, and what similarities and differences characterize their make-up.

In a book entitled *The Girls' Schools*, Dr Kathleen Ollerenshaw gives some facts about boarding schools. She defines public schools as those which belong to the G.B.G.S.A. (Governing Bodies of Girls' Schools Association). She shows that of these 154 schools, about sixty per cent had over sixty per cent of boarding pupils. If Catholic convents are included, there are 244 schools, over eighty per cent of which have some proportion of boarding. In addition, local authorities in 1960 were said to have 2,121 boarding places for girls, in schools they ran themselves; (this is apart from schools for educationally sub-normal or physically handicapped pupils). Names of schools are also given in the Girls' Schools Year Book, and in H.M.S.O.'s List 70 of Recognized Schools in England and Wales (the facts in these two sources are not always identical). Together with a further list from the Boarding Schools' Association, a total was compiled of 359 schools with boarding. This still leaves a number of private schools (Ollerenshaw says there are at least 141 girls' schools which were not 'recognized as efficient' in 1965, not all being boarding). The quality of these schools may be good or bad, but they will not appear in this study.

Schools were chosen to be visited according to a quota system, so that some semblance of representation in the right proportion of four important characteristics would be maintained. This proportioning is shown in four tables, as follows:

Table 1·1. Proportion of schools visited, by area of location

area	number of schools in list	number visited	per cent visited
North and Scotland	41	4	9·7
North-west Midlands	41	1	2·4
East Midlands and London	57	7	12·3
South-East	88	3	3·4
Centre-South	47	2	4·3
South-West, West and Wales	85	6	7·0
	359	23	—

As the twenty-three schools visited represents 6·4 per cent of the entire number, I would like to have visited as near to 6·4 per cent of the schools in each area as possible. But this was difficult to arrange, and the disproportion resulting shows too much attention to London and nearby counties, and not enough in the North Midlands. Unless some dramatically unusual boarding schools are systematically located in particular areas, which seems unlikely, these disproportions should not be too serious.

Table 1·2. Proportion of schools visited, by amount of boarding

boarding proportion	number of schools in list	number visited	per cent visited
boarding only	64	4	6·2
mainly boarding (over forty-nine per cent boarders)	101	13	12·8
mainly day (forty-nine per cent boarders, or less)	194	6	3·1
	359	23	—

The distortion of proportioning here can be said to be in a favourable direction. For though I visited over-many mainly-boarding schools, this could be thought appropriate in a study of boarding. However, as there are many schools in which the boarding element is not predominant, and the life led by such boarders may be affected by this fact, particular attention should be paid to findings from this type of school.

Table 1·3. Proportion of schools visited, by size of school

number of pupils	number of schools in list	number visited	per cent visited
200 or less	144	8	5·5
201–250	61	2	3·3
251–399	76	9	11·8
400 or more	78	4	5·1
	359	23	—

The disproportioning here is not seriously out of true. There is a slight neglect of the largest and smallest schools, and concentration on those of medium size.

Table 1·4. Proportion of schools visited, by size of fees

termly fee	number of schools in list	number visited	per cent visited
£125 or less	227	7	3·0
£126–150	66	7	10·6
£151 or over	43	9	20·9
	336	23	—

B

The fee discovered for each school was for girls in the upper school, and was either the consolidated fee published, or the tuition plus boarding fee. Data were not available for all schools on fees. The most serious disproportioning in arranging a sample to visit has occurred with respect to fees. I visited over-many of the more expensive schools. However, some of the schools I visited in 1967, which came into the most expensive category, might have quoted smaller fees for the reference books published in 1966. To some extent, therefore, the apparent disproportion is worse than is really the case. Nevertheless, it seems likely that not enough of the cheaper schools were visited, and this should be borne in mind when examining the results.

The sample of schools visited included one maintained school, two direct grant schools and twenty independent establishments. These latter may not all fit the Public Schools' Commission's definition of public schools as 'those schools now in membership of . . . the G.B.G.S.A.'; they do all fit the definition in the 1966 Girls' Schools Year Book (on p. 676) which counts as a public school '. . . one which possesses a governing body as opposed to a private undertaking'. This would include convents, and apparently the direct grant schools as well.

The history of girls' schools in the U.K. is described by Kathleen Ollerenshaw. A few boarding schools, including some I visited, have roots in the eighteenth and nineteenth centuries. These tend to have been associated with charitable foundations and trusts set up for girls from particular backgrounds, for example, military or regional. The late Victorian years saw the rise of energetic feminist educators, determined to give girls as good an opportunity as boys had, and to show that girls could do as well as boys.* Though there were signs of co-education in pre-Victorian times, the combination of Victorian outlook and feminist assertion made for the establishment of single-sex schools. Several of the present heads of girls' schools were trained directly by, or in the aura of,

---

* This apparently referred to academic fields then thought to be proper to males only. This desire to equal males at tasks hitherto considered in the male province, appears to lead to what I call 'masculo-feminism'. This exists alongside 'femino-feminism', by which I mean the esoteric 'women's page' world of fashion, manners and maternity literature. Masculo-feminism appears to be more confusing to the led than to the leaders of this movement.

these turn-of-the-century educationalists. There appears to be no coherent movement with its roots in the present, driving to establish girls-only boarding schools, but they exist, and answer new needs as old ones fall away. There is a distinct overseas connection among senior staff who have served abroad, and among the pupils one finds the daughters of English businessmen working abroad and of foreigners who value a British education. In these senses, and in that boarding draws together pupils from a wider area of the country than does day schooling, many boarding schools have an eclectic quality which should be taken into account when viewing the definitions of the public schools as socially divisive.

The People in the Boarding Schools

Having said a little about the schools visited, we can now examine some of the 'vital characteristics' of the people within. This will incidentally help us to see, in one way, how far the boarding schools form a watertight system.

Governors

At the head of the schools, according to their prospectuses, are bodies of governors. The names of governors are frequently given with their ranks and titles, and readers are presumably meant to notice this. I did, and present the findings from twenty prospectuses (most of these schools were ones I visited, though two were not).

Table 1·5. Some characteristics of boarding-school governors

total number of governors, visitors, etc.	*188*	*per cent*
number of women governors	67	35·6
J.P.s	25	13·3
Knights, Baronets, Ladies, Dames	19	10·1
Officers above Brigadier, Vice-Admiral	14	7·9
Archbishops, Bishops, Canons, Deacons	12	6·4
Dukes, Earls, Lords	11	5·8
sub-total: honours and titles	81	43·5
persons not otherwise distinguished	107	56·5

There seems some intention on the part of some schools to indicate that the board of governors is graced by a Duke or Archbishop, and possibly even the school by his daughters or near relatives. It must be presumed that the prospective clientele are impressed, or in some way reassured, by this kind of display. It may be a form of urge towards decoration, symbolically denying drabness in a country whose climate and surroundings present few dramatic contrasts. It should be said that the categories in Table 1·5 overlap; some Admirals are also J.P.s, and so on. It is possible that the number of women serving is an underestimate; usually sex is indicated by a title before or Esq. after a name; but in the case of doctors, there is no Esq., and some lady doctors may have gone undiagnosed.

Governors of proven or even inherited distinction in wider society may prove useful to schools. They may provide the schools with access to financial aid in time of crisis – which has been observed; they may convey 'tone' and attract a clientele consonant with the schools' chosen ethos (of one school it was half-jokingly said: 'half the Front Bench have their daughters there'). However, there are some feelings that a more elderly senior management can lead to disadvantages.

It is ridiculous to have . . . men, around 70 or 80. With a few of 45–50. There is no sense, they may have money but they *certainly* have no idea how to run a girls school. My own opinion would be to have a separate committee consisting of middle aged men or younger for the financial state and a committee of women for girls' requisities, as obviously men haven't much idea of this!   (14)

While this girl's views might be discounted by some, she is merely saying (and probably without having heard him) what the Provost of King's College, Cambridge, said in a Reith lecture in 1967. This research was not focused on senior management, but it can be suggested that where governors are used as royal seals to confirm decisions of a prime ministerial headmistress, or where they individually provide access to financial, professional or even educational (e.g. local authority) worlds, they would seem to be the more useful for their distinctions in other fields. But where governors take a closer interest in termly, perhaps even daily, affairs (at one school, girls' career intentions are examined by the governors), their age and perspective may not be able to harmonize with that of the pupils.

Heads

None of the twenty-three schools visited had a married headmistress with her husband present. Only three had been married or divorced. As Ollerenshaw suggests, and as many senior staff told me, there are two important reasons for this. One is the loss of men in the First World War; this left many spinsters, of whom the more able and talented ones made themselves careers in the field which to many pioneers of women's rights was the pivotal one in influencing the future – education. Secondly, there is said to have been some feeling among the feminists of the first quarter of this century that to choose a career was to exclude marriage, marriage being seen then as a role of subservience, a career a role of assertion. To rise to become a head requires unusual talent with good fortune, or a longer time of unbroken service, hard to combine with marriage. In recent years, however, some heads have been appointed from outside the teaching profession. Finally, there are now at least two girls-only boarding schools with headmasters.

Some school prospectuses give not only the degree a headmistress has, but also her university. In this way we know that eleven out of twenty-three heads were at Oxford or Cambridge, and two at London. Inquiries at the schools suggest that about half the remainder were also Oxbridge graduates. There are doubtless many reasons why heads should either be, or resemble, Oxbridge graduates. There may have been something in the Oxbridge atmosphere of twenty and more years ago, in which the drive to lead in women's education, and to strive towards the best, converged. These Oxbridge credentials with their aura of aristocracy and merit may be instrumental in making parents feel that their daughters, too, might go to Oxbridge, or somewhere equally congenial.

These points about heads and governors can but be noted and interpreted as thought fit, for often the facts will have fallen into place without anything having been overtly planned that way. Reasons advanced by the incumbents as to why they should have and should publish what become known as high status attributes, may be no more or less valid than reasons one suggests oneself. I discovered less about the schooling of heads, except that they had not by any means all been boarders. Some had been to and worked in schools related by chains of common founders and pioneers; one at least had been brought up with private tuition and at least two had been at grammar school.

Staff

Information was gathered by questionnaires, filled in anonymously, from all kinds of staff (not just teachers); 200 viable forms were returned, representing between a third and half of the potential number. As the exercise was strictly voluntary, with no nagging to try and increase the returns, it is impossible to judge what kinds of biases affect the compiled results. Returns at some schools were conspicuously better than at others; some schools were very busy, and visited at a rushed point of the term (though the questions were such as were done in about fifteen minutes by average sixth-formers). A few staff took a great interest, not only filling in ticks where required, but writing further explanations and remarks. Here is some information gathered about staff:

Table 1·6. Age and marital status of staff

	number	per cent of total
single	109	54·5
married	79	39·5
divorced, widowed	11	5·5
age: 20–29	52	26·2
30–39	43	21·7
40–49	43	21·7
50 and over	60	30·3

This may mean either that there were many more older staff employed, or that the older ones were more conscientious about replying, or that they had more time to do so (younger women had families who needed attention, or their lives focused elsewhere than the school). I believe all these three reasons were partly true. There is some information available on the job-stability of the staff:

Table 1·7. Length of present job of staff

years at job	1–3	4–6	7–9	10–19	20–29	30–39
number of staff	99	30	19	36	8	5

Those who have worked a whole lifetime in their present school are very few. However, those with over ten years in their present job are one quarter of the total. These staff span two or more successive generations of pupils; therefore old girls returning to visit will find staff there whom they know. This element of continuity provides a core of stability for the environment in which the teenagers live. Also, there is a large number whose jobs have not lasted long – half the total. These are not all younger staff, by any means (though one head commented, 'They *come* with a great big diamond ring, and only wait till they can put the deposit on the bungalow'). It may be, however, that the abstainers from answering the questionnaire were not distributed in the same way as those who answered. This would make the real picture different, but it could not be so different as to obscure the very large amount of new blood, and the substantial core of stability. Staff's previous job experience was as follows:

Table 1·8. Previous job experience of staff

	number	per cent of total
staff in their first job	47	23·7
previous jobs *only* in boarding	29	14·6
previous jobs *only* in day schools	64	32·3
previous experience in boarding	88	44·2
previous experience in day schools	120	60·9

Here again, it is possible that massive abstentions from one sector alone could significantly alter the picture. However, if the sample answering is considered anything like representative, we see that those staff who have only worked at boarding schools amount to thirty-eight per cent, nearly two-fifths of the total. Some of these will have been at day schools themselves (see Table 1·9); but those who have moved jobs and stayed in boarding, which shows an element of decision in favour of the system, rather than just experiment with it, are few – less than fifteen per cent. Over three-fifths have had some experience in being staff (presumably teaching therefore) outside the boarding schools; half of these are new to boarding work. Unless the answers here are very unrepresentative, 'the boarding system', at least with regard to staff, is heavily connected by shared experience with the non-boarding system. Observation suggests that relatively few have entered boarding work because they disliked conditions in previous, maintained schools (usually where grammar has turned comprehensive, with the resulting shake-up of ethos); more may take these jobs because they are available, and conveniently near their husbands' work.

Staff's own educational background has a bearing on the ideas they bring to their jobs, and on the extent they can contribute to the separateness of the system.

Table 1·9. Secondary and tertiary education of staff

	number	per cent of total	university
educated in day school	126	63·6	
day girl in boarding school	28	14·1	
boarder	44	22·2	
Oxbridge	33	17·4	
other universities	85	44·9	62·30
colleges or teacher-training, U.K.	60	31·7	
qualifications abroad	11	5·8	
total	189		

These results come not only from teaching staff, but also from matrons, bursars and others. The majority were themselves day pupils, even though one-third had either been boarders or had closely observed boarding. There is not such a tradition, evident in boys' schools, of old boarding pupils returning to teach. This is another facet of diversity of experience which dilutes the extent to which we can identify a self-contained system in girls' boarding. Of those who described their role as 'housemistress' (or combined this role with that of teaching) fifteen out of seventeen had themselves been day girls. Unless we assume that boarding-educated house-mistresses selectively abstained from answering the questionnaire *en masse*, we cannot say that the important position of housemistress is dominated by women passing on the boarding ethos learned in their youth. But there may be some truth in this possibility.

First, some housemistresses may have described themselves merely as 'teacher', though it is most unlikely that a particularly high proportion of these (if any) should have been boarding-educated. The second possibility is more serious. The question-naires had been given out in most schools by leaving them in the staff-room; non-teaching housemistresses, who might well have included several boarding-educated, may not have come so often into the staff-room. Visits to houses were not always made in the best conditions for giving questionnaires to staff. (In one house, very soon after supper, a procession of girls starting from the youngest came to say goodnight, formally, and the housemistress had told the head girl of the house that she was 'going to get that man out of here no later than 9.30'. In the event, I stayed later than that, but questionnaires were not on the cards.) In these ways, some boarding-educated housemistresses may have been missed; but not enough to overturn the conclusion that houses are not generally run by those immersed from the start in a boarding life. It may be, of course, that this is a handicap, in that those trying to run a boarding house who have not themselves known boarding life may not do so with an informed understanding. In one or two schools, how-ever, there is an emphatic air of boarding continuity, with staff who were boarders and appear to consider it as the best educational form.

In contrast to the heads, only a small proportion of staff were Oxbridge graduates. However, over two-thirds of those answering have university backgrounds, and this figure may be slightly increased by those with qualifications abroad. The sub-stantial proportions of university-educated staff are indicated in many school prospectuses, which often also specify their scholar-ships and additional merits. These may convey an aura of university-orientation, which might be what many parents are looking for.

Schools often appear to make the most of any Oxbridge connections they have. Origins of head or staff, fellowships or university posts held by governors, are publicized; iconic links such as pictures, lists of girls with university places, or houses named after famous educationalists associated with the school or universities are evident. When considerable overt play is made of the Oxbridge connection, efforts are likely to be noticed (only two or three schools to judge by here) to keep this up. A large sixth form may be worked up – parents will be told that they are expected not to withdraw their daughters before; streaming may be effected, with resources directed to the upper stream. Talented 'academic' staff may be given facilities before accessory subjects are aided; senior pupils may be given student status, with separate accommodation and some detachment from the authority and rules structure – and freedom and an onus to work. Many of these things will occur for reasons other than desire for places at Oxbridge; but it is less likely, with all due respect, that efforts are being spent specifically to get girls into Edinburgh or Bristol University, even if these are thought of (quite rightly) as congenial alternatives. For the most part, however, schools appear to strive for attainable goals, without undue emphasis on Oxbridge links in the past, or hopes of the future.

Continuing on the theme of examining the people within the schools, and for signs that they arise from and function within a system, we can look at some facts about the girls.

The Girls

The facts gathered here are more valid than those about the staff. Only a very few girls declined to answer questionnaires, or made a mess of the papers. We are looking here to see whether pupils' parents, brothers, sisters and holiday friends were at boarding school; such pupils would be embedded within, would in fact define, a system. Those whose contacts were not in boarding schools would give a measure of interconnectedness of this part of the educational system with the mainstream.

Table 1·10.
Family educational backgrounds of boarders and of day girls

| | | percentage whose: | | |
	total	father was at day school	father boarded	others
day girls	410	55	34	11
boarders	1,332	36	50	14

		mother was at day school	mother boarded	others
day girls	410	66	23	11
boarders	1,332	44	44	12

percentage with:						
	total	brother at day school	brother boarded	total	sister at day school	sister boarded
day girls	236	50	50	207	74	26
boarders	809	18	82	718	24	76

Many girls openly said they did not know what sort of schools their parents had been to. They did know about their brothers and sisters, however. We see that half of the boarders have parents who had boarded (slightly fewer among the mothers); this represents a great measure of traditional coherence within a 'boarding system'; it also represents a great measure of movement into the system over a generation. Many day girls (a quarter to a third) also came from families with boarding experience. Without further inquiry it cannot be known whether these are people who want boarding but cannot afford it, or who want principally independent schooling. To an extent, they represent movement 'out of the system' across a generation. It is quite possible, though we cannot but guess at it here, that many pupils now in the maintained day schools system, are children of parents educated in boarding schools. These would represent the proper measure of movement out of the system across a generation.

Once a generation has moved into using the system, boarding is evidently the style accepted for most or all children; over three-quarters of the boarders had brothers and sisters also as boarders; very few had brothers and sisters as day pupils. The boarding principle is kept to somewhat more strongly for brothers than for sisters. This shows more strongly among day girls. The figures suggest that among families sending girls to boarding the prior concern is for independent schooling, next, for boarding for boys, and then for girls.* A further comparison can be made (not given here) which shows that there is no difference in the proportion of boarding or day backgrounds in the families of younger or older girls.

For most of the girls, arrival at their present school was either at age 11 or 13. Previously, they could have been to 'prep' (independent) boarding or day schools; others will have been to state (maintained) primary schools. Again we can see to what extent the system is defined by similar experience outside of the present schools.

Table 1·11.
Preparatory school experience of day girls and of boarders

		have been to a co-ed school	have been to a prep school	have been prep boarders
day girls:	number	292	276	29
	per cent of total	71	67	7
boarders:	number	1,003	961	334
	per cent of total	75	72	25

The majority of girls have, at some early stage, been to a school at which there were boys. There is no statistically significant difference here between the experience of day girls and of boarders.

* One startling illusion from the figures is that (adding in the respondents themselves) families apparently have nearly twice as many daughters as sons. This is because the total number of boarders commenting about their sisters' education (718) may be referring to one, or more, sisters. The percentage figure refers not to the proportion of their sisters in or out of boarding; it refers to the proportion of their own number who have sisters in or out of boarding. The table thus shows that girls are more likely to have brothers than sisters in the proportion 809/718. The number of brothers, however, is presumably likely to be greater than the number of sisters, to give an approximately balanced population.

The question here was 'Have you *ever* been to a preparatory board-ing school . . ?' which includes spells of a year or less. Thus a small number of present day girls have boarded at the prep stage; some may have boarded because their parents were abroad; others may have tried boarding but found it unsuitable.

Only a quarter of present boarders had been to a boarding pre-paratory school. This pre-training in the ways and ethos of the system has been said by Royston Lambert in his book on boys' schools to be a most important element in supporting that system. The same situation clearly does not hold among girls. The present sample of twenty-three schools includes one maintained and two direct grant schools, and it is probable that many of the girls with-out independent prep-school backgrounds will have come from those three schools. So the important elements in defining a system here, by virtue of common experience, outlook and ethos, would seem to be those of independence and fee-paying, rather than of boarding. Royston Lambert makes a sociological case that pre-boarding experience trains pupils to adjust to secondary boarding. If that is so among girls, we might expect to find a correlation between the extent of experience of prep-school boarding and present satisfaction among boarders.

Statistical calculations show no direct correlation between in-dividuals' experience of preparatory boarding and present satisfac-tion as a boarder; neither is there any direct correlation between previous independent prep-school experience and present satisfac-tion. There is, however, another way of examining the data. If we list the schools in order of highest to lowest average satisfaction, and also list them according to the prevalence of types of prep-school experience, we find that there is still no link between satisfac-tion and prep-boarding incidence; there is some small correlation, however,* between the happier schools (on average) and those whose pupils had some experience of independent prep schooling. The upshot of this is that, using a criterion of present satisfac-tion in school, and the two most sophisticated statistical measures for this type of comparison, no effect of previous boarding on 'training towards adjustment' can be found; but there is some evidence of 'training towards adjustment' from having started in an independent school. The important characteristic defining

* rho $= 0.477$, significant at 0.05 level.

any 'system' therefore seems to be independence, rather than boarding.

The last point to examine here concerns the holiday friends of boarders, and whether these came from 'this school or this type of school', or from 'other schools, and elsewhere' defined in class-room explanations as: state schools, or people of unknown back-ground met, for example, in discotheques, or those in higher educa-tion. These are the results:

Table 1·12. Holiday friends made by day girls and by boarders

		percentage of holiday friends who are:				
	total number	from this or similar schools	from other schools or elsewhere	mostly girls	mostly boys	mixed
day girls	337	48	52	22	7	71
boarders	1,141	38	62	15	9	76

Figures are available (though not given here) which show that day girls and boarders say they make very similar actual numbers of friends in the holidays on the whole. Boarders make a greater proportion of their holiday friends outside the 'system' than do day girls. Why is this so? Are boarders 'boy mad' and making many more boy-friends, some of whom might be non-boarding products? The answers they give (remember that the questionnaire sessions were conducted with the large majority of classes in a serious and responsible mood) suggest that they are not 'boy mad'. Boarders make more mixed groups of friends than day girls. It is day girls who seem to show slightly greater desire for the company of their own kind, not only in sex, but also as regards type of school. The boarders include those who travel 'home' to their parents abroad, and they may be tired of the company of those who know their school lives so well. There are no grounds for finding that boarding presents an 'in-group' to boarders, who might continue to make friends only in boarding society. On the contrary, boarders say they branch out in making friends, finding them from outside the 'system' and having some preference for mixed rather than for girls-only company. In this respect, the circumstance of boarding appears less 'divisive' than that of being a day girl. Of course, this says nothing about whether independent schooling is divisive, or in what ways.

At what age do boarders make this branching out in friendship? Here is the evidence:

Table 1·13. Age at which boarders make friends from different backgrounds

background of friends	age: 13 and under	14	15	16	17 and over	total girls
this school and similar (per cent)	19	26	22	22	11	435
other type of schools and elsewhere (per cent)	16	23	22	20	18	706

Until girls are 16, there remains a strong trend to make friends within the system. At 17 and over, girls who are boarders are clearly more interested in making their friends outside the system. It should be noted that a large number are saying they find their friends within the system, even at the later ages, so the cultural effect of proximity in boarding is not without its importance. It is not, however, all-powerful; it does not lose out early on; but for sixth-formers, interest in the wider world seems to have taken over.

Summary

We are interested in the extent to which the boarding schools comprise a system, peopled by those from a certain class in society, staffed by adults who themselves were boarders, patronized by parents who were boarders, whose pupils start with primary boarding experience, and who make their holiday friends from within the system.

Starting at the top, governing bodies appear to contain about forty per cent of titled or distinguished people. It seems clear that the purpose of having such governors, apart from the advantages of their experience in management or contacts in administration, is to confer a tone or aura upon the school, as their titles and offices are clearly shown in prospectuses. About one-third of the governors were women, though the implications of this are hard to judge. It could be seized upon by feminists as yet another area for reform, and by anti-feminists as yet more evidence with which to tease the ladies.

The heads of schools were mostly single women, and well over half were Oxbridge graduates. This may be taken to imply the possession of an extra *savoir faire* in administration, or of scholarly distinction; at a guess, it might also serve iconically, as a saint's picture may help in intercession for a mortal, regarding her admittance to a higher place. In these times of very fierce competition for Oxbridge places, a head with an Oxbridge degree may make no more difference in gaining a place than the possible application of her encouragement in this direction.

Staff show a lower proportion of Oxbridge connection than do heads. Staffs include many more married women, in some cases both husband and wife working in the same school. Staff include a sizeable core who have worked for over ten years at their present school; half have been under three years at their school, and a quarter are at their first jobs (a few of these are not newcomers, but have remained in their present jobs for many years). Nearly half the staff have worked previously in boarding schools, but over half have also had experience in day schools – this applies especially to teachers. Just under a quarter of staff were themselves educated in boarding schools. In sum, the staffs do not present a picture of a homogeneous, in-bred group of people who know only the boarding system. A diversity of backgrounds is readily apparent. A diversity of views is also apparent if one wishes to attend to it.

Girls who are boarders come from families in which at least half the fathers, and slightly fewer mothers, were themselves boarders. This represents a substantial family rootedness in the system; but half the girls are also 'moving into' the system, whose parents had not known boarding. Among day girls, one-third had fathers, and a quarter had mothers, who had been to boarding school. This can be seen as being to some extent a movement away from a completely enclosed system. Half the day girls had brothers who were boarders, and a quarter of them had sisters at boarding schools.

Three-quarters of the total of the boarders' brothers and sisters were also at boarding schools.

The signs then are of substantial movements into, and possibly out of the system as well (to make sure of the latter, complementary investigations would have to be made in day schools). The boarders, perhaps surprisingly (to those who expect 'institutionalization' to operate), perhaps unsurprisingly (to those who see young people's interests as unfetterable), tend more than day girls to make a mixed-sex group of holiday friends; boarders also tend more than day girls to find holiday friends outside the system of boarding schools. Not enough is known about the informal details of this finding; for instance, day girls may be likely to keep to other day girl-friends from within the system (depending perhaps on the number of day girls in their school). Boarders may classify their friends as being out-system partly in wishful-thinking; their friends may be those who actually had boarded before, though who are now in college training, or work. Without research among old-girls, it must be concluded at least that the intentions, and possibly also the actions of boarders themselves, are not to remain tied (at least for the immediate present) to connections within the system.

It appears that the two extremes in the hierarchy – the heads and the pupils – have more links within the boarding system than have the staff. While most heads are formally committed to supporting boarding (unless they are in process of closing down their boarding departments) many pupils show a desire to look elsewhere. What their intentions will be when they in turn have to educate their daughters cannot be exactly predicted. A dislike for one's boarding experience would have to be very strong if it were to survive the transmuting force of a nostalgic regard for one's youth and one's activities then. The life-style of the young adult casting aside the recent fetters of boarding may give way to the middle-class mother wanting to ensure the same ethos for her daughter. Meanwhile, class attitudes in the country, as a result of the progress of comprehensive education, might change, relieving the demand for independent and boarding schooling. This would presumably also reduce the substantial numbers of day-schooled parents who at present send their children to board. Staff will still look for jobs pragmatically, finding them in boarding schools if convenient, rather than forming a dedicated corps of those devoted to the idea

of boarding. The number of such women, by all accounts, partly
depends on the spinsterhood caused by loss of men in war, and on
the feminist traditions in the first half of this century, and this
number is decreasing.

Two: Goals

Just as there are many pairs of eyes in each school, so there are many views about what schools should do. There should perhaps be more agreement among internal observers* as to what each school is doing; but even here there is room for disagreement. Thucydides, the Greek sociologist-historian, recognizes this problem of the observers' bias in reporting 'objective reality' when he writes 'different eye witnesses give different accounts of the same events, speaking out of partiality for one side or the other . . .'. He clearly recognizes that observer bias is not just a matter of different phrasing of the report, but of substantive differences in perception and interpretation. Not only can the same thing or situation seem different to different observers; we can also find a single thing which seems different to the same observer when he comes to it from various recent experiences. The famous example is of tepid water, which to a cold hand seems hot, but to a hot hand seems cold. If one hand has previously been cooled and the other heated, when both are put together into tepid water, it becomes very difficult to describe its temperature.

How then are we to try and describe what schools aim to do? For it is fairly obvious that various attitudes of the observer can and do affect his assessment. The only way to deal with this difficulty, and this way is not perfect either, is to record what people in the schools say themselves; school documents can also be studied. Statements from individuals should always be set against majority views on the same topic, and also compared with the attitudes of powerful minorities. One girl wrote:

Unlike most schools we are absolutely anti-games whereas most schools are terribly hearty and rushed out to games every day with great enthusiasm. WELL I ASSURE YOU WE *DON'T* neither are we very likely to. So there. (13)

This girl's opinion was shared by the majority of pupils at her school; in fact after three days in the school I had not seen one

* Than among outsiders.

hockey stick, until I came across what was possibly the last of its era being turned into a salad fork in the handicraft room. One might conclude that the school rated low the goal of athletic success; yet the available space and facilities were good, and some staff showed determined signs of wanting to raise the popularity of games. So it would seem wiser to state the collective views of different sectors in the school's population, and also to discuss what is actually going on.

In the studies on boys' boarding schools goals were categorized as 'instrumental, expressive, and organizational'. I believe this categorization can be made, but only on a basis of asking a large number of people to judge the nature of each goal. Taking the above example, it could be established that the staff in three schools have a goal of improving interest and performance in organized games. At one school, there might be a general agreement that the reason for this was to win matches for the school, keep people occupied during hours when many other staff are unavailable, and so on. We could agree that this would be serving the organization primarily – an organizational goal. In a second school, people might reject the first view as petty, but state that they wanted to improve games performance to win some tournament, increase collective self-esteem, essentially so that morale could be translated into more harmonious relations and better academic performance. Such a situation is where games are seen as 'instrumental' in achieving something else. As 'instrumental', they would seem to be a means, rather than an end or goal. The concept of 'instrumental goal' seems therefore to be somewhat careless, possibly misleading;* it could be seen as referring to short-term as against long-term goals. A third school might see more intensive games as an end in itself; the view might also claim that games are intrinsically enjoyable, and that this outweighs 'organizational' or 'instrumental' aspects. Here we could say that we see an 'expressive goal'.

It seems possible to me to arrive at judgements based on majority local opinion as to the possible instrumental or expressive nature of various goals. However, I did not pursue this line in my inquiry. I examined the school prospectuses, in order to elicit documentary or formal evidence on goals; and I used a questionnaire for senior

---

* It might be construed as an example of 'oxymoron', or an expression of which one part implies a meaning opposed to that of the other part.

girls and staff, similar to that previously used in boys' schools. This questionnaire listed fourteen different goals,* and people were asked if their school *should* try, *did* try and *actually succeeded* in doing each of the fourteen items. For simplicity in reporting, I have grouped the fourteen goals into three categories; these categories can certainly be assailed on whatever grounds the critic wishes. They will be explained after first looking at the content of prospectuses.

The Prospectuses

Twenty school prospectuses were examined. These are presumably the 'best foot' which the schools put forward in their first contact with parents. Much atmosphere is conveyed by the photographs (beautiful mansions, grounds, interiors, where possible; girls seriously at work, cleanly at play, even dancing in pairs, uniformed, in a large ballroom), information about the acreage, bracing air, lists of distinguished governors and other material. The principal object of search was, however, a statement of *aims*. Eighteen prospectuses put forward† goals, the ends towards which the organization says it will bend its efforts. Even here, this implication is not always justified, as three or four schools were reluctant to let me derive my impressions from the prospectus. New ones were being produced, this was an expensive matter which could get delayed more than they wished, but their ideas had changed. So even these prospectuses are not entirely valid as formal evidence; but they are what the parents see, so they were surveyed.

I wrote down any statement I could find about aims. Three schools' prospectuses made no overt statement about aims. In one, it was possible to guess at aims, as it included phrases such as 'drawing and painting are taught . . .'; but in the absence of the school saying why such things were done, they were not included in the present list. One staff member, aware of my interest in prospectuses, brought my attention to the school prayer, in which

* It is actually begging the question to think of these as *goals*. They may not all be seen as *goals* by some respondents, who might consider them as *means* (or intermediate, short-term goals, we might say).

† Statements of aims, overtly expressed as such. These are presumably what can be called 'formal'.

some formal aims were clearly implied. This particular analysis, however, kept to what was found in secular printed documents. In another school, it was 'assumed that all the girls are in process of becoming useful members of the community, capable of earning their own living'. Here were two assumptions (joining the community, earning a living) which were not directly claimed as goals; in fact it could be taken that these items were being left to parents to inculcate, or for physical maturation to bring about. Nevertheless, they were counted in, and the full list appears as follows:

Table 2·1.
Aims of boarding schools, found declared in their prospectuses

	total mentions
'social responsibility' consideration for others: 5; social service, useful membership of the community: 3; individual responsibility: 3; useful: 2; powers of leadership:1; steady: 1; dependable:1	16
'individual fulfilment' realize full potentiality of the individual: 7; develop self-reliance-confidence: 4; initiative: 1; individuality: 3	15
'all-roundness' thorough, sound education: 9; wide education, avoid extreme specialization: 4	13
'manners' courtesy: 3; self-control, discipline: 5; poise: 1	9
'careers' aim for high academic achievement, prepare for non-university careers	8
'happiness' help girls to be happy, foster a happy atmosphere	5
instil *Christian* precepts	5
enable girls to take their proper place in the *home*	4
'miscellaneous' confer a proper balance between freedom and responsibility	3
instil a response to beauty, taste	2
use freedom wisely, allow full opportunity for creative work, instil meticulousness, encourage originality, integrity	1 each
ALSO: the schools should be modern (3), healthy (2), homely, moderate cost (1)	

The list comprises over ninety declared intentions, which averages four or five statements per school. Thus a school mentioning social responsibility is likely to have mentioned three or four other ideas as well. The items low in the list are, of course, rarely mentioned. No suggested *means* or methods are listed above. Thus several schools said, 'contact with parents is encouraged, to discuss problems', or words to that effect. This was considered not to be an aim in itself, but a method whereby other aims – for example, understanding individuals' problems and helping them – could be promoted. The grouping which has been made may be done in other ways. Thus 'courtesy' could be put with social responsibility (though to my mind it lacks a component of initiative which characterizes the latter); or 'originality' and 'integrity' could be used to expand the category of 'individual fulfilment'. Continued argument about these allocations is not likely to be conclusive. It is safest to say that both social responsibility and individual fulfilment are widely held and stated as goals; there is no evidence to suggest that the one is much more commonly advocated than the other. Perhaps it should be noted that (only ?) five schools say their aim is to make girls happy; four refer to women's possible future domestic role, and two refer to aesthetic sensibility; also two mention physical well-being (through games, and eating the school's home-grown food or the neighbouring farm's creamy milk).

Such are the formal, overtly stated goals. A case could be made for adding here statements made by heads, which supplement and perhaps even alter what is in the prospectus. There is also an opportunity to interpret what may be in 'a school's' (collective ?) 'mind' when noting, for example, display cabinets full of cups, shields and trophies; are these to encourage athletic and other competition, individual performance, the school's prestige? Or how should one interpret the gilt-lettered lists on panelled walls of old girls entered, some with scholarships, at Oxbridge? The interpretation of such signs and symbols offers tempting possibilities for the visitor, who, having thought of some implication or interpretation, may congratulate himself on his clever insight with a resulting state of intellectual well-being which somehow convinces him that he must be right. In fact, he may be right; but this course, unless no other is available, seems to be open to error. One of the advantages of the research method was that time and opportunity was available to get the girls' and staffs' own views on which goals were important and to what extent. It is only after examining the results of the questionnaires that we can indulge our insight as to the possible explanations or causes contributing to the states of affairs that are found.

Questionnaire on Goals

Fourteen goals (fifteen for staff) were listed in a questionnaire. The papers were given in classroom sessions to 517 sixth-formers in twenty-two schools. Papers were also left for staff to answer anonymously, and 186 properly filled replies were received. For each item or goal, people were asked to make three judgements, as the following diagram shows:

Put ticks to show: How much do you think this school:

goal	should try to			does try to			actually succeeds		
	very much	medium	hardly at all	very much	medium	hardly at all	very much	medium	hardly at all
Get good exam results:	√			√			√		

As answered, the person responding in this way would think that her school *should* try very much to get good exam results, also that it *does try* very much to get good exam results, and what is more, that it *actually succeeds* in getting good exam results very well. The questionnaire then continues with the other thirteen goals. The format was carefully explained to the girls in classes, though not to staff, which doubtless explains why so many staff papers were returned with unusable answers (e.g. *two* ticks in the section 'should try to' for the same goal, etc., etc.).

The resulting evidence can be analysed in a bewildering array of tables. This would undoubtedly be the most thorough course to follow, but a balance has to be struck between comprehensiveness and comprehension. I have therefore grouped certain goals together; results can be examined in these families of related goals together, thereby involving fewer tables and figures. The goals are as follows:

Table 2·2. Goals listed in questionnaire and their grouping

goals primarily concerning the individual	goals concerning the individual and the community	goals primarily concerning the community
develop girls' *own* personality	get good exam results	keep the school running smoothly
prepare girls for jobs and careers	teach people to live together happily	keep up the school's public reputation
prepare girls to understand the opposite sex	put into practice Christian principles	keep girls occupied all the time
enable girls to decide for themselves what is right and wrong		
develop physical health		
develop cultural interests		

not grouped with the above
prepare girls to be able to
be good wives and mothers
make life in school something
like that of home
(*for staff only*) provide some
respite from pop culture

Results can now be discussed for three main families of goals. It can be objected, though, that the grouping above may obscure particularities that need to be brought out and looked at separately. In some instances, therefore, I will give the results for one particular goal from within a group. First, however, we can look at the relative priorities of goals, which can be done without even mentioning individual goals. This approach will inform us primarily about the groups of people who have recorded their views.

Priorities among Different Goals

We can see which goals most people think most strongly should be pursued, and arrange them in rank order. In this way, six lists have been prepared, three each for girls and staff. These lists show the order of importance in which people think goals should be striven for, are striven for and are actually achieved. These lists can be compared together (by means of rank order correlation); this shows how different groups of people agree, or to what extent one group thinks schools' efforts and achievements match their ideal priority of goals.

The table[1] gives the statistical results, from which the following conclusions are drawn. Girls' and staffs' priorities about what schools *should* strive for show no more than random similarity. But the groups have a fair measure of agreement about what the schools *do* try to do; they also agree to the same extent about the priority in which goals are actually achieved. The fact that sixth-form girls and staff, two independent bodies of observers both reasonably mature and certainly close to their data, have a considerable agreement on the order of importance of what *is* going on, is good validation for the questionnaire. In view of this corroboration, the lack of agreement between girls and staff on the priorities of goals that schools *should* strive for carries more interest.

Staff give more weight than girls do to the idea that schools should inculcate Christian principles. More will be said about that in Chapter Ten. The staff give more importance to the school running smoothly and also say that some attempt should be made to 'make life like at home' – the girls collectively do not expect this so strongly. Also, girls feel exam success should be striven for more strongly than do staff! This should perhaps be borne in mind when discussing efforts schools may be making to improve academic performance. There are also considerable differences between schools on this issue, and more will be said about this in Chapter Four.

How do girls think that their ideal priority of goals is being met? There is no agreement between the order in which girls think things should happen, and the order in which they think schools are trying, or are succeeding in their efforts. This is an overall (and statistically sound) conclusion covering twenty-two schools. There are certainly particular schools where girls think that what *should* happen *is* happening. Note that this is not a 'significantly negative' finding. Girls do not think schools are perverse. They do not think that schools are systematically pursuing those items which they themselves feel are unimportant; and systematically ignoring those things which girls think they should be putting first. They merely think there is no relation in the order of priorities between how things should be pursued, and how they *are* pursued and attained. Examples could be given from many fields, but one, that of sex education, is perhaps not discussed enough in proportion to the apparent strength of feelings about it.

They ought to give more sex education, rather than let girls go into the world and find out by themselves, by their mistakes. (16)

or at another school:

Sexual education – very bad, we don't get *any* help and learn from experience of very exaggerated form from others. Should be given by housemistresses *I think*, but mothers should do much more . . . otherwise it is very unfair to the girl – she doesn't 'get' all the filthy jokes going around and being new is very embarrassed when directly attacked '*Did* you understand?'. (16)

These examples are not given to create some major focus, but just to illustrate the discrepancy, shown in the statistics, between the order of priorities in which girls think things should be done, and that which they observe is followed in practice. I emphasize that the situation is not so bad that the girls think their ideal order is actually *reversed* in practice.

There is a significant similarity in the views of the staff between what they think a school should be doing, and what they consider it is actually trying to do. This similarity may be due to 'response set' in answering a questionnaire (though this did not apparently deter the girls). Staff also show a very strong similarity in their judgement of what schools try to do, and what they achieve. Here, staff and girls are of one mind. They do not effectively distinguish between what schools try to achieve and what they actually achieve. But even staff think the agreement between priorities of what schools should do, and what they actually achieve, is hardly better than random.

This complex series of conclusions could be summed up crudely, viz.: an actor playing the part of a girl says: 'School doesn't follow my list of ideas about what it should do, but what it tries to do it certainly achieves.' Then, playing the part of a staff member, the actor says 'School fairly closely follows the order of priorities I think it should – after all, I'm one of the people who see to this – and what we try to do we certainly achieve'. The theatrical critic who views this drama says 'Though there is bare agreement between staff and girls on the order of priorities which schools should follow, they agree fairly well about what schools actually try to do, and the order of priorities which they achieve'.

There is little surprising in these conclusions. One can see the girls as caught up in the possibilities of being customers, beneficiaries or victims of the system. They can be one thing to some of its aspects, and another thing to other aspects. Some girls feel like victims throughout, some feel like beneficiaries. To an extent, these (sixth-form) girls are the N.C.O.s of the community, and participate in running the regime. Various social forms of trying to involve girls more in social responsibility (by 'democratic' councils, and the like) or of detaching them from responsibility (by 'sixth-form' or 'student' houses) exist, and are discussed later. There is not a pervasive reason for girls to think of judging their own efforts when they deal with the question 'the school succeeds in . . .'; some also are aware of their customer role, which makes them critically aware of what they may be getting for their money. Staff, on the other hand, dealing with the question 'the school succeeds in doing . . .' are judging their own efforts. So we may expect them to mark these more highly than girls do. There remains overall the impressive agreement between staff and girls on the order of priorities actually in force, which highlights in turn their differing views about the order which should be in force.

Ideal Goals

A system has been devised[2] to show the results on ideal and achieved goals numerically. The goals have been subgrouped, as was shown in Table 2·2.

Table 2·3.
Goals schools should strive for, according to staff and girls

goals	per cent support from:	
	staff	girls
for individuals	78·7	77·8
for individual and community	76·6	70·0
for community	66·4	63·2
'preparing girls for roles of wife and mother'	53·7	61·5
'making life like at home'	73·7	57·8

We can begin to see now where differences of view between girls and staff actually lie. As said before, staff see more point in pursuing community goals, but they agree with girls in giving high priority to goals which concern the individual. There is very little difference in 'response set' to this question on ideals; over all the fourteen goals, staff show a more positive response (73·5 per cent) than do girls (70·4 per cent). This dramatizes the belief of girls that schools should give more attention to 'preparation for roles of wife and mother'; they also support more than staff do a high emphasis on exam results, on preparation for jobs and careers, and a concern for the school's public reputation. This last item may partly reflect discomfort some girls feel when they get teased by day-school pupils whom they meet occasionally out in town.

To some extent, the views girls give about what they feel *should* happen may be a reflection in some schools of what they regret is *not* happening. An example may clarify this:

The uniform is almost Victorian, so is the view of many of the staff, especially about careers for young girls, they all think being a nurse or a secretary is marvellous and any more ambitious careers are not a very good idea.   (17)

Here is a clear feeling that this particular school is not doing enough in the careers field. The point I am making is that this may make girls mark particularly strongly their belief that a school should make a big effort in this direction. In a school where people found the careers concern adequate there would be less need to say that that is what the school *should* be doing. So the results on ideal goals are a complicated mixture of what people would feel 'independently', plus their reactions to the deficiencies or adequacies of their particular situation. This desired goal of attention to jobs and careers was the top item overall for 517 girls in twenty-two schools; moreover, in each separate school it ranked high in priority, whereas some other goals (for example 'practise Christian principles' and 'keep up the school's reputation') were considered rather important in some schools but very unimportant in others.

Another topic where girls' views on what should happen are almost certainly influenced by what does happen, is the question of the relation of sexual roles in general. Partly to deal tactfully in this matter (in one school I had to debate tenaciously before being allowed to give only to the sixth form a questionnaire containing an item with the words 'get on with the opposite sex') the relevant goal was worded 'prepare girls for the role of wife'. We have already seen that girls and staff differed considerably on the importance of this possible school function. One reason why some girls may have emphasized some need here may be the approach which they observe in the staff's behaviour.

They call the police from the village if any young men appear on the grounds. Because of this swathing us in blankets, protecting us from the cruel exterior, when males come into the grounds its like seeing an oasis in the desert.   (16)

This goal is, however, not high in the girls' list of priorities. As a matter of fact, it is only tenth out of fourteen. It is a goal, however, where girls' and staffs' views noticeably differ, and the possible explanation of 'inflated need because of felt deprivation' is offered. Having implied perhaps that girls are criticizing their schools when they say they need something, or that the schools should pursue certain goals which they are neglecting, two things should be remembered. One is that staff may share the same view as girls on some topics, and that dissatisfaction with the state of things is one facet of a continual striving for improvement. The other is that girls express some desire for a 'decent front' for their school, a good public reputation.

Though I say things against this school, it is a very good school. Not only do you get a good overall education but you learn how to live with people, and above all you are taught good manner, which I think is important in a girl.   (16)

This is perhaps akin to teenage feelings about make-up, for the attractive presentation of the self (and of the community) in daily life. There is a possible harmony of concern both for inner and for outer appearances.

The ideal goal on which the greatest girls–staff discrepancy arises is that of practising Christian principles. Staff rank this sixth (out of fifteen) in importance. Girls place it last. One girl breaks into capitals:

CHRISTIANITY   DRUMMED   INTO   US: PUTS   US
AGAINST IT . . .   (15)

As the girls and staff closely agree on the high importance of developing moral discretion (ranked second for girls and third for staff, out of fourteen goals), I feel that there is something to say for the following explanation. To many staff, the phrase 'Christian principles' denotes moral values, therefore they approve it. For many girls, the phrase evokes thoughts about organizational rituals, and they find it unwelcome. At twelve schools the girls make this last in order of priority; but in one school, a convent, where an identification of Christian principles with moral values may be more likely to occur, this goal comes top!

The situations and attitudes so far described are obviously not the same in all schools. In some, as in the case above of pursuing Christian principles, results may go clearly against the trend. Schools are likely to be aware of it when they harbour such an exceptional situation. In other cases, schools may as well assume that their girls follow the general trend, and that the findings above are not scanty but widespread ones, based on a large number of girls at many schools.

Observed Efforts: Goals Schools are Aiming for

This is a question that I, as a visitor in schools for no more than a week each, have refrained from trying to answer myself. Instead, here is evidence of what the large groups of girls and staff (indicated by their questionnaire responses) think schools are striving for.

Table 2·4. Goals schools strive for, according to staff and girls

goals	per cent support from:	
	staff	girls
for individuals	66·6	45·5
for individual and community	81·2	69·9
for community	75·8	72·8
'preparing girls for roles of wife and mother'	40·0	19·9
'making life like at home'	61·8	29·9

Previously we examined views about what people thought *should* happen. Even if these views are influenced by reactions to what *does* happen, we may expect that sixth-formers across the country may hold similar views and ideals about school. If this is so, the range of results collected from different schools about ideal goals will not be as great as the range of results referring to observed goals. This would be because different schools try for different ends and are equipped differently to do so. The figures support this assumption. There is much greater variation between what schools actually are trying to do on any goals, according to the girls, than on what they think schools should try to do.

What do staff think is actually going on? They admit a 'shortfall' in actual compared to ideal striving in goals concerning individuals' benefit (66·6 against 78·7 per cent).* But staff evidently consider that *more* effort is being spent than they think is necessary on goals benefiting the community or community and individual. The girls also feel that these goals, which are not solely or directly concerned with the individual's benefit, get more effort than they need. The question of Christian principles is the one with the greatest difference.

I remember one day I took Communion because I *had* to at a 9.30 service at a Church at which we are not allowed to take it. I was called in by the house mistress and asked kindly not to do it again as we can only take it at 8 A.M. service.   (15)

Some might wish to emphasize the kindness which this girl was dealt with, but the point being illustrated here is that it seems that the organizational facets of school life are often said to be emphasized at the cost of the interests of the individual, and particularly with regard to the Christian life. Another girl thinks that it may not be a simple question of supporting organizational necessities in the ultimate interest of the individual, but of a deliberate intent to nullify individuality.

The school's ideal is to turn 300 nasty little girls into 300 identically nasty little girls . . .   (15)

This girl is at an age (see Chapter Four on satisfaction) at which boarders are least happy. But the same thought is offered from those of more mature years:

There is very little opportunity to express one's own individual ideas – everyone must be on the same level, and our views must be watched and censored, so as not to shock anyone.   (17)

* Comparing figures in Tables 2·3 and 2·4.

Girls find the schools' efforts directly on the behalf of the individual to be substantially short of what they should be (a difference of thirty-two per cent). They also estimate these efforts on behalf of the individual less than staff do (a difference of twenty-one per cent). As we have seen, this is not because girls have a conservative 'response set', or the tendency not to use extreme judgements. They think that schools' efforts for the community are greater than they should be. They are closer to the staff view in this respect. Girls, as we saw, do not strongly expect schools to try to 'make life like at home', but they are strongly agreed that very little effort is spent towards attaining this goal. More serious, perhaps, is the shortfall of effort girls perceive on the goal of preparation for the roles of wife and mother (forty-one per cent 'deficiency'). Staff also see a shortfall here, though to a much lesser extent (fourteen per cent). Girls say they need to know, and know about, boys. And this is the specific shortcoming that single-sex boarding presents, without apparently in many cases taking enough steps to explain or do something about the leeway.

We are cut off and suffer because of it. But we are *never* allowed any dances or social occasions with boys . . .   (16)

At another school, we also find:

We do not have dances or anything at all with other boys' schools.
(16)

At yet another school, girls said the head discouraged opportunities to establish a relationship with a well-known nearby boys' public school. Some girls' school heads spoke as though there 'are no other schools nearby', by which they meant public schools, for there were certainly maintained schools nearby. Several girls' schools were able to make arrangements with nearby maintained schools for senior girls to go there for science lessons when their own facilities were lacking. But formal social contact for dances was rarely or never noticed between a girls' public and a boys' maintained school. In this respect, most schools I visited were doubly divisive. The hazards of boy-friends are, of course, understood, and some schools allow contacts, trusting their girls. One school which encourages relationships also instructed the biology mistress to proceed with sex education 'up to modern standards,

C

including the pill'. I am *not* implying here that this school encouraged pre-marital sex; but in another school this had been faced up to by senior staff, even to the surprise of some girls!

... the school ... has a very broad outlook to life even to the extent of having morals from 1982 – I think this should be changed so that there would be a modern outlook but not so immoral! (16)

I cannot guess what this girl means by 'modern but not immoral'; however, the point is that schools do exist which give some attention to preparation for the adult woman's sexual roles. But the clear majority view is that this attention is more conspicuous by its absence. The future wife's role is not only that *vis-à-vis* males. Girls also write about domestic matters.

We're treated like little children, especially having 'lights out' so ridiculously early.... There's no domestic science – which there should be ... (16)

In another school, one with high academic goals set out in its prospectus, while many girls there accept these aims, some also feel a complementary lack:

We do not get enough teaching about running a house well, domestic science is only taken by those of a slightly lower standard. (15)

As is clearly implied in Table 2·4, the detailed results on each individual goal show that in every case but one staff think the school does try harder than the girls think. (This is not unnatural, as the staff are doing the trying, and in a sense they are just rating their own efforts.) The one goal apart is that of keeping up the school's reputation. Here, the girls feel that more effort is being spent than staff admit; but they both feel that more effort is being spent than they said should be spent. Some of the girls' attitudes here presumably come from the careful restrictions often applied over their appearance and possible actions outside school. A frequent rule is that girls may not bicycle; or if they do, it must be in threes – so that, in case of accident, one can stay by the victim while one goes for help. We are not discussing here *why* rules exist, merely how they may affect attitudes. Some girls also find ritualistic group activities in public distasteful.

School drill is dead boring, and all the parents see it dozens of times and they wish they did not have to see it again. (13)

This girl may or may not be right in her estimation of what parents like to see. At another school we see:

I feel that things like the summer display are utterly pointless. You just make a fool of yourself and feel stupid. (13)

These aversions might be put down to early teenage awkwardness, which it could be the task of the school to help surmount. This may be so; what is only being discussed is the feeling offered by sixth-formers (the two quoted were certainly not sixth-formers) that schools may be overdoing their efforts on behalf of their public reputation, a feeling, incidentally, mirrored to a smaller extent among staff.

Table 2·4 shows that goals involving both individual and community are thought by staff to be the most energetically pursued. The pursuit of these, and other organization goals, such as that of 'keeping the school running smoothly', can lead to a difference of interests between the individual and the community. A view is then developed that it is through the acceptance of this important goal, or through compromise between such opposing interests, that other goals are realized, such as the development of individual personality, and teaching people to live together. Another view takes the direct line that somehow systems should be devised that will cater directly for the individual's interest, without attending to the benefit of some abstract entity such as the community.

The detailed results reveal some considerable differences between findings from different schools. Unfortunately there were not enough staff answering from each school to set up reliable differences in staffs' views. This was, however, more possible among the girls. What do we find? Wide differences exist between how girls see their own schools striving to 'develop individual personality', 'develop cultural interests', 'prepare girls to understand the opposite sex', and 'practise Christian principles'. As to efforts towards the development of individual personality, the school with the lowest value was alone and at some distance (numerically) from the others; its prospectus was without any stated aims to be achieved by boarding, and the school was not in fact primarily organized for the boarders.

We [the boarders] are not allowed to go to school outings when it concerns school subjects which one is studying at school. This makes people discontented . . .   (16)

The same school showed a low result for the development of cultural interests, perhaps for lack of a visible community life because of the small number of boarders present at the week-ends. Of the two schools rated highest for promotion of cultural interests, one emphasized this in its prospectus, while the other was of high academic level and had access to an urban centre with whose cultural life considerable contact was kept.

Living near a large city is a great advantage, we go to plays, operas, recitals and concerts and become name-droppers – Segovia, Manitas de Plata, Yehudi Menuhin, etc.   (16)

On the question of preparing girls to understand the opposite sex, only one school produced a result of effort judged over fifty per cent. In this school there were several girls who travelled to holiday homes abroad, there were many day girls (whose answers do not enter the figures here) who led urban and more urbane lives, there was a link with a boys' school, and there were male staff who took both a formal and an active pastoral interest in girls' welfare. Whether these factors influenced the outcome, and in what proportion, cannot be decided. It seems likely they all influenced it. At the other extreme, three schools produced the unanimous response that hardly any effort was made to help girls to understand the opposite sex. These three schools included two small ones and one large one: one with the highest 'institutional control' and two with moderate control; none of the three was in an urban area, had a high proportion of day girls or had declared links with any boys' schools. These elements seemed not to be so much the original reasons for lack of effort in this direction, but to be the difficulties that relevant staff were presumably content to leave in the way of any alteration; for there were other schools showing similar characteristics, but which recorded more perceived effort towards understanding the other sex.

We can now examine what people say the schools actually achieve.

Attained Goals

These are the ways in which girls and staff consider that schools attain goals in various directions.

Table 2·5. Goals schools actually attain, according to staff and girls

| | per cent support from: | |
goals	staff	girls
for individuals	56·5	37·5
for individual and community	66·2	47·7
for community	67·2	54·1
'preparing girls for roles of wife and mother'	38·2	22·1
'making life like at home'	50·7	21·1

Clearly, the judged level at which goals are attained is substantially lower overall than people feel is desirable, and is also below the level they describe of actual effort. The deficiency is most strongly shown in the girls' views, particularly about the goals benefiting the individual. The staff agree with this estimate, though not so strongly. The detailed results show that there are no individual goals at all for which girls think achieved success measures up to the ideal. But staff find on two separate goals that schools actually exceed by very small margins their own hopes. These two goals are 'keep the school's public reputation good' and 'keep the girls occupied most of the time'. Both of these concern the organization rather than the individual directly.

The result of this is that staff see fulfilment of the efforts they thought should be spent (see Table 2·3) on the community. The girls even find only a small deficiency in attainment over what they thought best in this area (nine per cent), but they think schools fall down very considerably in offering the individual what they should (forty per cent deficit here). It is not likely to be sound to disrespect the girls' judgement on this. These are sixth-formers, and as we will see later (Chapter Four) generally in a more satisfied frame of mind than middle-school girls. Also, we have seen (Table 2·3) that these girls' judgement of ideals was quite similar to that of staff. Why do sixth-formers not develop a deep dissatisfaction over this lack of achievement of goals benefiting the individual?

One reason may be that, though these girls find serious shortcomings in reality compared with their idea of what should be attempted, they do not see it as a great deficit compared with what they see schools actually trying to do (Table 2·4). Their satisfaction may depend on comparing results with observed rather than with ideally desired efforts. Also, they may consider that the development of personality and other individual-oriented goals now lies in their own hands; one of their important preoccupations, as sixth-formers, is to pass exams. This goal I have placed in the intermediate category, benefiting both community and individual. The detailed scores show that girls do not judge an extensive failure of schools in producing good exam results. In fact, at some schools, this goal is marked as very thoroughly achieved.

What appear to be the greatest similarities and differences between schools? At a high level of achievement, girls from all schools consider that their communities are kept running smoothly. At the opposite end of the scale, girls judge that nowhere are they being successfully prepared to cope with wifely roles. The possibility of a 'sampling bias' must be pointed out here. These results were collected from sixth-formers; in several schools, there is a 'non-academic stream' of girls who would be likely to spend more time on domestic science, and possibly leave before sixth-form level. These girls might have recorded a better success for their schools in preparation for adult female roles than we find from these more academic sixth-formers. Nevertheless, they too will become adult women, and many will marry. Their problems of reconciling 'masculo-feminist' and 'femino-feminist' sets of roles may be more complex than those less academic 'simply-feminist' may find. This then, is the area in which girls judge least success from their schools. They are not alone in this. Though staff find schools successfully attaining (i.e. any response over fifty per cent) twelve goals, they find meagre success on 'helping girls to understand the opposite sex' (thirty-two per cent) and on 'preparing for roles of wife and mother' (see Table 2·5, thirty-eight per cent).

This matter of guiding pupils on the complex problems of how to be a woman in a changing man's world is not extensively treated in many prospectuses. One, of which there was evidently a male co-author, said that attention would be given to these problems since the majority of the girls would, the school hoped, get married.

This differs from the prospectus (not typical either, in this respect) which discusses the girls' futures saying 'marriage claims many'. It is possible occasionally to sense a wish for retaliation by some girls upon some staff who symbolize restriction; on them they wish the violent imposition of what they feel is normality.

I wish Boys would come and overpower all the teachers and the Headmistress and take over the school, that would be gloarious, especially if you found a boy you liked. (13)

Schools are judged by girls, then, as relatively similar with respect to being smoothly run, of making little headway towards understanding the opposite sex and of preparing girls for the roles of wife and mother (remembering a proviso on this last item about possible sampling bias). On all the other goals, fairly large to very large differences exist between schools. The greatest variance (a sixty-five per cent difference in strength of response) concerned the goal of 'promoting cultural interests'. I certainly saw differences on this item during my visits, but it would not have been possible without the questionnaire results to say whether this or some other goal was the one showing the greatest variation between schools.

Can we attribute differences in goal achievement to certain characteristics of the schools? There are two ways of commenting on this. One is to note which schools are marked by their girls as being good at achieving some goal, and then describing what appear to be relevant characteristics of those schools. Another is to take some particular characteristic (e.g. school size, 'institutional control', etc.) which is thought may affect success on some goal, and compare the whole number of schools by the relevant statistical method to see whether there is some connection between that characteristic and success.

Both these methods have been used. Let us examine, for example, the two schools which got the best response on the issue of helping their girls to understand the opposite sex. These two schools had very low institutional control (the rigidness of the rules and restrictions on privacy and freedom). They were both run by heads who appeared to be very much in touch with nearly every phase of school life. This does not mean that all schools with low institutional control will be more successful on this goal. It may mean that success will be more likely.

Making school life a little like home was rated a goal with a very low overall level of success. The one school with a fairly good mark here was a small one without day girls, who sometimes subtract from a community's coherence and intimacy. Of three schools with nearest to adequate response, none had a large number of boarders, and all had relatively light institutional control. Homeliness, it seems, was achieved least in the larger schools, especially if they also had more severe regimes. The fact of their being split into smaller houses does not appear to help.

As already mentioned, achievement of cultural interests was marked as attained to a very varied level of success, though overall a rather low one. Sometimes this is because sixth-formers are busy with roles in authority.

Every privilege which this school gives in VI form is a reward for authority. Only . . . prefects get an extra number of exeats. Work in art, music, drama, has no honour, no recognition.   (16)

Sometimes the cultural goal is affected by the idiosyncrasies of influential individuals.

The Headmistress disapproves of acting. The dramatic society is a sickly band of dedicated stagestruck females. However, the headmistress approves of music especially singing. It is rammed down one's throat. (15)

This unique method of singing may lead to a discord in the cultural scene at that school. The stated aims, social institutions and girls' descriptions at another school suggest that achievement of cultural sophistication (where 'culture' is more narrowly interpreted as love of music, the arts) is more likely where the overall culture (now using the word to mean the total shape and 'ethos' of society) is liberal.

I don't think there are many schools like this one. The freedom we have, compared with most boarding schools, is lenient – being allowed out at night with friends – boys included. I think this school is aiming at keeping everyone, at least in the sixth form, interested in culture. (16)

This is not to say that liberality in itself, as a laxity in rules, will foster 'cultural pursuits'. It may doubtless equally result in gross philistinism. What seems more likely is that in a highly controlled, severely regimented community (unless as in a monastery this rigour arises from a mature, widespread inner commitment), no amount of 'official' provision of cultural facilities or occasions will be likely to earn a response from the girls that the place is successfully 'cultured'. This is not to judge whether, after leaving such a school, girls may be more or less likely to take an interest in 'cultural' pursuits.

To compare the statistics of achieved success on various goals with a large variety of other factors, I first selected (from the detailed ingredients underlying Table 2·3) the five most highly rated ideal goals. These were:

> develop each person's *own* personality
> get good exam results
> prepare girls for jobs and careers
> teach people to live together happily
> enable girls to decide for themselves, what is right and wrong

These goals were, incidentally, also highly rated (first, second, third, seventh and eleventh out of fourteen) by staff. Next, the rankings of schools for the extent to which they actually were thought to attain these goals were combined; this gave an overall rank order of 'school quality'. This rank order of 'success on top five goals' was then statistically compared* with a large number of other factors recorded about schools.

Five schools clearly emerge from this procedure whose sixth-formers consistently ascribe good performance on the list of top five ideal goals. These five schools included four which made a similar good impression during the research visit. One did not, and this may illustrate the dangers of basing a judgement on such a visit rather than on the view of interior observers. The group of five poorest schools on this criterion include several characteristics. There is the large school, the small one, the one with few boarders whose week-ends are an empty husk of the community's existence; there is high and low institutional control, the expensive and the less expensive. Curiously, the three schools whose prospectuses showed no overt statement of aims were all in this group of five, none of which was in or near a large city.

In the intermediate range are some schools which made a very

* By means of rank order correlation coefficients and Mann-Whitney U tests.

good impression during the research visit. Some of the criteria by which they measure their efforts may not quite share the emphasis shown in the 'top five most popular' goals.

This school really makes you think for yourself, really we have complete freedom of speech and can do what we like. Our decisions are our own not the ones that are drummed into us. We have a lot of chance to prove our abilities at certain subjects (dancing, drama, games, singing, etc.) I think they are very good points and I particularly approve of the way we can think things out for ourselves and make independent ideas, knowing they will be listened to and probably accepted.   (16)

It is essential to remember that criteria of judgement vary; thus in this school there is less desire for exam success, or for emphasis on jobs and careers. So it may be very successful according to its own designs, rather than on all of the 'top five ideal goals'. Nevertheless, these top five have not been plucked from nowhere; they are the widespread ideals expressed by sixth-formers. So it is important to note that, statistically, higher success on these goals is certainly associated with lower institutional control;[3] it occurs where intercommunication between girls, and with staff (see Chapter Six), is more easy and fluent; and it occurs where girls showed greater aspirations to become prefects (see Chapter Three), thereby showing that they value active social responsibility in their community and identification with it. Higher rated success on these ideal goals also relates to the presence of high levels of satisfaction among pupils of all ages in schools. High success did not have any relation with measures of school size, federal or centralist structure, proportion of boarders to day girls, size of sixth form, teacher–pupil ratios, average pupil's satisfaction, nor a number of other criteria.

Conclusion

There is no neat summary possible to this chapter. The question of goals is even more complex than it has been shown to be here. Different bodies of observers emphasize different goals. They do not do this from some neutral and uninfluenced baseline. What people say they think ought to happen is partly influenced by what they experience does happen. The success they rate on various goals is in turn partly affected by the extent to which they desire such goals.

We can say that staff and girls broadly differed on ideal goal priorities. They broadly agreed on what they actually saw happening. Girls implied far more shortcomings in actual achievement than did staff; and shortcomings were thought, both by girls and staff, to exist more in goals concerning the individual than with goals benefiting the school itself as an organization. On a criterion of what the majority of sixth-formers most want their schools to be doing, it was possible to identify the broadly 'good' and least good schools. These statistical judgements agreed sometimes with my judgement as to the good and the intermediate schools. No schools at the bottom of this 'normatively' good list appeared to me as good. Overall, however, there were many unique factors which altered the general trends of inference for particular schools. The whole question of what parents' goals may be has not been investigated. These may in future be partly influenced by the findings of this chapter.

Notes

1. Rank order correlation coefficients for relative prominence of fourteen goals.

	girls *say school:*			staff *say school:*	
	should try to	*does try to*	*actually succeeds*	*does try to*	*actually succeeds*
girls say school:					
does try to	0·21	1	—	0·68†	—
actually succeeds	0·20	0·84†	1	—	0·70†
staff say school:					
should try to	0·40	—	—	0·55*	0·37
does try to	—	0·68†	—	1	—
actually succeeds	—	—	0·70†	0·83†	1

* significant at 0·05 level
† significant at 0·01 level

2. Marks are given 1, 2, 3, respectively, for the responses 'hardly at all', 'medium' and 'very much'. Averages can be worked out per school, or for the whole number of girls, or of staff. An average score of 3·00 indicates

that that goal should be, or is achieved 'very much'. The minimum score is 1·00. The range through which scores can vary is 2·00 points, with a zero at 1·00. The means have been converted into 'percentage agreement' by subtracting 1, dividing by 2, and multiplying by 100.

3. Rank order correlation coefficients are respectively:

for: goals/institutional control,   0·36 (N = 22);
     /communication index,   0·46 (N = 18);
     /staff personal index,   0·53 (N = 18);
     /aspiration to be prefect, 0·36 (N = 22);
     /satisfaction,   0·57 (N = 22).

Three: Aspirations

We have seen something of what girls think schools should be doing, and how far they think these desired goals are reached. As a reminder, the 'top five ideal goals' were:

develop each person's *own* personality

get good exam results

prepare girls for jobs and careers

teach people to live together happily

enable girls to decide for themselves what is right and wrong

What do the girls themselves want to attain? Clearly, what they want to achieve (or not) in school may relate to what plans they have for their later lives. Schools themselves, by their selection of pupils and by the culture and traditions they each inherit and develop, may also influence what girls want to attain. We can see something in this chapter of the girls' aspirations, both for their school careers and afterwards. To study aspirations in school, girls were given a list of five 'things' one could excel at. This list closely resembled what was presented in boys' schools, so that comparisons can be made. Here are the five items:

outstanding at games

a leading prefect

good at art, music or drama

good at work, an outstanding scholar

very good at domestic science; highly capable at household skills

Girls were invited to put a tick down for their first choice, and another mark for their second choice. Items left alone thus ranked as equal third. A scoring system* enables us to look at the results in a convenient form. People were then asked, if they found nothing in

* Three marks for top choice, two for second, one for others, enables a mean score to be calculated for each item. The maximum is 3·00, minimum 1·00. These means have been converted to 'percentages' by the formula:

$$\text{per cent} = \frac{\text{Mean} - 1}{2} \times 100.$$

this that appealed to their ambitions, to write freely about how they did want to excel. Relatively few took up this opportunity, but one wrote:

I think they are a pretty poor lot to choose from and I think you ought to have things like getting on with people etc. (15)

Further ideas were collected from the continuation of incomplete sentences, such as 'when I am twenty . . .' and 'if only . . .'. These questions on aspirations were put to fourth-, fifth- and upper sixth-form girls. This is a wider group than those who answered the questions about goals. What then is the main burden of the statistical results?

Table 3·1. Relative strength of aspirations (expressed as a percentage choice) for five different topics (N = 1,264 girls)

aspiration	overall percentage choice	difference in percentage choice between top and lowest school
good at work	50·1	58·2
good at art, music or drama	46·9	45·6
very good at domestic science	23·6	39·6
outstanding at games	16·4	23·2
a leading prefect	9·4	15·1

The result is clearly in favour of work, with artistic abilities a close second. Very little desire to shine in authority is shown; nor are games popular. Why do girls want to excel at work? The reasons vary.

While I am at school my parents are having to pay out a large sum of money, so if I do not work hard I shall be wasting their money and my time. (13)

Elsewhere, it would seem to be the school which puts the emphasis on work:

The teachers' motto:
Slave, slave, slave, work, work, work, and do as you're told first time all the time. (13)

Many girls see their present immersion in work as a means to an end. The ends may be loosely or more clearly defined.

I would like to be good at work because you can get a lot farther in life if you are brainy. (11)

Be able to get a steady, well paid job . . . get more out of life, appreciate books, music etc. to their full value. (12)

I would like to be an outstanding scholar . . . because my father wants me to go to university, I want to live up to his expectations . (13)

. . . I live here so that I can get my 'O' and 'A' levels and so become an M.P. which is my ambition. I want to go to L.S.E. and take P.P.E. (13)

Four different reasons for devotion to their studies. An important factor in producing an emphasis on work is undoubtedly the school. For the school with the greatest interest in work (seventy-eight per cent choice) was very different from the school with least drive towards academic work (nineteen per cent choice). At the other end of the scale, there is also a difference between the school where people most want to be prefects and that where they least want to; but the difference is much smaller. We would be safer to think that wherever a girl goes to school is not likely to make such a difference about her desires to take up authority in a community. In this respect the pupils' acceptance of some traditional idea of feminine roles must make for different possibilities in running a boarding community than is the case for boys who may be more willing to take up authority roles. On the other hand, where a girl goes to school is likely to play a considerable part in determining her desire to excel at work.

I collected a lot of information about girls' backgrounds, and from this we can see that schools where there is a high aspiration to do well at work systematically show some associated characteristics.* Schools whose girls most want to excel at work tend to have client parents who themselves had less boarding experience (this is consistent with a pattern of 'upward social mobility').[1] Next, those schools where the parents had mostly themselves been boarders usually had a greater proportion of pupils who had been to preparatory (independent) schools;[2] schools whose pupil body had mostly started with independent preparatory schooling tended to have them show less ambition to excel at work.[3]

* Rank order correlation coefficients are respectively (for N = 20): (1) 0·57, (2) 0·79, (3) 0·48, for the relationships described.

This information is all consistent, and can be illustrated by some reference to the sample of schools. The group included a local authority, and a direct grant school, where girls would have had less prep school experience. These showed a relatively high ambition to do well at work, quite conscious of the relevance to bettering themselves. The schools with mostly fee-paying parents certainly included some with a heavy accent on work aspirations, especially where an Oxbridge tradition had existed or was being striven for. But there were also expensive schools whose girls showed more diverse interests, in arts especially, which reduced their choice available to show their ambitions at work. Finally, there were schools frankly calling themselves 'comprehensive' or 'for the less academic child', where the accents were shared between the arts and domestic science.

In the same statistical analysis* it also appears that schools with high work aspirations were those with higher institutional control (or less individual freedom within the rules, and provisions for privacy);[1] higher work aspirations occurred in schools where pupils said that boarding had a poor or detrimental effect on family relationships.[2] This link is an independent one; that is to say, it is not recognizable that higher institutional control is linked with a detrimental effect of boarding on family relationships.[3] Probably again the family relationship problems among the girls supported by a local authority were more frequent and severe; these are the girls who are striving to do well at work. They are not necessarily all at schools with high institutional control, but this latter factor also contributes to higher academic efforts. Finally, it also appears that high striving for work occurs in schools where girls say they are less happy.[4] This measure of girls' happiness seems to be a co-product of the poor rated effect of boarding on family relationships, and high institutional control.

Some further questions can be asked about academic aspirations. Are the girls who want to excel at work the older ones or those in the higher forms? Or are they the more 'brainy' girls as measured on two separate tests of abilities? Does higher work aspiration arise in schools where there is a larger sixth form, or a better teacher–pupil ratio, or even a better teacher to sixth-form-

* Rank order correlation coefficients are respectively (for N = 20): (1) 0·41, (2) 0·51, (3) 0·06, (4) 0·46.

size ratio? The answer in all these cases, for all practical purposes, is No. (More carefully, there are no grounds on which to say Yes.*)

An aspiration that does depend to some extent on age is the desire to excel at arts. When we examine this, we may see that a plausible explanation may lie in the different ways in which an individual can interact with the community at different ages. Let us also see what other things are associated with a preference to do well at arts, or what is related, to develop a more sophisticated sensitivity in an artistic mode. First, let us look at the connection with age.† The youngest girls seem keen on pop music, which appears to be an art form best appreciated in groups.

I like Pop Music . . . I try to appreciate some sort of good music i.e. Bach, Mozart, etc. but it is rather boring. (13)

The seeds of a later sophistication may exist at the earlier age; but younger girls have much less privacy, fewer occasions on which to embark on the private inner voyages into the realm of art. Such voyages as occur tend to be communal rather than private; and the realm into which they venture is probably not what they, as well as myself, would call that of 'art' as it is meant in this question. Sometimes there is group discouragement of one who violates the fashionable code; one girl tells us what the majority want:

I don't like pop music as such, e.g. cattawalling males, etc. But I like folk songs and rhythm and blues songs. Anyhow people don't listen to songs for the words, but just to hear the pop-idols. A sort of sex-symbol. (13)

Another younger girl shows what can happen to those who have atypical inclinations:

Music and poetry mean a great deal to me. In school the girls in general tend to regard poetry as a bore, and music as a bind. I *enjoy* both. Poetry (as painting) is something beautiful, something which I often write (I *am* considered 'funny' because of this, but I *don't care*). (14)

* Product moment correlation coefficients between work aspiration and age, and form: (-0.04, -0.01, $N = 1,173$); with tests: (0.07, 0.08, $N = 831$); rank order correlation coefficients with sixth-form size and both teacher-pupil ratios: (0.30, 0.03, -0.14, $N = 22$).

† Product moment correlation coefficients between art aspiration and age, and form: (0.17, 0.19, $N = 1,173$).

The effort to 'don't care' about what other people think and to underline it, is that which socially detaches those who want to develop a further aesthetic sensibility. They have to make space in their social relations for the enlargement and development of an inner world of perception. In this connection, those schools which are set in beautiful houses in large country sites often make use of these circumstances. Thus at one school with a classical hall and twin curved stone staircases, an impromptu evening performance of motets brought forth silent figures from doors and corridors who sat quietly to listen to an internal magic which was made more possible by the knowledge and feeling of the beauty and silence outside. These same girls were later capable of an explosive dormitory riot with screaming and lights flashing on and off that gave the impression of a *son et lumière* battle scene to a witness a quarter of a mile away.

The middle teens can bring a phase of eclecticism and experiment that can be one of the most exciting periods of discovery of a lifetime, and can affect the aesthetic and personality characteristics of the adult.

All music is fantastic, from Beethoven to the Stones. I adore the Classics, as well as folk music, such as Bob Dylan's. Pop music is also wonderful, and as all music betrays people's feelings, and can be used to show your own feelings, so it can. (14)

The opposite mood, of constriction, it should be said, can be found as well.

Self expression is good in a way, but it shouldn't be allowed too much, and should be controlled. I don't feel I know enough to be able to write anything about it. (14)

What happens to the potential love of arts, of creative expression? This depends a good deal on the school and the facilities it offers and the culture it fosters. In Table 3·1, we can see that there was a wide variation in response between the top and the bottom school, with regard to artistic aspirations therein. At one school high on the list, a matron took drama classes, and the head joined in the school orchestra; at another there was a tiny 'bijou' theatre, used for performances, and a special new room for guitars. At a third, there was excellent provision for pottery and girls who arrived knew that they would have to sign for it straightaway, if they were to get on the 'active' list two years later. There was also a sculpture teacher, and several part-time staff to teach musical instruments. Another school with high artistic intentions had methods of self-expression in all subjects explicitly embodied in its educational philosophy.

On the other hand, schools showing a lower interest in arts included one where the art rooms were locked, for administrative reasons, at week-ends; and one, with high institutional control, where the pattern of community supremacy over individual privacy persisted even for seniors:

There is no privacy because someone will always come and ask why you are not joining in with the rest of the people. There is no place where one can go, except out into the grounds but it looks rather peculiar if one person is out walking alone.   (16)

The achievement of artistic self-expression in the group arises in formal occasions such as with choirs, or in private enterprise. Seniors seem to have written nothing about group aesthetic experience (but younger girls have):

I remember . . . we went up to one of the music cubicals . . . and sang out of a Joan Baez song book. Played the harp too. I felt glad to be alive, glad that I came to this school. Made me feel wanted.   (14)

Later, the assistance that company can provide can explode through a 'sound barrier' to the greater need for privacy:

After exams I let myself go a bit by doing crazy things, like running across a pitch in my dressing gown . . . with friends and we all go mad together. It gets rid of the strain of working so hard during exam week!   (14)

Then, another girl:

I love all animals. Walking alone on warm nights. Enjoying life even the sad bits.   (14)

Art can then be used as a medium of working through and out of trouble.

If I had any worries . . . I would . . . probably go and write something to get the whole emotion out. Hence the vast amount of poetry I write at school.   (17)

It is not a general rule that walking alone and writing poetry occur most among the girls who say they want to excel at arts. But it does seem more likely to occur with this aspiration than, for example, with those concerned with work, being a prefect or games. Further, we can hear girls describe how organizational factors associated with being a prefect or promoting exam work sometimes clash with the artistic world.

Every privilege which this school gives . . . is a reward for authority . . . work in art, music, drama, has no honour, no recognition.   (16)

In the previous chapter I mentioned the report of a headmistress who disapproved of acting, but who rammed music down the girls' throats. Thus there are many circumstances which cut across the association of age with an interest in artistic expression. It is important to note that the aesthetic goal has served two related purposes. It has provided the individual with a private world in the crowded community, one where meaning and emotional reference is quite personal (only with a very close friend could a girl reach understanding in sharing an aesthetic experience); secondly, the art has been given a personal symbolism, becoming a language private to the individual. Music is no longer, as for the younger girls, like a biochemical stimulant, or a social solvent like alcohol; it is now a psychological medium by which the individual communes with whatever world she has herself chosen. This aspiration is thus the chief one of the five offered which is not restricted to the school scene. It offers a 'psychological window' connecting with another realm of experience and emotion.

Music to me means home, freedom, beauty, especially jazz. I love it, its also romantic and seductive, I like to listen and relax and forget about work here and school life.   (16)

These remarks may not apply so strongly in the case of drama, which is a social art. One should mention also, that 'Pop' is manifest as music, when it clearly appeals more to the smaller girls; but it is also manifest visually, as posters or pictures of more or less 'psychedelic' sparks and hairstyles which suggest that electrostatic storms are sweeping the brains of their owners. This visual pop scene is favoured by older girls who can work quietly while looking the other way, as these pictures scream silently behind.

We know that artistic aspirations are systematically associated with a variety of other conditions.* Schools in which there is a higher level of artistic ambition also tend to show the lowest institutional control;[1] they tend to have pupils who are more ready to discuss their personal problems with somebody in the community;[2] and who are daughters of parents who themselves had had more boarding education.[3] The schools with greater artistic aspirations tended to be those whose pupils had mostly been to preparatory schools[4] (remember, the others were focusing on academic work), and thus they showed less desire to excel academically.[5] Finally, schools with higher recorded artistic aspirations also contained on the whole happier pupils.[6]

We know that desire to do well academically showed no link with doing well on tests, but artistic aspirations were slightly (though significantly)† linked with good performance on a test of imaginative fluency.

The wish to do well at domestic science is socially benign, and in this sense similar to the artistic urge, but without quite the same individualistic (non-competitive) overtones. Domestic science comes a comfortable third in demand, but in relation to its overall popularity there are rather wide differences between schools. Few girls have written anything of note about domestic science ambitions, except as an afterthought to something else:

I would like to be good at *sculpture* and *art* because that is my ambition ... I can't think of anything that would prevent me from getting where I want to except that I am rather stupid. I would like to be a good cook because I hope to be a successful housewife.   (13)

Preference for skill at domestic science‡ is clearly associated with the smaller boarding schools. These usually lack the financial resources to support good science departments, and they tend to cater for less bright girls; this is shown by a link between high domestic science aspirations and low scores on both the tests given. Also, this

* Rank order correlation coefficients between level of artistic aspiration and the following six variables in order are respectively: (1) 0·52, (2) 0·40, (3) 0·68, (4) 0·54, (5) –0·47, (6) 0·52 (N = 22).

† Product moment correlation coefficient: 0·14 (N = 840).

‡ Rank order correlation coefficients between domestic science and boarding size, and two tests are: –0·51, –0·40, and –0·68, respectively; with sixth form proportional size: –0·37 (N = 20).

preference usually occurs in schools with the smallest proportional sixth forms. This may be thought obvious, but is not necessarily so. In a smaller school with a smaller sixth form, it would be easier to become a prefect. But this form of aspiration, or that for excellence at games, does not appear as the third choice, or as the preferred *métier* of many girls in the smaller schools. There is some small sign that in all the schools, large and academic ones included, there is a tendency for greater domestic science preference to be found among younger girls.* This is doubtless because it is the plausible choice for those who are not likely to stay on into academic sixth forms.

We come now to the aspirations to be a prefect and to excel at games. These are fields of excellence involving competition or dominance over others (rather than in the first place against an objective standard, as with academic work). Notably, both these ideals are low in popularity, nor is there any great variation between different schools. The youngest girls, for a start, accept their mischievous norms, and write nothing about wanting to become prefects.

I would try and dodge being a prefect.   (13)
If I became a prefect which I hope I won't because it might turn me into a snob but if I was I would smuggle tuck . . . and argue with the staff to do desent things for a change.   (12)

Older girls also are often not comfortable in the prefect's role; enough of them do not aim for this place in authority, so that we find that at any age the chances of wanting to excel in authority are equal† and small.

There is too much emphasis on sixth form running the school, setting a good example, and supervising, especially in the house.   (17)

There are also in several schools incongruous situations devised for those who have to officer the community.

. . . there isn't much time to think because when your not keeping the dormitory under control, you have to catch up on sleep missed because of the necessity of getting up at 5 o'clock in the morning to sit in a cold bathroom to work because of the ridiculously early hour the seniors have to go to bed.   (16)

* Product moment correlation coefficient: -0.16 (N = 1,173).
† Product moment correlation coefficient: 0.04 (N = 1,173).

Some schools, particularly where an effort is being made to raise academic levels, have created 'student status' for those who would otherwise be senior prefects. These girls get more privileges, have more opportunity to work harder and stand outside many of the rules. The lower sixth prefects then complain sometimes that their authority is let down by the upper sixth students giving a bad example. In spite of many circumstances making the prefects' lot unenviable, some girls accept it:

If I see any [infringement] I will say or do something about it and not turn a blind eye. If everyone turned a blind eye no one would ever improve or find themselves.   (17)

The schools in which a noticeable number of girls want to take up responsibility show certain other related facts.* There is a greater willingness to talk to staff about personal problems (not just to anybody, but particularly to staff);[1] these schools contain fewer rebellious and more compliant girls (see Chapter Five);[2] the schools are rated as succeeding better on the top five ideal goals,[3] and the girls are happier.[4] In all, this presents a picture of a community pulling together. Notably, there was no link whatsoever between desire to become a prefect and primary schooling as a boarder[5] or in an independent preparatory school.[6] A theory has been put forward elsewhere for boys' preparatory boarding, that this training in the boarding system and its ethos prepares boys even before the senior school to accept the system and perpetuate it. No evidence is found here to support this pattern amongst the girls. Many have been to preparatory schools, even as boarders, though few want to become prefects. Those who do want to become prefects show no sign of coming more, or less, from the ranks of those with preparatory 'training' for the system.† There is some very slight evidence‡ that girls who want to become prefects tend to score better on a test of verbal problem-solving. It is just possible that this skill is allied to the social skills needed in a prefect and this may explain the link.

* Rank order correlation coefficients are: (1) 0·69, (2) 0·39, (3) 0·36, (4) 0·37, (5) —0·17, (6) —0·13 (N = 22).

† Product moment correlations between aspiration to be a prefect and previous boarding experience (—0·04), and previous preparatory experience (–0·03) (N = 1,172).

‡ Product moment correlation coefficient: 0·1 (N = 830).

There is an interesting absence of a relationship that could have existed, and might well have been expected, but did not materialize. Heads were asked to rate girls on two scales; one scale showed how much a girl gives to the community ('is a useful member of the school'). Would girls who said they wanted to be prefects (and who on other measures were seen to approve the school and perhaps communicate well with staff) be rated by heads as better contributors to the school society? This was not so.* Possibly heads gave better ratings to girls who were at the moment feeling rebellious, banking on their often repeated observation that the more 'spirited' younger girls often turned out later to be good supporters of the establishment.

So far we have examined aspirations within the school sphere. What do girls want to do afterwards, and can any of their present aspirations be related to future ambitions?

Aspirations for the Future

It will be easier to understand some of the following quotations if it is remembered that several methods were used to collect them. One, mentioned already, involves completing a half-sentence; another approach was to ask girls to look back on their lives, and describe what was likely to have happened, or what they would have liked to happen.

Though there has been no counting of proportions, and though results of this type of inquiry are notoriously vulnerable to subtle effects put across in the first place by the investigators, it seems as if girls looked ahead to a bright young adulthood, followed by secure marriage, children and work. Careers and professions seemed less common as a central focus; instead, 'good jobs' seemed to be the kind of thing that would finance the gay pre-marital years, and thereafter serve for part-time or temporary occupation. There were some signs of fear of the future, but for the most part the views seem secure enough.

When I am twenty five . . . I never want to be 25 because I want to stay my own age.   (11)
When I am Twenty five I am going . . . to another country with my

* Product moment correlation coefficient: -0.09 (N = 668).

father as I am not going to get married. My sisters will get married, but I am going to look after Daddy. (13)

Most writers suggest no altruism, but the idea of marriage.

When I am twenty five I will most properly get married. (13)

Proper ideas seem to include some that may have included jibes at myself (frequently a five-o'clock-shadowed investigator).

When I am twenty five I shall make sure my husband shaves propally under his chin. (13)

Occasionally, some worries, ranging from the global to the personal, are shown.

When I am twenty-five, the world will be completely different and may not exsite at all. (13)
Nowadays I have begun to worry about my future carrier. (13)

We can see that the ideas of marriage, and of some future career, exist strongly even amongst the youngest girls; this reflects back on the previous chapter and a half, on the goals and aspirations dealing with work, careers, preparation for personal development and the skills of living together.

The range of careers envisaged is wide and susceptible to fantasy and self-doubt.

When I am twenty, I hope to be a famous ballerina, and married. (13)

No further worlds to conquer! Someone with smaller vistas says:

When I am twenty five I will be sure to be just as horsemad, cat mad, rabbit mad and dog mad as I already am. (13)

But the 'sensible solution' is expressed by another girl writing:

When I am thirty I hope to have joined the R.S.P.C.A., and to be some kind of animal worker and have married a man who is a farmer. I hope to have had my first child. (13)

Most of the writings mentioned little about husbands, who seemed at this stage to be unspecified in detailed requirements; little detail was also sketched in about children. These, as animals, are perhaps written about as objects to nurture, with the focus being on the writer's own needs. Possibly this lack of plan about others represents a commendable state of open-mindedness. In a few schools, some more extravagant flights of fancy were produced. One school had artistic and exotic norms (or abnorms?) for behaviour.

When I am twenty I shall know French, Italian, Spanish and German fluently, this is an age when I would like to start learning Chinese, that is my lifelong ambition. I shall also think about catching a millionaire to marry.

But when I am twenty five I shall have married, had two children and I shall emigrate to China, perhaps become a Communist (though I don't agree with the principal) and learn more about that mysterious country. (13)

So much for Chairman Mao. That extract has the ring of a Rose Macaulay, with the comfortable omnipotence that can be bred in an unruffled English mansion, which considers foreign people and places as queer and fascinating, to be viewed and perhaps visited and collected as mementoes for retelling. At another school, a similar assurance was met.

Went to Oxford, where she got a 1st class degree. Had an affair with HRH Prince of Wales at Cambridge (but did not marry him as she was unsuitable). Was the first woman to swim the frozen Arctic. Came back to Britain for the Miss World 1999 – she won it. Married a millionaire, but dies in poverty, after trying to commit suicide. (15)

A second extract, written in the same school, provides a further divergent outlook.

. . . School did not do much for her except give her a variety of complexes and teach her a lot. . . . She left University . . . after some months she decided to buy a horse and ride round the world. She spent five years doing this and paid her way round and also killed off 18 horses in doing various things like chasing the Abominable Snowman off Mount Everest, trying to persuade it to come underwater swimming. . . . She had several dangerous adventures and spent time in the harem of the King of —! [author's own blank]. . . . She had learned to lassoo in Patagonia and then . . . with a party of head hunters . . . lassooed them all in one lassoo, suspended them all from a tree and proceeded to ask them about the art of head hunting. (16)

This last section may be an intended parody of the research; curiously enough, a story in an old girls' book at another school does tell of one of the old pupils who learned lassooing in Patagonia, though without the other adventures attached. The girl above's school was one where even the seniors experienced great restraints on their access to the outer world. Their escape may then be devised inwards, so that an extravagant story can be put together in five minutes in a crowded classroom. The point concerns not the 'actual ambitions' implied above, but the agile familiarity within the world of fantasy.

Though it is of interest to examine the 'further out' gleanings, the mass of ideas was more prosaic. Among the older girls there was often a practical and realistic concern about careers.

When you get into the VIth form your worries become very big and by that time the biggest worry is what I am going to do when I leave school because I don't know and nobody can give me any good suggestions. (16)

This is not an isolated view. The chapter on goals suggests a widespread feeling of shortcoming in this area, and at another school one girl explains:

Here there is no one except the headmistress to deal with problems concerning careers. There should be someone to advise us. Practically everyone applies for University without any idea of what career they will follow once they have left there. This is a great worry to many people and there is no solution to it. (17)

At least at one school the apparent determination to improve the success ratio at A-levels seems to involve discouraging the participation of a few of the weaker candidates. They may then have to transfer to another school (they exist) which is less careful of this particular index of its reputation.

The more thoughtful girls see clearly that they have some ideas about what they would like to do and be in later life, and their ideas are implied in the formulations on goals and aspirations we have already seen.

When she left school she went to a domestic college and then took a course in beauty culture . . . worked as a beautician in London, later opening up a beauty salon of her own. She met a lot of famous people and then married a farmer. . . . She had eight children varying largely in ages. (16)

Glamour, useful, flexible work, then stable marriage; these are the ingredients carried to an extreme above, or stated more modestly, in a much freer school:

When I am twenty five, I hope to be married with children but to have gained a wide knowledge of life first – having had a respectable profession for three or so years.   (15)

There is some possibility of a 'pressure cooker' effect, of the school with high institutional control evoking more extreme post-school ideas than the relaxed school. But at a school where the social control was low, though the intellectual atmosphere relatively demanding, a most thoughtful and inventive view combined a girl's ideas of how she could use her school experience in furthering her future hopes, and with this I close the chapter.

A public boarding school for girls isn't too bad a place for someone, who wants to be an actress, to grow up. Of course there would be advantages in going to a day school and living at home – one would come into contact with more varied characters and social classes of grown-ups & also not just girls of ones own age. But one can catch up on these sorts of things during the holidays, & I think it is useful to have a general knowledge of human behaviour – which you can get just as well from a single-sex society before going on to details of characterisation. And besides at the age at which one comes here one is picking up most of what one knows about lovers and sex-motivated behaviour from books anyway. Living in a boarding school one learns not only to live with people – to deal with people – to be a peacemaker during lessons . . . but more than all this you learn to be independent & you learn to know what's going on inside people's minds.

It is, to my mind, vitally important for an actress to be able to walk into a crowded room unafraid, to be able to hold her own in a quarrell, to know something of the powers and arguments of logic, to be detached, to be open minded, to be able to observe without relating it *all* to herself. It is no good getting type cast in character; actors in their profession as well as in private life have to have as full personalities as possible & going to a boarding school, if you're that type of person & the school's like this one, can help.   (15)

Four: Happiness and Success in Schools

Many people will feel that it is dull, perhaps even sacrilegious, and certainly grimly lacking in sensitivity, to trap a blithe and free thing like happiness down in a statistical net. It will seem rather like pinning dead butterflies into narrow and polished drawers. Yet it is not happiness itself that is being dealt with in this way; rather it is the numbers of those who are happy. If it would make one any happier, I could write this as a chapter on unhappiness, about which few would mind a statistical mesh. However, I feel more positive in treating the extent of happiness.

Happiness is the chief short-term criterion which I think should be applied to evaluating the pupils' sojourn in the school. But as others will raise the questions of academic and social training (basically: 'Did she pass her O- or A-levels?' and 'Is she now a lady?'), two other criteria are applied. These arise from head-mistresses' ratings of pupils on two scales, which will be explained later. It is quite possible that still further criteria will be found missing by some critics. Why ask about expectations, hopes, goals and the rest, if one does not establish how all these relate to some useful result, say that of girls becoming integrated citizens in a 'social mix', able and inclined to climb down from the cliff of privilege on which life has arranged for some of them to be born? These, and other questions, are not to be dealt with directly in this book. There may be some material in the next chapter which tries to describe some of the nature and quality of daily life in schools, to satisfy further curiosity in this area.

We must now consider what happens to all the hopes and expectations dealt with in the previous chapters. The first step was to get the great majority of girls encountered to answer the following question:

Do you enjoy being at school? on the whole, yes
                                mixed feelings
                                on the whole, not so much

Each girl ticked the answer most appropriate to her feelings. I now assume, from the similarity of the terms 'enjoy being' and 'happiness', that we can talk about the results in terms of levels and occurrence of happiness. We shall see that happiness varies in a large variety of circumstances. It will not be proper to attribute causal explanations always with certainty, but we will be in a better position to think about these after examining the statistics. In any case, when reading the descriptive material later on, it is essential to bear in mind the statistics of happiness and success, of how many do in fact say they are unhappy or happy.

I must point out, partly as a 'political' move, lest the schools feel that I was going round canvassing unhappiness, that the 'bad' alternative is moderately worded. It will net all those who feel genuinely unhappy and are eager to make this fact known; but it may also get a few responses from girls who might otherwise shy away from saying outright that they are unhappy. The effect will be to emphasize the amount of what I shall call 'unhappiness' (i.e. enjoy school . . . not so much). This is, paradoxically, under the guise of being mild, loading the scales on the negative side.

What are the levels of happiness among different parts of the population?[1]

Table 4·1. Happiness of girls expressed as a percentage among boarders and day girls of different ages

age	12 and under	13	14	15	16	17 and over	total girls
boarders	70·5	61·5	55·5	52·5	62·5	62·5	917
day girls	69·0	74·5	67·0	56·0	61·0	55·5	302

If every girl in any group said she was happy, the 'percentage' would appear as 100. A percentage of fifty means that as many are unhappy as happy, while some are non-committal. So we can see fairly clearly that the youngest girls are happiest. The novelty or the ability to enjoy school soon reduces – somewhat later for the day girls – and the nadir is reached for those aged 15. Three possible groups of causes can be put forward to explain this low point of happiness at this age. Two causes concern girls themselves, namely, the developmental change affecting nearly every phase of her existence, in making a woman from a child; and the relationship between the individual and the mass media, which exploit the emotional turmoil by a variety of products to satisfy needs which a girl may take time to evaluate and bring under her own control. The third possible cause is that in many schools, up to the age of 15, not much extra privilege and freedom is offered over that available to a 13-year-old; many may chafe against this, especially those who are not going to remain on in the sixth forms, and emerge into the realms of relative school privilege and candidacy for future 'honours' of university entrance. Also at 15, in some schools girls may find themselves in positions of minor authority, able and required to control and punish the younger girls if need be, but are also themselves liable for punishment, and can be seen, by their dormitory juniors for instance, weeding flower beds or whatever, for their own infringements. This 'role conflict' can add to the awkwardness of the middle-school years.

At 16 and over, satisfaction seems to increase. Perhaps four elements contribute to this situation. Many less academically capable girls, who were not going to get high exam rewards out of their school careers, will have left. The remaining seniors now find a situation of somewhat greater freedom and privilege (not in all schools – there is a great range in this matter). Many seniors stay on for academic reasons, and at some schools, where organizational duties do not intrude, the situation is geared to allow the best opportunities possible for girls to get on with their work. Finally, seniors are more mature, and perhaps more able to look to deferred instead of immediate gratification of their emotional needs. This places them less at the mercy of the entertainment media which set out to whet girls' appetites for boys. The seniors have different problems with their boy-friends, whom some of them miss, but apparently this does not have the effect of making them less happy overall than the 15-year-olds.

At some ages (13–15) day girls are happier than boarders in school. But at 12 or under, and at 16 or over, day girls are less happy than boarders. What is the overall result of this?

Table 4·2. Happiness in school of day girls and boarders

	day girls	boarders
number of girls	416	1,332
enjoy school (per cent)	44	37
mixed feelings (per cent)	39	42
enjoy it, not so much (per cent)	16	21

The day girls include significantly more who are happy[2] than do boarders. Remember that the schools in the sample included six which were mainly day schools. From these, equal numbers of day girls as boarders were studied. Seventeen schools were either mainly-boarding or boarding-only. Thus we would expect the social structures of the majority of schools here to cater principally for boarders, with perhaps day girls feeling 'left out'. There is some evidence of this in some schools, where day girls say that boarders keep their secrets, and don't let day girls into their circles of friends. However, overall there is no escaping the fact that day girls are more inclined to say they are happy than boarders. One factor may contribute to this: some girls are boarders because they are considered to need to be away from home (loss of parents, travel, broken families). Many of these girls are not likely to say they are happy. It is not known how much this single factor contributes to the observed difference in happiness from day girls.

What other factors, apart from age or boarding status, can we see as linked to levels of happiness? And are there factors which one might expect to associate with levels of happiness, but which do not do so? One way of looking at these questions was to calculate the levels of happiness recorded in each school, and arrange them in rank order. Are all schools similarly happy? Certainly not. The highest score was seventy-nine per cent and the lowest 39·4 per cent. There were seven schools out of twenty-three where the level was below fifty per cent. This means that more girls were unhappy in them than happy. These facts will doubtless be seen as suiting their case by both proponents and opponents of boarding. They will both be helped to decide by considering some further facts.

I noted which schools were visited during summer terms (s), and which in the winter and spring terms (w). By means of a statistical test[3] we can see that the level of happiness tended to be better in the s than in the w schools. This is a plausible result. Despite anxiety in the time leading up to summer exams, the weather allows girls to go out then, and they get more freedom of movement than when they are cooped up in winter. It may be a coincidence that this result was found, or it may also include an element of the researcher's own morale, improved in summer and reflected in happier classroom sessions with the girls. At any rate it illustrates that one must take care in attributing the causes of results one finds.

Visiting season was also associated with an index of communication fluency (see Chapter Seven), but with nothing else. Was satisfaction significantly related to the level of institutional control, as suggested by our explanation for happier summers? It was,[4] and this means that the more lenient schools produced the happier responses. Was it by accident that I had visited more lenient schools in the summer, thereby producing the 'summer happiness' as an accidental result? No; there was no correlation between season of visit and institutional control. We are left to conclude that organizational control affects happiness, and so does season of year.

With what else was satisfaction associated? Two indices of whether girls would consult others about their personal problems were related to satisfaction – where there is more happiness they are more ready to discuss their problems. In particular, however, happiness was linked to what girls felt about their home backgrounds and relationships (see Chapter Six).[5] Where girls tended to say that boarding had a good effect on family relationships, they were happier. It is important to be careful not to infer from this a direct chain of cause and effect. However, if a school is less severe in its control it is more likely to contain happy girls who say that boarding has a good effect on their family relations. But this is not all. There are other chains of cause and effect which cut across this. One is that schools with smaller boarding communities (with a very few outstanding exceptions) tended to be happier.[6] These schools with smaller boarding communities did not necessarily imply more lenient regimes. Thus a small school (of boarders) might be more likely to be happy, whether severe or not; a lenient school might be more happy, whether large or small. The effect that girls think boarding has on their family relationships is independent of the size of the school, or of the severity of its control. There are, however, some very slight (but significant) indications that, where individual girls are happier in their relations with their family members (with mother, father, brothers, sisters, in that order),[7] they are also happier in school.

There appear to be no systematic links between any one of the circumstances A to D, and any of the others. They seem to contribute independently to helping girls to be happy as boarders. We can guess what would happen to the happiness of a girl from an unhappy family who went to a large and severe school; however,

D

if she went to a small but severe school, or to a larger but lenient one, it is much harder to predict.

This whole complex situation can be summed up in this diagram.

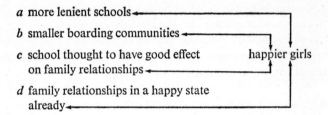

a more lenient schools

b smaller boarding communities

c school thought to have good effect on family relationships   happier girls

d family relationships in a happy state already

We also know that happier schools tended to be ones where there was a higher level of aspiration to excel at arts, a lower drive to do well at work and exams, a greater feeling that the school was succeeding in attaining the five ideal goals, and even a slightly higher desire to become a prefect.[8] Happier schools also tended to be ones where more of the pupils had an independent preparatory school experience, but not where they had any more, or less preparatory boarding experience.[9]

So far we have been discussing what characteristics are associated with the happier schools. A different type of analysis is necessary to look for what betokens a happier girl. Of course, by definition, a happier girl is more likely to be found in a happier school. But as Table 4·1 suggests, there are large numbers of girls who are not all that happy, even in the happiest schools. There is very little evidence to link levels of individual happiness with previous individual educational experience, with tested ability or with different aspirations. There was a small connection between the girls' own feelings of happiness and two ways in which headmistresses rated each girl. These two ratings form the other criteria of success, and were defined as shown on page 99.

The happier girls (by their own rating) tended to be rated by heads as better at fitting in socially, and in making the best of academic opportunities.[10] This is a straightforward finding that, where a positive person is encountered, signs of her satisfactory position in society are clear to others as well as to herself.

Rating A. 'Fitting in socially'

1. Is (and always has been) a really useful member of the school, has never worked against the stream. Makes a great contribution.
2. On the whole is a useful member of the school, though occasionally has shown bad patches.
3. Is neither a great help nor a hindrance to the life of the school.

4. Seems not to have identified usefully with the life of the school at all.

5. Is (or has been) a really difficult member of the school.

Rating B. Making the best of her academic opportunities

1. Has made the very best of the teaching and academic facilities available to her to develop her academic performance.

2. Has used the teaching and academic facilities here quite well.

3. Has not concentrated on trying to develop academically though she has not squandered her time or opportunities.

4. Has wasted opportunities to develop academically, through interests elsewhere, lack of time or negative reasons.

5. Has neglected every opportunity provided to develop her academic abilities and performance.

We have seen something of how many girls feel happy or not. What do heads indicate about how the girls are doing?

There is a tendency for girls to be thought of as making better use of academic facilities ('taking') than they are of fitting in socially ('giving'). Furthermore, day girls are thought to make just as good use of academic facilities as boarders. (There is no statistical difference between the two subgroups.) It is sometimes said for boarding that it allows boarders to make more efficient academic use of their time. This has not emerged as it might be expected to have done. It may, however, be said by heads that they rated day girls on their effective use of time *while in school*. As the boarders spend more time in school, their overall benefit might still be argued to be higher than that of day girls without this showing in this particular form of rating. There is no doubt, however, that heads appear to think, overall, that day girls include more outstanding contributors to the community than do boarders. If we lower our standards of comparison, heads give as many ratings above 'good' to boarders as to day girls. It should be noted that heads do not notice distinctly more or fewer rebels among day girls, or among boarders; the difference occurs among the 'pillars of the establishment'.

Tables 4·3. Headmistresses' ratings of day girls and of boarders

percentages rated as follows:

| | *fitting in socially*[11] | | *making best of academic opportunities*[11] | |
	day girls	*boarders*	*day girls*	*boarders*
best 1	33	22	38	37
2	33	40	42	42
3	26	28	12	12
4	6	6	8	9
worst 5	3	4	0	0
total of girls	192	701	192	698

It might be that more results were collected about day girls proportionately during summer visits or that the day girls represented some other disproportion of ages, or whatever characteristics, compared with boarders. These possibilities have been examined and ruled out. The conclusion is clear, that day girls include more who are happier, and more who are rated as pillars of the establishment. They do not, however, get rated as making better (or worse) use of the academic facilities.

What else may we find associated with individual happiness? One thing I looked at was possible effects linked with kinds of Christian name. The majority of girls have nicknames it seems. Do those who do not state their nicknames either have such nasty ones, or in not having any indicate that they are not socially well accepted, and would they include more unhappy girls? The figures show no sign of this. One reason is that it is not really possible to judge whether a nickname which a girl acknowledges is felt to be nice or nasty. A girl who may be called 'Flea' might find this pleasant and affectionate, or stinging and hurtful, depending on who uses the nickname and how.

What about rareness of names? I examined the results from fourteen schools, dividing them into a severe, and a lenient subgrouping. The level of happiness indicated by girls with unique names in their age group was worked out, and compared with the level of happiness among girls with more common names. Commoner names were Susan, Elizabeth and Jane; rarer names included ones like Camilla and Anthea. Over all ages, boarders were equally happy whatever the commonness of their names. However, day girls with rare names seemed to include more who were happy than day girls with commoner names.[12] Day girls are arguably in the most 'lenient' situation compared with boarders. Would boarders with rare names be happier in lenient schools, with rarity of name making no difference in strict communities? There was no sign of this. Instead, there is an age difference to be found. This is very small, but occurs among boarders and day girls, in severe and lenient schools. This shows that while girls of 15 and younger are no more or less happy, however rare their names, for girls of 16 and over, possession of a rarer name is somewhat likely to indicate a happier girl.[13] The interpretation one might offer is that, where individuality is more important to a girl, or some evidence or feeling of detachment from the community is wanted (as among senior girls of any kind, or possibly among day girls), a unique name is a categoric sign of this independence.

We have seen several factors which contribute to affecting individual happiness, and the level of happiness within the school. The next chapter will contain many examples which will typify trends explained above. Equally important, there will be things people have written which do not stand for the overall or typical situation. It is particularly valuable to hear these atypical feelings and views but it is equally important to be able to know just how generally they apply.

Notes

1. As before, happiness is rated on a 3-point scale, on which the range of the mean can be from 1·00 (happy) to 3·00 (unhappy). This has been converted into a 'percentage' by this formula:

$$\text{percentage} = 100\left((1 - \frac{(x-1)}{2}\right)$$

where x is the 'mean happiness' score. This means that a school where the mean score was 2·00, made up all of non-committal replies, would get the same result as one where the population was evenly split between outright happiness and unhappiness. This would be blurring an important social reality between a humdrum and a 'two camps' situation. In fact no such bipolarity occurred.

2. Chi Sq. $= 9·34$, for $df = 2$ significant at 0·01 level.
3. By a Mann-Whitney test, $U = 29$ for $N = 7 + 16$, and $p < 0·05$.
4. rho $= 0·64$ significant at 0·01 level.
5. rho $= 0·45$ significant at 0·05 level.
6. rho $= -0·87$ significant at 0·01 level.
7. r for satisfaction and good relationships with mother, father, brothers, sisters, respectively (Ns in brackets) 0·17 (1,303), 0·15 (1,271), 0·13 (902), 0·08 (778).
8. rho $=$ (respectively) 0·52, $-0·46$, 0·57, 0·39.
9. rho $=$ (respectively) 0·48, 0·21.
10. $r = 0·18$, 0·15 ($N = 705$ in both cases), respectively.
11. For fitting in socially, Chi Sq. $= 9·65$ which for $df = 4$ gives $p < 0·05$; for making the best of academic opportunities, Chi Sq. $= 1·43$, not significant.

12.

rare names (one only)		*commoner names (two or more)*	
happy (per cent)	54·8	43·2	Chi Sq. $= 4·02$, for $N = 296$
other (per cent)	45·1	56·9	day girls $p < 0·05$

13.

rare names (one only)		*commoner names (two or more)*	
happy (per cent)	49·5	50·6	Chi Sq. $= 4·70$, for $N = 405$
other (per cent)	38·9	61·1	girls $p < 0·05$
			aged 16 or over (both boarding and day)

Five: School Life: Arrival and Formal Social Control

Introduction

By now any reader might justifiably be impatient and say, 'Yes, yes, but what's it really *like*?' This invites some account of the quality of life to be found in the schools. First, and crucial to understanding the validity of this chapter, one must realize that there is no one 'it', or single nature of life in school. There were twenty-three different schools and over 1,500 girls from whom information was collected, so there are that many different realities of the school regime. This is not to say that some general resemblances do not exist. The preceding chapters have been preoccupied with these patterns.

We come now to look at the variety of individual experience in the schools visited. Extracts from the girls' writings will be quoted to try and illustrate points all along this spectrum of sensibility. It will not be right to suppose from separate examples that they represent a general rule of what happens. Where possible, it may be pointed out that certain types of situation exist commonly; this is especially possible in the sections of this chapter which deal with aspects of social structure. But we are not going to deal here with systematic relative comparisons of what kinds of structure or event are more, or less, widespread. It must be understood that this chapter (and the next one) tries to represent relative qualities, rather than relative quantities of kinds of situation and experience.

I will start with some account of the experiences girls have described of their arrival at school, and how they became enjoined in the life there. Where a school has, or tries to have, a certain way of life, it will clearly help to continue this if newcomers either already know about this life style, or may be readily incorporated into it by some process which quickly instils knowledge of the relevant rules and attitudes expected among the pupils. Next comes the topic of 'social control'. This is subdivided into two sections. 'Intra-formal social control' considers the aspects of life about whose nature the prospectus or school rules of the 'formal system' does not legislate.

This in practice refers to how the society of the girls makes itself a reality of which the individual girl has to take note. Girls may regulate what attitudes, tastes and actions are popular, or unpopular and more difficult to get away with, with regard to other girls, or to their views on life in general. Girls may also 'informally' help to regulate attitudes towards the formal system, for instance by setting a mode as to how much mischief is to be admired and what the limits should be.

But before the more subtle question of intra-formal social control, which will be dealt with in the next chapter, comes that of formal social control. This will examine ways in which the schools 'officially' arrange for pupils to behave. They do this by rules which are publicly made known by the leadership of the staff and by providing material and social circumstances which make a certain range of behaviour more possible and other actions more difficult.

The studies on boys' boarding schooling have looked into what have been called 'instrumental control, expressive control and organizational control'. I consider that the English language, because it is not inflected, allows ambiguous expressions to be coined very easily. Thus 'instrumental control' might possibly mean 'a type of control which we shall call instrumental', which conjures up views of staff using 'instruments' like racks, perhaps, or canes, sticks or even carrots, somehow to control behaviour. However, 'instrumental control' may also mean 'control (of an unspecified kind) over some area of function we can call instrumental'. This is, I believe, the sense in which the phrase has been used. It boils down to 'control over instrumental functions', which is a curious phrase. An example which might be given of 'instrumental functions', i.e. those which directly serve other goals rather than being a goal in themselves, is that of exams. Now, 'instrumental control', as one might apply the term in the case of exams, does not refer to control *of* the exams, for example by invigilators or time limits; it means the use of the institution of exams 'instrumentally' in order to serve other ends. In other words, 'instrumental control' seems a phrase which repeats the same idea twice. This is what is known as pleonasm.

'Expressive controls' would seem to mean 'controls which serve to regulate areas of function which are undertaken as ends in themselves'. Thus controls of this sort – for instance, the decision that prayers will occupy so much time per day – are regulations which are themselves 'instrumental' in promoting 'expressive', or essentially short-term goals. Following these lines of reasoning, it has not been easy for me to distinguish 'instrumental, expressive and organizational', either as analytic categories, or for that matter as distinct types of phenomena into which I could group observed aspects of structure or function. It has seemed to me that it might be more important to note that in boarding-school life, every part of it has *some* instrumental, expressive and organizational aspects interdependently mixed. It might be possible to define those notions, somewhat as was done for grouping the types of goals in Chapter Three, and to get pupils and staff to rate the instrumental, etc., content of various aspects of school life. This has not been done here. Thus two schools might have exactly the same amount of time spent on prayers; while at one the members might assess the situation as primarily organizational, with expressive aspects of secondary importance, the other school might feel the other way around, that the expressive aspects are more salient. The matter is really one for the people on the spot to judge, rather than a visitor, however well trained he is.

I have tried to explain my position on these matters, as some sociologists may wonder why the examples and situations which follow have not been analysed according to the above conceptions. If, in fact, these three categories are clear and distinct, the material should fairly easily fall into place without this having to be under-lined; otherwise, it seems to imply that importance should be given to the view that phenomena are more validly to be understood as parts of a unitary whole, than of a tripartite scheme of things. Readers may care to choose the framework in which they prefer to see the matter.

Arrival and the Daily Round

For some girls, their career in secondary boarding school begins before they arrive. They may have been to preparatory boarding, which will prepare them for being away from home; they will most likely come from families which were of, or have reached, middle-class financial positions, which will prepare them for many atti-tudes they may meet in their schools. Some girls will have read books by Enid Blyton, or others, which make a minor epic of boarding-school life, the hardships, comradeship and minor adventures of its *dramatis personae*; this occasionally corresponds in part to what they may actually find, though much of this literature conveys a pre-war flavour.

Here are three sources of pre-school information that have been recorded:

My mother was here and told me all I had to know.   (11)
Before I came we used to read comics and when mum said to me, your going to boarding school . . . I thought that it would be great.
                                        (a local-authority-assisted pupil, 11)
I have read books about boarding schools and they are nothing like what it is here.   (11)

Another source in some schools comes from letters from existing pupils, sent unofficially to friends, or as part of a scheme for welcoming new girls, with varied effects:

In our House it is customary for the godmother to write to her new girl in the holidays offering answers to any problems she may have. (17)

But at another school:

Before I came here I received a letter from a girl who was already here. She told me it was a horrid school and she advised me to beware of certain staff and senior girls.   (12)

'Horrid schools' will clearly not be able to prevent the informal spread of information, but if they are to undertake some introductory correspondence it might clearly repay some care.

The first impressions of arrival have clearly been vivid and many girls have written profusely on the subject.

We came a day earlier than most people, because we were new; we found our way round in that extra day. We had godmothers when we were new . . . and they told us what to do.   (11)

(This school has very good marks on indices of satisfaction.)

Elsewhere, actually at a school which shows overall much less happy results:

I was made very welcome, and people were more friendly to me when I first came than what I expected, especially the seniors.   (11)

And things and people girls notice:

When I first walked in the front hall I felt completely out of place . . . I was greeted by the headmistress who was very kind. Then I was shown to the room where I was to sleep that term. Here I met my first friend. (11)

. . . everything seemed strange, even the way we went into prayers and stood. (11)

When I first came . . . I imagend them not to notice us little first years . . . I soon made lots of friends . . . at first I felt a bit homesick because the doormatres are so big to wards my little bedroom at home . . pocket money was a large sum of 5/– . . . so I was deeply amazed. (11)

At night I felt very strange sleeping with a lot of other girls . . . the only trouble being a first year is all the older girls look down on us as babys. (11)

My house mother is called Iris and she is nice, the first thing she told me was how to make my bed and other things. (11)

Everybody seemed to be hurrying this way and that and telling us what to do. Everything seemed to hurry along the corridor and rules seemed to dart at me from dark corners. (11)

I received my lacrosse stick and I didn't know what it was. (13)

The penultimate quotation came from a large school, as does the next from another one:

The school seemed so big with endless corridors and hundreds of rooms. I thought that I would never find my way around. Everybody was nice to me and showed me what was what. But I felt that I hated it with all my heart because Mummy and Daddy were not here. (12)

Lest one suppose that that was an enduring impression for this girl, one should note that she goes on to say:

After half term . . . I realised that it was not much good spending all my time moping around . . . I have lots of friends and we have great fun together. (12)

At the same school, another girl is unhappy, and for an unexpected reason:

. . . I settled down, but every Sunday when I went to chapel, the tears would well up and I cried softly to myself for I was homesick for the junior school, not for Mum, I had been used to leaving her, but the junior school. (12)

The main impression, however, seems to be that while the entry of many newcomers is smoothly managed, a few have a miserable first few days, but then are likely to settle down. The quantitative findings of Chapter Four confirm that the first-year girls are relatively happy as boarders. This good adjustment appears to stem importantly from finding good friends among peers, rather than by forming relationships with staff.

I didn't have time really, to feel homesick, I was so confused when my parents left me. After I'd unpacked my case, I just stood watching the other girls arrive, most of them were chatting and laughing, a few were tear stained and others looked as frightened as I was . . . I thought it exciting after a day or two, we were all busy making friends and losing them.   (12)

Several girls mention the presence of relations. This seems to help, but there also seems a tendency not to depend on this asset too much, perhaps for fear of losing other friends by seeming to be at too much of an advantage.

. . . that night I was jolly homesick, and as my cousin was already here, she came and comforted me. She still does sometimes.   (12)
When I was first new I found that things I did were often wrong and my sister used to say 'you shouldn't do that' and I would be most surprised and say 'But that's silly'.   (12)
I was extremely excited but very sad at seeing my parents going away. I felt that I could stick it out with the help of my older sister.   (12)
As my sister was there I felt I could stand up without being frightened . . . we looked at the notice board to find which dormy we were in. Then my sister showed me where it was and then left me to my fate. Our dormy head was very nice and showed us what to do.   (12)

New girls must discover where to find things, places and people, what to do when, what various places and procedures are called, and any or all of these things may seem strange. New impressions are also not just a matter of discovering facts, but equally importantly of discovering deep feelings which are sometimes subject to rapid shifts and realignments.

It seemed strange to be ruled by bells. . . . It was odd to have to register in the form room. Also the names Divinity and Biology are queer as I used to call them Scripture and Nature.   (12)
It was almost the opposite of what I had expected because a lot of the

bedrooms had got no heating in them at all, and half the beds were falling apart and there were not half enough toilets or baths. (11)

As already mentioned, the settling down process clearly involves learning facts, adjusting to friends of one's own age, but also a broad range of different kinds of experience with staff:

When I first came to the senior school our teacher was very helpful and kind. (11)

I was welcomed into my housemistresses' room. I could see she was always busy by the way she wrote every piece of information down. (12)

The Headmistress tries to make day girls and boarders be friends but she takes boarders out but not day girls so how can we? (11)

I often feel afraid of meeting up with a mistress. (11)

There was a horrid matron who was awfully nice until all the parents went away and then she was terrible. (11)

You should expect to be told off by our housemistress every ten minutes for nothing. (12)

[But in the same school] I would hate to go to another house because the other house Mistress and matrons are so Bichy. but our house-mistress is so soft you can do anything (up to a point). (12)

[Elsewhere] I was surprised at some of the staff. They made me as a boarder, very unhappy in my first year. (12)

[And in the same school] I was taken to a dormitory which looked like a hospital ward and as I was accepted into the community of the school I was amazed at the attitude of the staff to us. They thought we were *a whole lot of silly* stupid queers. (12)

Fortunately, the position at that school is not uniformly as these two girls indicate, as on two indices of pastoral care (see Chapter Seven) and on satisfaction, the school shows very fair to good statistical results. Elsewhere, and again against the statistical pattern, which suggests that the next girl will be likely presently to change her mind, we hear:

I found that when I first came the housemistress and matron were both very kind and understanding. . . . At school I got on very well because my form mistress is very sweet. I enjoyed school here immediately. (12)

This school ranks nineteenth out of twenty-three in level of satis-faction expressed. The girl quoted from may have been inclined to look for sympathy among staff, as she had not got on too smoothly with her peers:

In the dormitory I was bullied quite a lot, because I was told if I didn't
do a cartwheel after lights out I would be a coward.   (12)

It is possible that the company of one's peers, ever-present, is
the more important social group (than staff) among whom to make
friends, if as a new girl one wants to get on well and be happy.
This observation introduces the topic of intra-formal social control,
which will be treated in more detail later. Before this, I shall discuss
the matter of initiation rites.

Initiation rites and ceremonies are a matter of deep interest to
social scientists, to whom they figure as important social mechanisms for bringing about a relatively abrupt change of status, and
for whose researches and books they provide dramatic highlights
especially if they have included circumcisions, flagellations, lustra-
tion, cicatrization, or some other gory or public assault on the
bodies of the ordinands. Did I learn of, or even witness in English
girls' boarding schools, anything I could call an initiation rite?

In only one school visited was anything of the sort described.
The phenomena did not appear to have any official support, though
the staff were aware of what went on, and found it harmless enough.

When I first came we were as we call it Cristend that was pushed into
the pond by one of the girls in the form above us then we are made or
called proper members of our school.   (11)

Described like this, given a name and acknowledged as a mark of
qualification for acceptance, this is more a thing that could be
called an initiation procedure than sundry more informal challenges
to do cartwheels or other minor mischief devised by girls elsewhere.
At the same school:

. . . it is a custom to tell the first years that 16 days before the end of
term we start crossing off which is climbing a ladder to the top of the
dining room and cross off the pictures. I am sure this is not true. I am
afraid of crossing off if it is true because I am scared of heights and
the dining room is terribly high.   (10)

Many girls wrote about this matter, giving essentially the same
story. After their first term, they see that it is not true, they no
longer talk about the matter, and no longer feel they are new girls.
They are 'let in' – to the secret, such as it is, and with it, to the

society of their fellows as full members. I can suggest an explanation of this phenomenon, that it serves to keep new girls in suspense until a certain time when, emphasized by the Christmas holidays, the whole thing can be forgotten, until it is revived next year, and the very same girls who were only recently made mildly anxious now inflict the same feelings on the next intake of newcomers. None of the other schools visited produced such a clear example of an initiation procedure. Here is one mild example, mentioned by only one girl at her school:

Some people are given what is called 'new girl treatment' – apple pie beds and other tricks are played on them. After their first term they are usually treated as one of the school.   (13)

It also seems possible that some knowledge of sexual matters may be required as a sign that a newcomer 'belongs' to the company of initiates.

I didn't get on very well with people at first, cos they kept asking me to do stupid dares. like stripping in the window, etc. . . .
Then they used to tell jokes I didn't click to, they called me 'innocent, spas etc.' But eventually you get to know the things they talk about its OK.   (13)

And a peripheral finding from a remark in another field:

The juniors should have one or two sex lectures, but most of them are adequately taught in the dormitories, the first thing found out about new girls is how much they know.   (16)

Clearly, factors affecting style and content of dormitory conversations will include the number and ages of girls in each room, the supervision and the condition which the oral tradition in the school has reached. Not all of these examples can be described as true initiation rites, but they do appear to be situations through which many newcomers must pass in order to qualify to lose that label.

Enough initial experiences, procedures and situations have now been described. After these, the girls are accepted into the 'normal' cycle of school life. It would be exhausting and not very instructive to discuss the minutiae of different routines and regimes. Two extracts only will be given, to say something about the nature of daily life as it impinges on two girls, at different ends of the age range, and at different schools.

At 6.0 A.M. I woke up with the noise of two owls calling to each other. Lay awake thinking, till 7.0 when the dreaded bell rang, and the day begins.

I dragged myself out of bed, got the water-jug and went to the bathroom where someone from every dorm was waiting for water, some with frilly mob-caps covering curlers, others with hair all over the place, everyone looking like something from outer space!

After getting the water, I crawled back into bed. at about 7.20 the housemistress walked in and gave us a row for being lazy so we had to get up. She went out again, and we all got back into bed, and started getting dressed under the bedclothes. Soon the silence bell went, so we got up, dressed, washed, etc stripped our beds and emptied our hotties. Then, the second silence bell went, so charged downstairs, got our cloaks, and went over to school.   (12)

So a day begins, and in more than one school, girls have specifically mentioned how the day is divided up and milestoned:

> For five disturbing years
> The school bell daily clanged
> I went by hour
> From house to school and back again
> Bullied by bells.   (16)

Formal Social Control

We will come to see, through studying this section, that it is difficult, probably impossible, to say exclusively what is meant by 'formal social control'. Let me start by considering that this refers to 'the organization's overt ways of regulating social and individual behaviour'. A little careful scrutiny will show that the title phrase is ambiguous; it sometimes refers to the *means* whereby an organization affects an individual's freedom; it also sometimes refers to the *situation* in which some means or methods have had an effect. We should probably recognize that our analytic difficulties in trying to describe and categorize what can be observed about formal social control are at root philosophical.[1]

It could be said that formal controls sometimes serve organizational functions. Thus a rule that games shall be played for so many hours per week could be interpreted as serving the organization (the school) by occupying people who might otherwise somehow threaten the smooth running of the society. However, it could further be held that 'the school' is not like some super-person, feeling threatened, irritated, exercising power or whatnot. One can argue that something which is explainable at one level as serving the organization, actually serves the convenience only of individuals within the organization. Thus, by conducting games, one teacher controls many pupils while other staff can relax or go out or do other things. This does not particularly help 'the school', but it helps staff. If they become refreshed and able to teach better, this in turn helps the girls. At the first stage, it is a convenient approximation to say that something is done 'for the organization', but I consider this an insufficient analysis; because 'the organization' does not exist except in the actions and minds of its members or its observers, and it is in these minds that one should eventually seek to understand or explain group or organizational behaviour. Similar difficulties of overlap of meaning occur with attempts to analyse controls as having expressive functions; while all controls must presumably be 'instrumental' – unless they fail to effect control, in which case they are not really 'controls'!

To start describing formal control, one should look for the most permanent members of the society and see what they prescribe. This means paying attention to what governors, heads and staff devise as a social structure, and the ways they devise for getting the less permanent members (the pupils) to behave as desired.

First there is a question of public advertisement; the school makes (fairly) clear through its prospectus what kind of society it is, and parents who take an interest are likely to cooperate with the regime. Some schools, for example, say they emphasize sports or arts, or are non-denominational or orthodox Anglican. Some parents will enter their children for a school knowing they disagree with some of its aspects but, since large fees are involved, they have good reason to inquire into and know about what they are 'buying'. Some schools say, for example, that once entered in the junior school some pupils are expected to stay through to the sixth form. This provides the school with an assured clientele, at the risk of having to 'carry' some pupils with poor academic prospects. Other schools make it clear that they are 'academically oriented' and may recommend parents to 'place their daughter somewhere more suitable' if it is felt she may not make the academic grade. This may be interpreted uncharitably as a jettisoning, primarily for the school's good A-level record, of those with poor prospects – an 'organizational goal';* it could equally be said that such moves are made in good faith by schools, which keep up a high academic pressure in the interests of highly selected and academically capable pupils.

Once the pupils are selected and enter, the families are often sent lists of required clothes, instructions on the school's particular ways, advice, rules and other information. On arrival, pupils are met and talked to; in several schools they see rules pinned up or are given legislative booklets. There may be mottoes, school songs or prayers, or a variety of ways of publicly or privately informing pupils of the formally expected modes and limits of behaviour. Some of the private channels of information, if for example they are delegated through senior girls, may shade into the area understood as 'intra-formal control', which will be considered later. For example, at one school some seniors thought to underline the awe in which newcomers should suitably regard their predicament by a story of how a ghostly baby's head would roll along a corridor at night. This would not be a detail envisaged by the formal system, though it might serve to enhance, for a time, some respect for and dependence on the seniors who hold and exercise authority for the formal system.

Among the 'instruments' of formal control we can include the physical, temporal and social structures of a society. By physical structure one means the provision and allocation of rooms and room. Generally there is less individual room for juniors, more for seniors. Juniors sleep in large dormitories (though not always), while seniors more often have smaller rooms, sometimes individual study-cubicles, carrels or separate compartments of some sort. Seniors often have better studying space, and sometimes eat in smaller dining-rooms, or may stay on in the dining-room after others have left, and have coffee in relative peace. Inequity in distribution of space can be used in the privilege system, which we shall presently look at.

---

* To describe this as an organizational goal is not necessarily adequate; it could be that the school is interested in getting good A-level results for its *pupils*, rather than for 'itself' (e.g. for staff kudos); we would then say this (getting rid of a girl) was an 'instrumental' means.

The temporal structure is the system of routine devised. We have already heard one girl's cry of how she feels 'bullied by bells'. Not all, of course, mind the bells, but they have been written about in several schools as a salient and not too welcome feature:

. . . it seemed strange to be ruled by bells. It was difficult to keep quiet in the silence bell.   (12)
Being a boarder you find that life is run by bells.   (13)

At one school, however, the school bell became one of the foci of collective affection and identity. Situated out of doors, it was an old ship's bell, marked with its initials and known by them as a name; girls took it in turn as a duty to ring it and did so with some gusto. Apart from the actual machinery of setting time, comes the important question of how it is allotted. Like physical space, it can be treated as a commodity for use in the privilege system. Not all schools give seniors a liberal hand with time:

[school] expects us to behave like adults where work is concerned . . . then they treat you like a 7 year old and expect you to go to bed at 8.30 or 9 P.M. lights off at 9.30, and given times for letter writing, walks, prep, amusement, and *no* unorganised time of any length at all in which to do what you want.   (16)

Girls' time is not only organized in the normal course of events, but can also be reorganized as a punishment:

. . . I was in trouble with my best friend for talking to some fellas who used to come into our grounds and of course we would get caught and would have to sit in the front hall doing work until about 11.30 P.M. (13)

Differences in attitude to time were quite clear in the schools' treatment of my own visit. At some, like that above, I was not allowed to continue talking with girls late into the evening, and I was reprimanded if I overstepped limits; at other schools I was able to talk to senior girls till past 11 P.M., taking the view which was put by one head, that 'Time is not here to use us, but we to use it'. Yet, even at schools with a flexible attitude to time, it was the rare exception which did not expect girls to come to lessons punctually, and sometimes give punishment for tardiness. In this example, it seems as if time has somehow been retributively exacted from a transgressor, and symbolically destroyed, causing some upset.

I was late for a lesson. . . . Oh gosh I thought now I'm for it, and I was.
. . . we had to write an essay on punctuality and manners . . . we gave
it in . . . and . . . she ripped it up before looking at it. I think that was
really horrible as she had not even looked at it.   (11)

At the opposite extreme came the school whose head, mentioned
above, set the tone; by prolonging morning prayers with extra
announcements or necessary homilies (rules and disciplinary steps
were always explained carefully, at length, to everybody) the routine
of the morning could be set quite askew. There it did not matter,
but at another school the question of a spare ten minutes and of
who should use it – the catering department for a mealtime, or the
chaplain for a service – was the occasion of a distinct organizational
rift which had serious effects on the public value attached to the
pastoral care functions in the society.

More subtle and complex than the physical and temporal aspects
of structure is the social structure. Here we can instance sub-
societies within the main society, such as houses, each separately
run by a housemistress, often physically accommodated apart,
occasionally (and this is getting rarer) catered for separately, with
separate authority and privilege systems. We can point to sub-
systems within the overall system, thus the financial system, the
'pastoral system' (matrons, chaplain, housemistresses, etc.), or the
pupil system. We can think of the various types of hierarchy that
exist formally, thus the authority hierarchy, the status ladder (which
may closely follow authority, though not always: for example, in
one school where foundation scholars have high status, even when
they are relatively junior and without much authority), and the
privilege system. The privilege system includes scales of rewards
and of punishments.

All sorts of reward systems can be devised. They can try to work
through promoting group solidarity ('house pride') and cover a wide
range of behaviour, or they can be specific, as in one instance where
girls each have a weekly chart on which marks for each subject are
given, in red (good) or blue (bad), the whole chart amounting to
an easily read visual symbol which can be a proud sight for those
who have worked well. Visual symbols are clearly important, and
instances include badges worn (in enamel) or in some schools sewn
on to the uniform, signifying various achievements of status or
performance (thus: junior prefect, 1st XI hockey, etc.); also cups

awarded to teams or houses; also the names of distinguished old girls put up in gilt lettering. An example of the use of a visual symbol was one school where 'the Dormitory Picture' was given every term as a prize. Each girl started term with fifty points, and deductions were made for misdeeds. At the end of term, an average score per dormitory was computed and the winner got the picture. It is worth noting that there were plenty of other pictures in most dormitories, some of them even nicer; but there was only one prize picture, which thus had symbolic value apart from its intrinsic merit.

Punishment and reward systems are sometimes purposely devised as interdependent. Thus, withdrawal of rewards (privileges) is used as a punishment. This is a case of formal and obvious interdependence, when it is publicly made clear what the consequences of good or bad behaviour (as officially defined) can be. But it is really a point of this chapter that, even without openly stated links, aspects of the social structure are nearly always intermeshed, so much so that it is sometimes difficult to classify various aspects apart. For example, in one school an aspect of privilege was to gain permission to visit the nearby village or town; but this piece of freedom was also one criterion of the status hierarchy. We can see in some examples how sanctions are intended to apply in both directions; and they do not always work as smoothly as intended.

The privilege system on the whole is greatly abused. It is used as a method of punishments. . . . When someone does not gain a privilege which the rest of her form have, she may assume a harmful don't care attitude, or . . . [if] a timid person, retreat even more into her shell. If someone as a junior committed some sin, it is remembered even 4 years later *and affects* her privileges.   (17)

In another school:

[our school has] . . . a ridiculous system called a privilege list. If one is liked and considered responsible and helpful (i.e. a bloody sucker) one is promoted on to the list. Being on this list one can I go for walks in fours . . . [but] one has first to submit to being sworn in. This compiles a list of rules (e.g. not to go further than holding hands with a boy . . .). This said and done are then broken the first weekend after being put on the list. If you are not on it then the staff pick on you and mentally beat you up.   (16)

It is fair to record that not all girls develop so jaundiced a view.

In the same school as one of the above extracts is drawn from, we find:

The privilege system is a good idea, girls should be awarded more responsibility as they progress up the school, this does not seem to be typical of all boarding schools.   (16)

While at another school one girl appreciates freedom as a privilege, at two others girls recognize the dilemmas of limits, and comment more pithily than I can:

I think we are given much more freedom than other schools. We do not have very many rules. . . . We do not have a strict uniform. If we call the staff names most of them take it as a joke. (Not rude names of course).   (13)

This school has the highest 'score' for happiness of its girls. But what is worth considering is that it was also top of the list of average scores for 'aspiration to become a prefect'. It seems an example where freedom has been communicated as a companion of responsibility. Secondly, elsewhere:

Freedom at school is I believe to be limited to enable a pupil to appreciate freedom when it comes. School is in itself a form of Freedom, freedom to learn, make friends and develop ones opinions but the restrictions are of value.   (15)

And thirdly, a more jaundiced, though candid judgement:

This school is meant to be based on a trust system. I think this does not work because (a) we are not in fact completely trusted. (b) we are not completely trustworthy.   (15)

This girl's pinpointing not only of the design of a system, but of how it is applied, reminds one that, although sociological analyses are relevant, so is the elusive quality with which they are used. Thus we should remember that it is possible for even a clumsy and inequitable system to be run with some success, if the staff are good enough. However, in such a case they would clearly be likely soon to change the system design. But a good system design does not in itself ensure harmonious results if the people running it are not of the appropriate quality.

Something should briefly be said about a few other aspects of the social structure before going on to comment about how, and to what effect, structures function. The authority and status hierarchies have already been mentioned. Most, though not all, schools have a prefectorial system. A few schools have been experimenting with either abolishing prefects altogether, or keeping a more junior rank of prefect while last-year girls go into 'student status'. This latter is done so as to allow them to practise responsibilities in the non-school world – they get some freedom to go out. However, there is sometimes a side-effect, namely of neglect of responsibility as it is expected to be fulfilled within the school. Thus elder students sometimes take liberties which lower sixth-formers complain may be setting a bad example, or not setting a good one. The reasons for setting up a student-status, off the top of the authority ladder but securely high in status, are often bound up with the idea of giving girls the chance to work more efficiently. The range of structural designs in this area is obviously great, from the upper sixth-formers in one school who talk realistically about Chelsea, allowances and university, enjoying social parity with adult staff and visitors to the school, to the sixth-formers in another school who, as we have seen, go to bed at 9.30, must still wear 'bullet-proofs' (lisle stockings) and have their work-efficiency reduced by prefectorial duties. Usually, however, authority, responsibility, privilege and status increase with age. If any of these should get seriously out of step, there will be 'status disequilibrium' which will be troublesome for the individual. We have already come across examples, particularly at junior authority level, where girls may be seen being punished by those over whom they will soon have to exert authority. There can also be imbalance if, for example, a girl is a house prefect, but not of the same school rank as prefects from other houses.

The houses in some schools can be microcosms of the school. In each house there is a small staff, girls representing the age range of the school (except in junior-only, or in sixth-form houses), a system of house privileges, punishments, authority, and so on. Houses sometimes serve as foci for motivational systems organized by the school. Thus houses are given marks according to the behaviour of their girls, and official kudos (or symbolic rewards) given to the winner with the best average. Some such systems treat it as better to have 'knowledge of results', so house 'scores' are posted up as they are continuously computed. This enables girls to see who must try harder, or supposedly brings loyal and keen members of the house to put pressure on those miscreants who are spoiling the house averages. There is a possibility that girls may 'see through' such a system and become disenchanted, even if they mechanically follow some of the prescribed ways.

Well all us little juniors have to slave away to get STUPID good house-marks for the seniors. The teachers give bad marks as well as the seniors for bludy stupid reason.   (13)

This school ranked eighteenth (out of twenty-three) in level of happiness, and this may possibly have had something to do with the competitive house system, and the way it was run. Unfortunately, also, a competitive scheme can be misused; for example, the prefects, or even staff, who give marks can gerrymander their own house's success. Two such examples were met, in one of which the staff member of one house was accused (by another) of helping the house win by unfair generosity to its girls. Systems which do not declare scores until the prize is just about to be awarded are less open to abuse. They are also less conspicuous as motivators. Inter-house games can also be used to maintain inter-house identification and competition, which is thought to lead to 'keenness' or other good qualities.

What aspects of girls' behaviour and lives do formal controls set out to regulate? There are two sorts of answer to this. One concerns quantity, and we will see below that different schools set out formally to control pupils' lives to markedly different degrees. The second type of answer concerns quality; examples will now be given to show that at various schools nearly every conceivable aspect of girls' lives is brought under attempted control. Consider sensory experience. The world of vision is probably the most important of the senses by which we relate to the world. Schools affect what girls see. In many, there is the intent to provide gracious buildings (even if the intimate furnishings are battered or sparse) to promote a particular sort of aesthetic sensitivity. Several schools try to control what girls may read, placing limits at various degrees of dross, or of scurrility. Some discourage 'teen comics, magazines, James Bond books; one housemistress told me she refused permission for girls (over 16) to see an 'A' certificate film on their free afternoon, when in principle it was allowed for them to see films. This modern variant of the fig leaf syndrome centred not on the fact that a woman in the film was seen murdered on screen, but that she had been a prostitute. Lest this be thought of as a peculiar aberration of public boarding schools, it did not take a large sample of direct grant schools to find this kind of control being attempted over day girls:

Dance halls have recently been made strictly out of bounds. I think people are more tempted to go now. . . . Dance halls are out of bounds even in the holidays. Aren't we allowed to grow up?   (15)

Girls are quick enough to discredit the motives and the sources of regulations, if they do not accept the reasoning offered:

. . . the day girls are supposed not to do things like cinema and circus etc but this is only for the germs sake. But you could pick up the same germs if you just walked down the street.   (12)

It is possible here that a staff motive in opposing cinema attendance was concerned with the exceedingly taboo subject, which has avoided public discussion even in the frankest modern press, and on which I was not allowed to ask questions in any school where I broached the matter, of minor molestations inflicted on girls and women who go unescorted in dark public places. Whatever the explanation of this taboo, the point is that some schools try to specify what girls may casually see, or examine visually.

The same applies to listening. Radios are allowed in some schools, and sometimes as a part of seniority and privilege. A genuine administrative problem exists here, of ensuring that the radios are all properly licensed. There is also the question of noise control where tens or even hundreds of girls might all want to listen to different programmes. Some schools try to influence the type of music that may be played, though hardly any could resist the pressure to get at a television to watch a pop music programme, which seems to be so strong a motive in young teenagers as to rival the legendary all-consuming 'maternal instinct'.

We are only aloud T.V. at weekends and then the housemistress says if we watch much more we shall go square eyed we have so pettie rules it makes everybody feal so small.   (13)

Elsewhere:

The most exciting things . . . [include] . . . when we watch 'top of the

Pops' for ten minutes after drawing room . . . I looth drawing room it
is so booring we are read a book by the housemistress. But I really like
this school.   (12)

One result of restrictions in these fields is illicit reading or listening, or exaggerated behaviour in display. Transistors are hidden
in teddy bears, and in the school with a large dormitory around
which a hot water pipe ran, it was said that if the iron bedsteads
were pulled up to touch the pipe, girls all along the row could listen
to one radio placed upon the pipe at one end. I was unfortunately
unable to verify this story, though I did see the pipe and the iron
beds. In one school, week-end opportunities to 'let go' were
evidently seized by some girls with all their being.

At weekends the form is awful. Radio (recently allowed) record player
(form privilege this term) blaring. . . sweet papers on floor, waste paper
basket overflowing, desks upside down, hunks of bread and butter all
over the place, cakes, bottles of pop, biscuits etc on desks, rags being
around, records being on the floor and everybody screaming.   (15)

This raises the question of the fate of the dissenting individual,
on which I shall touch in dealing with 'intra-formal control'. What
else do schools sometimes control? They control eating; at one
school even the termly 'dormitory feast' was evidently a few biscuits
and Ovaltine brought in on a tray by a housemistress not long after
'official' lights out. Usually there are controls on under-eating
(sometimes tried by enthusiastic dieters, wanting to get into training for the middle-aged middle-class slog against food), as well as
on over-eating. The cult of the tuck-box may not be so widespread
in girls' schools as it evidently is in boys', as perhaps girls have less
need for this gastric symbol of absent mother love. How girls smell
is also sometimes controlled, with rules about make-up which will
include scent. I never met a school, though, which aimed at an
olfactory uniform by prescribing the same scent for every girl – or
even including this officially in a scale of perfumed permission with
the seniors allowed to choose more rare and expensive fragrances
and the juniors kept on cheap lotion. Girls' visual appearance was
nearly always subject to control, though. Haircuts and styles are
in most schools kept modest. It is impracticable for girls to keep
up anything elaborate, and some schools do allow variety within
limits; but complaints may focus on this issue sometimes which

probably derive their energy from a more generalized dissatisfaction with other aspects of that school's life.

> We do have dances. We are not allowed to meet boys . . . or . . . to speak to them. . . . If our hair touches our collar we have to have it tied back which is ridiculous. (16)

School uniform, with house particularities, as for example cloaks with different coloured inner linings, is found in the most permissive schools. Cloaks formed perhaps the most popular item of uniforms, though pinafores at one school were objects of personal involvement – almost battle-scarred histories of each owner's school career – and affection. Bullet-proofs were probably the least popular item. There was evidently not much need to control underwear, as few girls would hazard expensive oddities here. At one school it became fashionable to sport coloured bloomers, which was not officially resisted; but at another, a rule enjoining the wearing of white knickers could be enforced as all the girls sat cross-legged on the floor during part of morning assembly, during which time offenders could be spotted by staff elevated on a dais.

At one school even personal temperature came under scrutiny, and each girl had it taken daily, except on Sundays and Ascension Day; the reason for this latter omission I could not discover. The procedure was said to be more useful for giving the staff member an occasion for person-to-person contact with each individual girl every day, and 'social diagnosis' took place that was considered much more important than the thermal diagnosis. This was probably true. Unfortunately, the questionnaire concerning pastoral care responsiveness was not allowed to be given at this school, and we cannot see how this daily contact may have affected the girls' stated readiness to take their problems to staff. At another school, personal contact was assured more literally, as the head shook hands with every girl whenever she took chapel. Some schools maintain a drawing-room ceremony at which either a form (in rotation) or the whole house (possibly omitting some seniors) come and see the housemistress and say goodnight formally, shaking hands or even curtseying.

Relationships within the school, of course, come under control, as do the thoughts people have. Most schools seem to aim at healthy friendships among girls of equal age, and to a lesser extent across ages. Schools vary in the extent of 'pashes', 'crushes' or 'cracks'. Attempts to 'break down form barriers' proceed only so far, lest it be thought that these crushes may therefore become common. Such emotional relations appear to cause unease to all concerned; to the participants (whom I never persuaded to be articulate about the matter) there is a sort of spiced unease, pleased at least that something warm is happening, though anxious about the meaning of the 'relationship' and how it will be taken by onlookers. The onlookers also often sound uneasy, perhaps with a tinge of jealousy. The difficulty may be that public opinion will not approve of relationships which are sensed as being highly ambiguous – a mixture of pseudo-heterosexual affection (the older girl as man-the-actor, and the younger as woman the protected admirer), and a mother-child relation (older girl maternally nurturing the younger). Formal control steps over such relations can include movement of girls to different dormitories, even houses, private talks, and lectures to the school by the head, probably at prayers or assembly.

People's thoughts are affected by all the controls on what they see, hear and do, the kind of relationships they may have both in school and out of it, and by the kind of (aesthetic) sensibility they come to develop under these conditions.

Communications with the outside world, almost by the very nature of boarding, come under observation, if not control. Letters are sometimes looked at externally in case they suggest illicit origins. One example was given of a girl receiving invitations from some organization to 'all night parties in London', and it is clear that, however rarely it may actually happen, letter correspondence is open to abuse. Most schools keep a light hand in this area, and some sort of supervision without censorship can be effected by having staff or senior girls sort the mail and be responsible for giving it out. Censorship over letters, especially as it would be likely to be combined with other signs of strict control, would probably prove very unpopular.

At my last school*. . . there was not 1 minute of the day when there was not some rule restricting you, even in free time – you had to report to [staff] every ½ hour. . . . We had to leave [letters] open for the [staff] to inspect before posting. They could open your letters. There was no privacy . . . and I HATED it.   (16)

* Not one of the schools visited during the research.

This extent of control is more possible when there are no day girls present. With these to act as couriers, however, such controls are sidestepped. Needless to say, a whole book of quotations could be put together of thoughts about the restriction of access to boys. Two schools were visited, however, which allowed quite extensive contacts. At both, the boys, preferably relatives, had to be introduced; no stories of pregnancies were related – though they were recorded, very rarely, from schools with more careful controls.

Communication patterns within the school are often influenced by design. Most attempts related were concerned with 'trying to break down form barriers'. These barriers are strengthened by the punishment system.

When I first came there were terrific form barriers. . . . Discipline was fairly rigid and everyone followed the group, [A new headmistress came] and most of this has been changed [by her]. Form barriers are no longer in existence, and there is very little discipline. By discipline I mean punishments given for crimes. There is plenty of self-discipline.   (17)

This seems reliable witness to one source of influence on form barriers. Another approach is to try and get girls to mix more, for example at meal times. At one school dining-room seating was arranged so that older and younger girls were neighbours. Unfortunately for the official intentions, the girls said that their own ('intra-formal') canons discouraged older girls from fraternizing with younger ones ('currying favour') or vice versa ('sucking up'). The result was mealtimes in silence.

At another school, an effort to randomize seating plans was made by giving girls numbered tickets which would determine their seating order. After queueing for tickets and food, girls found their friends, swapped tickets and sat more according to their choice. The system was not entirely nullified, however, and may have promoted some mixing. Elsewhere, it is of interest to consider the school which is second in the ranking list of 'index of communication' (see Chapter Seven), which means that girls were very ready to discuss their problems with each other, as well as with staff. A feature of mealtimes was that the head made frequent announcements to comment on individuals' misdeeds, but always linked this with explanations of punishments and of their aptness and justice.

This seemed to contribute towards a shared awareness of each other's problems. Mealtimes were very noisy indeed, and though the level of happiness rated was 'only' in the middle of the list, possibly because many girls came from very difficult home backgrounds, the school had the top ranking in the 'rated success on the top five ideal goals'. I also seemed to find in this school that efforts to restrain discussion on questionnaires so that an earlier class did not gossip with one met later in the week, were less successful.

An opposite style in communication to this shared pool of intimacy was met at a school where the head addressed at least some messages to staff about how they should control girls via correspondence with the senior mistress, pinned on the common room noticeboard. Paralleling this, housemistresses put messages on boards in their girls' common rooms. In one case, the noticeboard was across the room from the door and the housemistress would have had to enter it properly to put up a communication. Her messages were thus symbolically in the girls' midst, and in content they offered advice and information rather than commands. In contrast, in another house the board was almost at the door. Notices did not enter the girls' milieu, but may have served symbolically as a frontier, even a barrier between them and staff. The messages tended towards curt instructions rather than information or advice. During the research visit, the girls were incensed when describing their rules and took two notices down which they gave me as souvenirs. This made the housemistress exceedingly angry with me, possibly because she felt me acting as a threatening agent who removes a protective fence. The girls felt embarrassed at her remarks to me, and apologized for the incident – which illustrates a hazard in investigating a delicate system of controls and relationships.

Institutional Control: 'Measuring' Formal Social Control

We have now dealt sufficiently with the nature or quality of instances and patterns of formal social control. Other examples will be clear by implication throughout the book, of ways in which the official 'formal' part of the system seeks to control the life of the society, by determining aspects of physical, temporal and social structure. But what about the breadth or extent of control in any one school? Can this be 'measured'? Closely following the work on boys' schools, an index of institutional control was devised. This gave quite arbitrary markings to aspects of life for which control existed in any school. This scale covered 'compulsory activities, personal appearance and possessions, movement and activity, social relations, time and privacy' and some questions on any controls extended over day girls.

It is very important to understand the workings of this scale. For example, if girls were not allowed home at any occasion during term, twenty-five points were put down; if girls over age 16 were generally put to bed before 9.30, ten points were added; and so on. Now it is likely that schools with many severe controls will get a high mark – the maximum possible was 231; lenient or permissive schools would have a low mark – the minimum possible was seven. However, a school which was lenient on the whole, but which had one or two particular restrictions for which the scale gave very high marks, might in this way get an overall score higher (more restrictive) than a school which was in fact more restrictive on the whole, but just happened to allow liberties in the particularly highly marked areas. The effect of this is that we cannot put much faith in small differences of total score. A school with an institutional control score of 100 would not arguably be distinct in severity from a school with a score of ninety or 110. The border of ambiguity may indeed be greater than this. On the other hand, it is possible to assume that schools severe in some respects would more likely be severe in others, while permissive schools would also show this characteristic throughout the regime.

One can therefore list schools in rank order of institutional control score, and assume that the internal consistency of the scale is not so poor as to dramatically render invalid the rank order we find. Refinements of the scale (which would require more work than possible with one visit per school) might mean some re-adjustments of the rank order, but these should not be great. How did the schools work out then?

Table 5·1. Distribution of institutional control scores among twenty-three schools

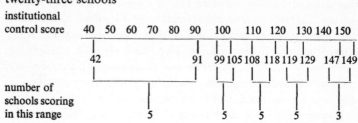

The 'spectrum' of severity of control runs from forty-two to 149. It suggests there are a fifth of lenient schools, between three-fifths and three-quarters of medium-strict schools, and three very strict schools. In view of what most girls wrote of the strictest schools, the scale is designed with an over-stretched range, for a school which scored over 200 would clearly present an unbearably ferocious regime.

Having 'measured' institutional control, at least approximately enough to arrange the schools in a fairly valid rank order, what other factors can be statistically associated with higher institutional control?

Table 5·2. Factors associated with higher institutional control

schools which had higher institutional control tended also to have:	(statistical test)*		
a larger proportion of entry from their own junior school	Mann-Whitney U = 36		
intention to keep personal problems private	rank order correlation		− 0·57
lower readiness to discuss personal problems in general	,,	,,	,,	− 0·70
lower readiness to discuss personal problems with staff	,,	,,	,,	− 0·49
lower general level of happiness	,,	,,	,,	− 0·64
parents who had themselves been to boarding school	,,	,,	,,	0·64
higher aspirations to excel at *work*	,,	,,	,,	0·41
lower aspirations to excel at *arts*	,,	,,	,,	− 0·52
lower approval of school (judged by fifth-formers)	,,	,,	,,	− 0·44
lower success on five ideal goals (judged by sixth-formers)	,,	,,	,,	− 0·36
lower results on the test of divergent ability	,,	,,	,,	− 0·36

* All these values give *p* significant at 0·05 or smaller.

Most of these statistical findings are fairly easy to square with what is observed during visits. Several of these circumstances seem to hang together and are quite possibly causally related. Parents who themselves have been at boarding school are evidently likely to patronize the stricter schools. This may be partly to copy the pattern of their own youth, and partly because many of them choose their own old schools for their daughters. Some of the older schools (with one or two notable exceptions) tend more than the newer foundations to cling to regimes from the past. It would seem easier for an old-founded school to change to new ways if it is smaller, and change is possibly associated with a new head. In many ways a new head can effectively mean a new school. This finding suggests two tides of parental motivation in choosing boarding. There may be those who feel bound to repeat a style of life they valued, and others who make this choice as an innovation – who are more likely to choose a more lenient school. There are some signs that when a client body with a great deal of boarding experience choose schools which are lenient, the schools tend not to be just non-strict, but more 'positively libertarian' in some aspects at least.

The girls in stricter schools are less happy, and in them they are less willing to discuss their problems with others. Probably no one of these elements causes the others, but they are all interdependent. The stricter schools appear to generate more desire to do well at work, and the girls actually show lower levels of scores on the test of divergence (or imaginative ability), which accords with the lower aspiration to excel at arts. These aspirations may result in fact from the reflection of 'artistic' leanings as more likely to be found in a freer organizational structure; they may also link with the possibility that parents who choose the stricter type of school may encourage academic more than artistic inclinations. Two 'success' indices, wherein different bodies of girls imply judgement on the schools' performance, show that the stricter schools are found less successful in what by implication is the girls' own view.

It may be of interest to note with what circumstances institutional control scores seem to have *no* systematic links. Strictness seems unconnected with the rated effect of boarding on family relationships; this reinforces the idea that family ethos is to some extent paralleled by school ethos, so that school strictness or freedom will neither particularly reinforce nor disagree with the pattern of

E

family life and relationships. There appears to be no link between strictness and the ratio of sixth form–whole school size, or with the teacher–pupil ratio. It might perhaps have been expected that, if there were fewer staff per girl, the rules would have to be stricter to keep order. This kind of effect, if it existed, must have been swamped by other effects and no trace of it was found. There is no correlation between the desire to become a prefect and the strictness of the regime. Nor is there any connection with levels of ability on the 'convergent' (problem-solving) test or, more strangely, with an index which assesses whether girls tend to be more rebellious or conformist with the regime.

We have now seen something of the nature of the life and society into which the girls are admitted. Many statements have probably been made that it would have been more correct to phrase as suggestions, or intuitive interpretations. Some attempt has been made at measurement, however, as the formal control system declares itself, and is therefore on record. The same is not true of the patterns which spring up between the cracks of the formal structure; these patterns cannot be measured, but only described, and this is what the next chapter tries to do.

Notes

1. To say directly, or even to imply, that 'a society', or a social unit, like a school, 'exercises control' over something resembles what we can say about one person exercising control over another. We usually (unless we take the remotest behaviourist, or purely 'sociological' view of personal identity) recognize a person as one who exercises some 'free will', or choice of action. This recognition of the individual as a locus of initiative (however restricted or beaten it may sometimes become) finds ultimate expression in the phenomenon of religions. Religions usually acknowledge that free-willing (or free-being) individuals have a unique capacity, or chance, to recognize or even just search for a sensing of Being of limitless free-will, or 'power'; they also derive from their particular experience of God a set of rules by which people agree to regulate their behaviour. The unit-members of a religion are, to the best of my knowledge, always individual humans. No religion I know of is made up of unit-members which are societies. This is ultimately because it has not yet been possible to recognize a live consciousness, a free will, a corporate initiative, within a society or an organization.

   It is not difficult, even in this book, to find descriptions of organizations, be they clubs, schools, companies, societies or churches, which seem to impute that a 'unit' of free will is located in the organization – that is, quite apart from the separate free wills pertaining to the individual human members of organizations. I believe that if such imputations occur, they are mistaken. This means that whenever we say that 'the school controls such and such behaviour', there is no multi-human unit called 'the school' which acts upon separate people. The people who run the school may see to it that rules which they approve continue to affect the lives of the members. The result is that rules impinging on members appear to come from a communal or historical unit which seems to act like a source of power. So we 'anthropomorphize' social units, speak of them as though they had distinct minds, intentions, powers. It is curious that social scientists speak of 'animism' and point as evidence to children who think that the sun goes to sleep every night, or that cars rest when they are tired. This way of thinking is treated as an immature failure properly to construe reality; yet other social scientists, sometimes even the same ones, themselves think about societies in a similarly animistic way.

The upshot of all this should be a reminder that when one reads below, 'the school does such and such', this is a shorthand way of saying 'the staff or officials continue (for their own reasons whatever they may be) to act together so that it is as though a corporate "mind" does such and such . . .'. This realization affects the way we can analyse different areas of formal control; with goals, for example, we might begin to think of formal control having 'instrumental, expressive, or organizational functions'. We may think of formal control of expressive functions as being ways in which individuals have or do not have freedom to do things that they find good in themselves, which may serve no other purpose; for instance, watching a sunset. Formal control may enact, for example by rules displayed or read out, that girls must, or perhaps must not, watch sunsets. Perhaps religion is the area of that kind in which most formal prescription is to be found; though it is arguable that religion is not 'expressive', but also serves organizational functions, in that it keeps the population occupied; it can also be seen as 'instrumental' if it is used to serve some other end – for example, it could help to comfort a distressed individual or buttress her confidence for an exam; or it could be used 'instrumentally' to provide moral justification for some step the administration might wish to take.

Six: Intra-Formal Social Control

Within the 'formal' structure of control, which is publicly declared, there exists a related, more covert structure. This may involve staff, but the part which will principally occupy us here is that which is created by the girls. They set up their own standards of behaviour, and ways of making the limits known and respected. Many of the comments shown here were collected in response to the question: 'If a girl "told on" the form about something they had done wrong, and as a result everyone had got punished, what, if anything, would you think or do about that girl?' Other replies came from the question: 'What should a girl do if she wishes to be popular, or not do if she wishes to avoid unpopularity?'

There will only be space to deal briefly with what is really a huge file of material, and I will quote from what girls have written on three areas: the machinery of control – largely psychologically based; the 'norms' or canons which are set up (these are not 'rules', but unwritten recognized standards); and the 'underlife' – that is, that area of girls' behaviour which consists in getting round or poking fun at the formal rules, and which even the most articulate sociologist would find it difficult to describe as anything broader than 'mischief'.

First, the machinery. We have seen how new girls meet the school world. There is constant discussion, much of it about their fellows and who is 'settling in' and how.

When new girls come in and they are generally different, i.e. individual, they are generally flattened down and rubbed into the characteristics which everyone has. (16)

Advice to a friend who might be coming to the school. . . . Don't talk about your Mother and Father being Lord and Lady so and so. You will just get beaten up and some people can be jolly bitchy, excuse that expression. (13)

Here we see some evidence of required behaviour; and of the types of intra-formal control – physical and psychological – that can be exerted. Psychological forces can be used collectively by the group, and this is a situation we may choose to see through a sociological perspective.

Some girls who are not so nice are really quite nice if you get on the right side of them. The trouble is if the popular girl does not like her the rest of the form does not like her.   (11)

There is advice also for the popular girl, for whom life has its own difficulties:

If you are too popular you may get swollen headed. You may cause arguments because so many people will be wanting to be your friend.   (13)
The disadvantages of popularity are you get chosen to do other people's work, to help them with music, to help them with their drawing. You also have to do all the jobs for the teacher, you usually get chosen as form captain.   (13)

This last fate, of being singled out by the formal system to participate in *its* machinery, is something that we have seen as a prospect to be avoided, in the chapter on aspirations. What these extracts suggest is the existence of 'homeostatic' forces which tend to keep a system stable and to correct any parts or members which stray out of the ordinary too far. The group's control tries sometimes to extend not only to what girls do, but also to what and how they think.

Most people have great interest in the actions and affairs of others and when, one dull weekend when the majority were ensconced in easy chairs . . . with the occasional monosyllabic discussion of others' characters and deeds to relieve monotony, two girls preferred to walk in the grounds for an hour in discussion and conversation which wasn't concerned with boys, clothes or pop music, and occasionally might have run into the tetrasyllabic, these two were regarded as slightly insane, and, thus, greeted with disbelieving stares and stupefied questions as to 'Why?', 'What?' and 'Where?' when they returned.   (15)

At the same school an older girl says the same kind of thing:

It is difficult to be an individual at this school; if you say what you really think which others disagree with, you are treated as a sort of outcast until you agree with them.   (17)

There is great philosophical difficulty in being clear as to what we mean by 'individual' here. Is it accepted that deviants or eccentrics are highly individual? And if so, can we think of those who 'choose' (in what sense do they choose?) to follow the ways of the majority as not 'individual'? There are probably at least two senses in common use of the word 'individual', which it is worth remembering at this stage. What this girl presumably means is that it is difficult to be the person one wants, if it is too different from whatever everyone else wants one to be. An example of the hazards of independent thought follows:

Everyone dislikes Mr Wilson, and if any girl likes him, they are battered down.   (16)

How are people battered down? And for what kinds of behaviour? We shall see three aspects of control methods: physical, psychological and collective. If a girl 'told on' the form:

I would get this girl and get her secretly get her in a corner and tell her what I thought of her and I personally would hit her head on a tree and make her cry and send her to coventry.   (11)
I would personally tell her off and put her in Coventry for a month or perhaps have a water fight with her. As a form I think we would put her in Coventry or duck her in the wash rooms and do it in different heats of water and lock her in the store room to let her cool off her temper . . . and perhaps chase her with comics and keep hitting her . . . or give her the rounds of the kitchen with a hair brush or a bell bottom belt.   (11)

This flight of disciplinary fancy (or possibly it was true) was not produced in a traditional public school, but by a state-supported pupil in a newer foundation.

Girls who tell tales are called splits . . . they are not spoken to and apple pies are made sometimes their mattress is put in the cupboard and their bed is made on the springs.   (13)

These are physical discomforts visited on offenders, which are also 'psychological' in that they are clear demonstrations of neighbours' displeasure. There are a large variety of non-physical methods too. In answer to the same question about a tell-tale:

. . . well I wouldn't do anything anyway. Sometimes people write poison pen letters which are the worst thing out.   (14)

A younger girl is less inclined (to want) to stand back from collective action.

I think the form would make the life of the person quite miserable . . . if the rest of the form decided on anything I would definitely join in. (12)

Elsewhere:

All the girls would have a council of war. The whole house would go against her likely. We could all be terribly nice to her and make her feel guilty. You can turn someone into a nervous reck this way.   (13)

At still another school:

The class as a whole . . . would call her horrid names as she went past, laugh at her, and maybe some nasty person would knock books off her desk and then laugh etc.   (14)

An example presumably of the 'horrid names' would be:

I would call her a bloody little bastard (maybe bitch) – excuse the language – then ignore her completely – maybe give her a cold stare now and then.   (14)

Finally, at yet another school, even an older girl can be found willing to join in:

. . . I would probably join in with them in 'getting even'. Putting her in Coventry and putting things down her bed taping up her room and generally making things difficult. This sort of thing doesn't last long. She wouldn't be trusted by the group afterwards.   (16)

Note that 'sending to Coventry' does not always mean leaving a person to her own devices – which some people might find more of a relief than a punishment. There is the aspect of hostile action, as well as of verbal shunning. Not all girls are uncharitable, however, and the seeds of forgiveness can be found in girls at every age.

. . . I would punch her, say nasty things about her, spread her name around the school and if she is sorry, forgive her.   (11)

Forgiveness and understanding might be difficult to stand up for and show, and may need to be communicated privately, as the following five examples from five separate schools show:

I would ignore the fact [of a girl who split] and try to be sympathetic and explain away their faults. I think it depends on who split and what the form would do to that person.   (13)
I wouldn't think much of her but in a way feel sorry for her being that sort of person.   (14)

If she was a best friend I'd probably talk to her on the sly.   (15)
It would depend on *why* she did it. If out of spite – retrospective
action. If conscience, admiration.   (15)
I wouldn't be very aimiable towards the girl for a few days but I
wouldn't hold it against her. I would in many ways respect her and if
everyone was being mean to her I would feel very sorry for her.   (16)

A full appraisal of the social forces arising in a community needs
to take account not only of coercive but also of protective tendencies. These latter may arise as part of the virtues of the system,
through the efforts of the staff by the example of fair-dealing they
can set, and through their own advocacy of fair play and charity.
There are plenty of examples of talks and speeches, often in public
assemblies and religious ceremonies, which because they occur at
a group occasion for which presence is usually compulsory, can be
parodied and described as occasions of 'repression'. One of the
casualties of repression in such an analysis would surely be the
truth. It would be more reasonable to suppose that some good
ideals are being propounded publicly, and that this may have something to do with good social behaviour when it arises, or at least
when girls prefer to think they would act in such a manner. It
remains to be said, however, that the examples quoted do suggest
that the intra-formal system can be as coercive as any formal
system, and that any protective ideals that the formal culture may
encourage, or which may stem from other sources, often need
courage if they are to be put into effect.

So much for the fates of non-conformity with the ways of pupil
society. What are the benefits of conformity?

The advantages of popularity are mainly that people are generous to
you and that you get no rebuke. This is because any person who does
not believe in your popularity can not show her feelings because of
other people.   (13)

The conception of popularity does not always refer to a central
figure to whom all attention is given. It more often seems to apply
to the average condition of being on good or likeable terms with
one's fellows. Friendship can be struck up immediately on arrival:

I remember when I first came I went into my Dormey after saying
Tatar to my Mum and Dad I went in to find somone crying her hart
out and within a short time we became best friends.   (12)

Among the younger girls there appears often to be a great deal of fluidity of relationships, with proximity, interdependence, jealousy and shared interests making for a high turnover of 'buddy' pairs, with some genuine relationships emerging. Sometimes there is a degree of witty observation of the process which can make for creation of a small epic in which two, sometimes more, may share:

. . .my worst enemy was awful but now [she] is my best friend. During the weekend we had what I call a 'World War III'! We have had quarrels three times and this was the third so it was counted as a War. We are now back in friends again so it has just blown over. We are now awaiting World War IV which will probably start next term! (12) I go around with a nice bunch of girls we all like what I do, pop music, mod clothes, amusing people and last but not least boys. I have a girl in the bunch I like perticuly, she's a great kid.   (12)

At another school, one girl observes many things about friendship, and another shows the strains that can arise when the formal system members decide to keep a great degree of 'order' in the intra-formal part of society.

. . . everyone gets 'paired off'. . . if you want to talk to anybody else, just cos perhaps they know more than the friend, then the friend gets all jealous. A best friend can share troubles and depression and so make it better. Also 2 people can be happy and have fun together whom you know you can rely on for anything.   (15)

But at the same school:

. . . one is forced to choose a friend, and to 'go around' with them. As one is not allowed to have friends in a different year (if one does the housemistress has you both in and generally dissuades you from continuing the friendship) and there may be as few as 2 or 3 in your year in your house, one has very little choice of friends and yet you are expected to be loyal and devoted to this girl as if she were your perfect friend. . . . Most of the time I don't care but sometimes this situation becomes desperately depressing and having to live in close proximity to a person you don't really like becomes a very great strain especially as you are expected to display a liking which you are not in fact feeling.   (16)

The benefits of conformity can range from very positive situations of real friendship, solace in trouble and enhancement of the good times, to mechanical and sometimes irksome proximity-relations. Not all schools produce the same effects; without having 'measured' the matter, and so without being able to generalize, there are some signs that where formal control over friendships tries to maintain barriers between ages or between houses (the first possibly in an attempt to avoid crushes, the second perhaps to try and increase house-feeling and hence competitive spirit leading in turn to better individual performance) there is not enough scope for selecting compatible pairs for true relationships.

An extreme example of what can be felt in a community with tight formal divisions highlights these points:

Friendship is walking over to school together. Friendship is sitting together at lunch. Friendship is having someone to talk to about the weather. Friendship is having someone to wash your back for you. As is patently obvious friendship as described above is shallow, superficial and stupid. In this school one has to make friends with people in the same house. People in other houses are discouraged by Housemistresses. Thus an individual has to make friends (if this is what she chooses) with one or more of perhaps five or ten females be they cretinous, bitchy, bloody-minded, 'very nice' (very rare) or whatever abilities they may possess. The moral of this is 'IF YOU WANT A FRIEND DON'T COME HERE'.   (16)

It must be said straightaway that this school also has an active old girls' organization with sub-groups which keep contacts going, so at least in the past there may well have been many real friendships fostered in the school. Although some might say that this school has not changed significantly over the years, it may be plausibly speculated that quite a real change has occurred: that whereas previously national mores and communication media made it possible for a regimented social system to be run without psychological tension, in latter years the staff may have felt it more necessary to pull the psychological strings tighter to try and maintain the organization as it was. The result of this would be the feeling that genuine and relaxed personal relationships, based on an interested exploration of others' characters, cannot easily thrive.

Elsewhere, if there is a more fluid system, there is some sign that really rewarding friendships are formed, even though these may also turn out to be mere crushes; only very rarely did I come across signs that such ties were 'unhealthy' or crippling, except once, for example, when the object of the impossible affection of a junior girl was a young staff member.

We have now seen something of the machinery whereby the intra-formal system tends to control behaviour. It has its hierarchy of popularity (and another of status, which has not been dealt with), its penalties and rewards which operate to set up and safeguard its norms. What are the norms then? What are girls required to do, and what kinds of behaviour are unpopular? Many answers to these questions are implied in quotations already given, but a few more will provide more direct illustration. We can examine what behaviour is liked, and what is often disliked:

> . . . one girl . . . had no friends and most unluckily is on our table and she always starts arguments by kicking people. We always groan when she has more food because she is so greedy and she cries at least five times a day. (12)

Some behaviour can clearly be considered *de trop* once a girl is disliked, which might be forgiven, ignored or even laughed at in others; but evidently misery can itself be disliked by others, thus setting up a vicious circle which may only be eroded by time rather than broken, though the formal system can take a hand by moving a girl to a different group (dormitory, house, table, class, etc., depending on the circumstances). Elsewhere:

> . . . there are some nasty girls one of whom for example banged my head against another girls bed very hard indeed for no reason at all. (13)

Usually, however, the misdemeanour is not physical, but psychological or social.

> . . . people make themselves unpopular through big headedness, or if they are eager to talk about their holidays or boyfriends and if you try to say something about yourself and they just don't want to know. (13)
> One girl who is very unpopular . . . makes out she knows everything about sex, boys, fashion, but I really think (so does everyone else) that she is better than everyone else at these things.
> . . . It is true we do break a lot of school rules and smoke, but anyone who is undercautious . . . and is too eager to break such [rules] as smoking, and makes out . . . that she is the best smoker and knows how to inhale, and no one else can do it properly [is likely to be unpopular]. (13)

The theme of requiring girls to take some risks with the rules is repeated in several schools. The 'goody-goody' is unpopular, as at an opposite extreme is the braggart deviant.

. . . you should break rules sometimes and not always be a Goody Goody and do not be stuck up. Don't tell tails or everyone will hate you and don't be wet and weedy.   (12)

To take 'unfair' advantage over others is sometimes warned against, and we have seen examples already when girls seem to obey this advice:

If you have a sister at your school, or knew some girls before in the form above, do not go and accost them as old pals.   (12)
Don't try to be clever, don't make out you can do a lot of work. Talk to people a lot, but not so much at first let people find out what your real character is. Don't . . . make up lots of stories about how great life is at home, get into trouble just to say 'I'm the naughtiest girl in the school'.   (14)

In other words the advice is: 'keep in line'. Even with mischief, do not take it too far. This does not exclude mischief completely, of course, and we shall come to examine this 'underlife' presently, as within the area of things which *should* be done.

Dear Sister,
   If you are coming to this school you must not be modist and frightened of people . . . and not be like a snail in a shell that will not come out. (12)

In a few schools there are signs of initiatory procedures, the undergoing of which enables new girls to prove themselves socially:

You may not be at all popular at first, and everyone will hate you unless you talk at night; you are considered a goody-goody, and you are supposed to be sent out and get a punishment before you really become a member of the house.   .   (12)

At one school there were signs of what at first might be called 'uninhibited' behaviour, but which an older girl realizes is an instance of individual behaviour being determined by the group, when she says 'the cult of being different is getting very fashionable'. Four younger girls at this school, however, write with considerable *élan*:

Have good taste in clothes and be fun; be exciting with lots of new ideas . . . *hate* games and *love* pop music. One must not be *too* hygenic. Must wear hair loose and not with a hairband. Not take any notice of the school list and bring lots of bloomers and stockings . . . *do not* use the clothes list as a true clothes list . . . don't be horse mad, hearty, too bumpseous; don't take notice of the clothes list . . . do know the facts of life. . . . Do bring a torch, lots of grub, clothes, good books and comics. If you do what I [i.e. 'we'] say you will be a BANG.   (13)

During the visit to this school a national charity day occurred, and little plastic flowers were sold. They appeared on different girls in a variety of positions – in the hair, on the shoulder, elsewhere on the torso, on the hips, one at either knee, thereby showing a range of expressive ingenuity. Few schools visited, however, allowed this extent of expressive freedom. Most schools strictly prescribed how visual symbols of free expression might be displayed – on boards in common rooms or studies. Even in dormitories, pin-up pictures of pop stars were discouraged in many schools, limited permission usually extending to family photographs only. Interestingly enough, where no symbolism of covert intra-formal ideals is realized by the rulers of the formal system, not only freedom but encouragement may be met; one girl wrote a story of a dream encounter with a pop star, the denouement of which consisted of his writing his name in her book. This story appeared officially in the school magazine, while overt material (for example, had the story ended with physical relations with the male idol) would more likely have been disapproved. Among the girls, however, restraint is not always advised:

. . . have some thrilling experiences to talk about which would hold the classes attention and make her more interesting . . .   (14)

Be boy mad if you want to get on with the majority, and like pop music.   (14)

Most signs of status are connected with boys, looks and ability at games. Receiving letters from boys is a status symbol . . . Being able to dance (not ballroom) in a different more exciting way than anyone else is generally admired.   (15)

In another school:

. . . if you are a senior, and a junior has a crush on you, it is regarded as a status symbol.   (15)

Obviously, girls are not unaware of their growing sexual

sensitivities, and their culture pays lavish, and sometimes imaginative attention to this area of experience. At one school the head found and confiscated a points-rating scale that was being circulated among the girls. This scale produced a score (much in the same way as did our institutional control scale) by awarding points for such items as 'petted above waist', 'petted below waist', 'told someone you love him' and (in homage to feminine power perhaps, bringing top marks) 'told by someone he loves you'.

Some girls, in several different schools, speak up for an individual to 'be herself' if she would be liked and popular in a genuine way:

It is better to keep quiet and not force yourself on anybody until you have been accepted . . . try to be an individual and people will respect you.   (14)

Have your own opinions and don't agree with *everything* popular girls do and say, – they will think you are a weed.   (14)

You must not try to do as the others, try to help, have good ideas.   (14)

In a place such as this, there is opportunity for finding a 'real friend' . . . of course, here, as anywhere else, there are many circles of friends who are not 'real' friends but purely a social group. This I see no value in. Most people here probably do just experience 'acquaintanceships' but I have experienced 'friendship'.   (16)

This girl was more fortunate, and shows that there is a considerable difference between schools and individual predicaments found therein. In some schools the 'social groups' as distinct from 'real friendships' do not just share contiguity (as the girl who describes back-washing friendships as shallow and stupid indicates above), but they can cohere quite strongly. Some references to 'gangs' were heard, sometimes crystallizing around one leader, and on one occasion there were two 'gangs'. These not only had rival leaders, and were conducting skirmishes which promised hostility and violence, but they also mutually symbolized their gang-membership by possessing one of two types of soup-tin label. The head very wisely recognized that cohesive forces of membership were invested in these physical, visual symbols. She called a meeting at which the two leaders were seated on either side of her, and at which the soup-label symbols of membership were ceremonially torn up. This not only demonstrated where membership was 'consecrated', but also 'poured it all into' the paper vessels which were then destroyed. The gangs were thus publicly, and it is said effectively, dissolved. This instance occurred among younger girls, and it is perhaps more common among them than in those approaching the middle-school years, from whom the following advice about individuality was heard:

To be popular or unpopular, girls would just have to be themselves and I don't see why anyone should change their character to suit others, but gradually you have to change and you do, not knowing that you do.   (14)

This was written by the daughter of non-fee-paying parents, 'integrant' into the boarding-school system. She sees that behaviour is moulded, either by most people wittingly or unknowingly giving in. A slightly older girl in another school points out that conformity includes not just what someone does, but also what a person thinks – or at least expresses.

To be popular it is necessary in most cases to be leading and lively in conformity. For the widely-acclaimed, a 90 % lively interest in boys and clothes is required, plus, perhaps, the ability to be a critic, preferably a knowledgeable one, of the non-conformists and staff. For the non-conformists, unless the ability to be absorbed by private interests in the presence of others is possessed, life is difficult, due to its extreme organisation, for girls are, on the whole, both inquisitive and critical, and for the less strong-willed, the general trend is the one to be followed, for there is 'safety in numbers' and 'what's wrong with the prototype end product anyway?' so the train of thought runs, if it runs at all. (15)

The conformity spoken of here is to the intra-formal system, the society of the girls. As has been pointed out, in many schools this requires an amount of mischief to take place, of staff-baiting, of testing out the rule-boundaries between formal and intra-formal systems. Most incidents reported to me were mild. Whereas colleagues visiting boys' or co-ed schools said they were liberally supplied with anecdotes about intimate sexual activities and other socially awkward-to-mention subjects, my own research visits were not similarly regaled. This may be because there was less to say; it may also be because the visitor was a man, and one who may have shown reticence to collect intimate information elicited as it were 'by advantage' of the research situation; or I may unwittingly have suggested an unsympathetic exterior or some other barrier to communication. At a very few schools girls frankly allowed some insight into their 'underlife', but my guess is that there was not a great deal of serious illicit activity.

What was told, and often with semblance of great daring and promising me to conspiratorial silence (i.e. as to the exact individual giving me the information), looked like this:

In the dormy we have a hide out, it is a loose floor board.   (12)
We all got out of bed . . . and started to open tins and bottles. We had masses of food and it included tins of cold chicken, cold baked beans, cold sweet corn, chips, cheese footballs, ritz biscuits, about three cakes and lots of fruit. There was coca-cola, shandy, and ginger beer. The feast lasted two hours . . . and at 3 o'clock . . . we were feeling very full and tired . . . and climbed sleepily into bed.   (12)

If this was a flight of fancy, it was effectively enough written, and corroborated by others. But most accounts were unfortunately of more meagre feasts. In one school, it was Nescafé made up with warm water, biscuits and fruit; in most schools, food is not allowed in the dormitories, except fruit – to discourage mice, it is said. Girls are supposed to be hysterically afraid of mice, though in one school they were popular as pets and there was a considerable smell in some rooms. Judging by the arrival of a cat in the aisle, a mouse may once even have been taken to chapel in a pupil's pocket.

Two other types of mischief, running away and seeing boys, are related.

The most exciting thing I've ever done in school is run away but I got caught when I got to the Isle of White.   (13)
That person from Cambridge is still here, he was in our house last night. The H-M had [him] in her room last night, Zoe and I betted she was buttering him up. We had a water fight, Jane and Zoe soaked me and then we soaked Zoe.
    Sue has just pretended to be sick. The milkman should come soon, then everyone will rush to the windows and wave madly.   (14)

Elsewhere there was evidently more occasion to get out:

. . . the best thing I remember in school is the Sundays when I use to go and met blokes in a hedge and at Nights go for and have a fag!   (14)

    Elsewhere:

Great! I'm going out on Saturday. Must get more cigs. We've run out, had the last six last night in the bathroom with the window open. It was freezing.   (14)

Girls reported two sorts of reaction to their rule-breaking from members of the public. In one, some older woman assumed to be a vintage old girl, would report the least infringements of behaviour or standards of dress. Telephone calls from such women were reported at second hand, at several schools, though I never spoke to a girl who had been reported herself in this way. The irritable old lady might be a projection of girls' consciences. The opposite was told of help received in breaking school rules which the stranger knew were not illegal in the broad sense; for example, a shopkeeper hid a girl under the counter when a school staff member appeared. Other public escapades were rarely reported, such as occasional trips to the seaside, cinemas or to pubs with boys. Two girls went out interviewing householders and accepting drinks while they conducted an *ad hoc* sociological questionnaire. Finally, in one school girls were trying out 'levitation', which occult practice as conducted could be alarming to more naïve or impressionable minds.

The prevailing impression was, however, that for girls (unlike reportedly for boys) the development of an 'underlife' into proportions of an epic – a continuing saga with heroines accomplishing dangerous and admirable exploits – did not occur. More characteristic was the 'spy out of the cold' episode described as follows:

I myself was not very misceivious, in fact rather a goody goody, but I thought the others were *really* daring and must be clever to take such risks. On one occasion I realised that I was wrong. It was when I decided to 'be a devil' and, with them, sneak out during the night. I was with the 'professionals' . . . we crept downstairs in our dressing gowns and were going to buy some chocolate from outside the station. Well, I was bubbling with excitement when much to my utter astonishment, one of the 'chief criminals' said: 'Lord, if I'm caught – I'm turning back . . . call me chicken if you like . . .'; with that she went back! Another, also very used to sneaking out at night put herself flat against a letter box so as not to be seen by a car that was coming – I was quite struck with the utter stupidity of my friends who would spend so long the next morning telling us all about it . . . she had put herself in the full glare of the headlights that were coming along, and on seeing a girl in her dressing gown standing thus, a policeman climbed out and soon presented us to the headmistress!! Such are the brains of the so-called 'shrewd dare-devils'.   (18)

My impression is that although some readers may know of

situations where really active and significant underlife systems are to be found, girls in boarding schools seem to 'lack' this field as an area in which to develop an epic. By an epic, I mean the case for instance of sports in some boys' schools, which provide an arena for action in which heroes can develop, where there is reference to a special history of a game and its literature, which offers exceptional performers a part in it as a career. In a few schools, for some pupils, 'culture' in the sense of music or poetry perhaps serves such a purpose. But at the risk of unpopularity at the hands of masculo-feminists for suggesting this, it would seem that girls are potentially, symbolically or actually preoccupied with preparing for the epic of motherhood. This may reduce the need to develop other epics, for example for boys that of the brotherhood of membership in a single-sex school (which can persist after leaving school), or of cricket or of an underlife-society.

Some questionnaire results from sixth-formers have a bearing on these points.

Table 6·1. What upper sixth-form boarders found most rewarding in school

item	rewarding* (per cent)
close relationship with particular friends	67·0
the general level of teaching	59·5
opportunities for drama, music, the arts	56·0
living together with other girls	52·0
opportunities for sport and games	46·5
opportunities for organizing and running things	46·0
being able to get round some of the rules	37·5
contacts with individual staff members	36·0

Source: 214 sixth-formers in twenty-one schools.

* The scale ran from 3 (max.) to 1 (min.); thus scores were converted as follows: $\left(\dfrac{\bar{x}-1}{2}\right) \times 100 = \text{percentage}$

Apart from the interest of the responses to the other items, we see that individual friendship is the most rewarding facet of life reported. This, however, comes from girls who are in the upper reaches, who may have forgotten the feelings of compression into

a group of peers that is complained of by younger girls. The somewhat awkwardly worded item on 'getting round some of the rules'
failed to capture any great enthusiasm for underlife. Perhaps this
should be seen as a large figure though, coming as it does from a
socially select band in the sixth forms.

Another question asked 'Which of these items do you think the
school promotes?' and there followed a list of eighteen items. There
were 638 replies analysed, from fifth- and sixth-formers in fifteen
schools. Approximately ninety per cent thought their school promoted 'the ability to run a home well'; over seventy per cent said
their school promoted snobbery, and eighty per cent felt that 'too
much interest in the same sex, for some people', was caused.
Snobbery and interest in one's own sex are phenomena which
concern the pupil society, though one is not saying that they are
either specifically caused or restrained by the girls. They are more
likely affected by aspects of formal structure which have already
been described. It does seem, however, that there is little sign that a
coherent underlife, challenging or snubbing the rules, or even a
'sisterhood' of epic proportion exists in many schools. Such situations may exist in a few schools, but not enough to affect the overall
results above. It may also be true that the prevalence of underlife
has been underestimated, due to the reticence of girls in giving
evidence. In that case it really *would* be an underlife, secret and
submerged. This would be in a different sociological category from
the usual kind of underlife which snubs the formal system, but
which is not shy of, and may indeed have need of outside attention
which would help it to cohere. The investigation gave every (decent)
chance for underlife information to emerge, and unlike what
colleagues reported from boys' schools, rather little emerged.

One sign of a rich group culture, private to itself and making its
existence distinct from what is outside, is the development of a
jargon. This has been reported in several boys' schools, in prisons,
armed services, and has been described from the special esoteric
societies by which some African tribes used to segregate their
youngsters in a 'boarding group' in preparation for their publicly
taking up adult roles. In the girls' schools I visited, I found no rich
jargons. There were some special words, and these often referred
to places within the school. There were some novel titles for senior
staff, characteristically referred to in the third person, thus the

Mahdi and the Moke (both heads). Nicknames of girls were widespread, and a list of over 600 can be given. Here are some examples: Baggy, Bambam, Bouncy, Bubbles, Bunny, Doodles, Farto, Flea, Hairey, Kipper, Maxie, Moo, Paw Paw, Pussy, Randers, Tick, Turnip, Wopsy . . .

There are plenty of examples which are merely accepted shortenings of full names like 'Chris', while others stem from combinations of the characteristics of the names and of their owners. Some further unmentionable names were offered, but I have not reported these, as there is nothing to be gained thereby, nor was there corroboration from several girls that such (obscene) names were used, and they may be inventions of single respondents to the item on the questionnaire. All the above examples were widely corroborated, and many could be found in several schools.

Items of clothing earned names, thus 'trolleys' for underwear, 'B squared' for brassieres and the 'bullet proofs' already mentioned previously. One school produced an unusual verb, 'clicking' for putting away crockery after meals, and several had esoteric words for toilets – Charlie, Alps and the Halfway House being three. Food only earned uncomplimentary epithets, many of which are variants met in boys' schools and elsewhere; thus 'Mersey Mud' is chocolate custard, and 'Benjie's Kittens' is shepherds pie. On the whole, however, no school was found with anything like a rich verbal code of its own – that is, more than a dozen words not in current teenager parlance (of the time) such as 'trendy' or 'rave' or 'dishy'. It is probably relevant to note that, where jargon existed, it was not specific to the school, but shared with the wider young population. Some few schools showed a 'debby' turn of interests, but most were plugged in to the 'youthsville' of the current mass media. One distinction was the widespread use of the word 'yobs', for working-class youths who dress and style their hair in a certain way. I inquired of 'integrant' girls whose fees were subsidized, and some of whom might possibly identify their brothers with the category labelled 'yobs', but could find no signs of disgust or discomfort.

The intra-formal systems have now been briefly described. No 'measurements' were made, and inter-school generalizations were not therefore possible. There are intra-formal methods of inducting newcomers into the pupil society, of rewarding 'correct' and punishing unwanted behaviour. Intra-formal norms, or unwritten rules, become clear and can be described by most girls. There is much evidence that girls are very interested in the world outside the school – they miss their parents, their pets, and their boy-friends at a later age; they listen to pop music and attend to its stars; they use the jargon of teenage cultures rather than developing extensive vocabularies special to the school community. There would appear to be few extremes, for example, of licence or of repression, though perhaps the 'extreme' of boredom is sometimes reported. Perhaps the three most appropriate adjectives to describe the field, which it must be remembered is not uniform by any means, are unexciting, though interesting, and conservative.

Seven: Pastoral Care

In her book on girls' schools, Dr Kathleen Ollerenshaw describes a question put to headmistresses of boarding schools on possible differences between girls' and boys' schools. Some mentioned that 'discipline concerning out of school activities has to be more strict ... but inside the "confines" of the school, discipline for girls can be much less strict'. The heads made 'a slightly wistful observation that ... [they] rarely have a separate house and their life is thereby harder and much more closely wrapped up in the school'. No mention is made of 'Pastoral Care'.

Royston Lambert has described how, in boys' boarding schools, the presence of married housemasters can be one ingredient of a system which provides effective pastoral care. This depends on a good network of communications; the master and senior boys must know a very great deal about the lives, worries, hopes and satisfactions of all pupils. With this knowledge, they are in a position to anticipate or notice suffering; they may choose to prevent, alleviate, ignore or even intensify the trouble. In some schools, decisions are sometimes made to allow younger pupils to battle through certain situations by their own efforts; elsewhere, every effort is made to reduce unhappiness and alienation. Sometimes the staff and older pupils try to mould not only the feelings, but also the attitudes and thoughts of those in their care. This process can be called 'education', or it can be called 'total institutional control'.

What is the pastoral care situation in girls' schools? I asked heads and staff what kinds of worries girls had, and what might be done for them. Sometimes one heard of ways in which adults and children enjoyed life together, though this aspect was under-emphasized both in the questions I posed and certainly in the comments I was offered. There were a few notable exceptions. The main body of information came from the girls. They were asked questions of this type:

If you had a problem *about work*, something that was worrying you, is there anyone in this school to whom you would go for advice and help?

A second question tackled another area by starting: 'If you were troubled or upset about some bad news from home . . .'; a third question referred to 'personal, emotional, sexual or moral difficulties'. Girls were not asked to name likely confidantes in person, but to give their position, thus teacher, head, friend, sister, etc. They were also told that, if there was nobody to whom they would want to go, or if there was more than one for any given class of problem, to say so. I am very aware that the results of this type of question can be extremely sensitive to the attitude communicated, or even held by the research worker. Therefore I made every effort to try to suggest a sympathetic interest, without any implied expectations of answers, or of how they would be judged. These questions were put in a standard form in all of the twenty-three schools visited. In some schools where there was time other writings were collected, for example 'sentence completion' items which were started off with 'if only . . .' or 'my worst time'.

The word 'sex' deserves some mention here. It is plain that in most schools girls are expected to remain virgins until at least after they leave school, and preferably until they get married. The precautions surrounding this matter are often extensive.

I often think I detest school, but really I like it. The staff drive me crackers sometimes, though – they're so narrow minded! Mention a boy's name and you practically get expelled!   (14)

One housemistress told me, barely minutes after we were introduced, and in a manner that seemed to suggest a triumphantly just accusation, 'I hear you have been asking girls in another school about their *sex lives* . . .'. This was unfortunately untrue; it would probably have been a much better study with such questions included. It would also probably have involved 'political' difficulties, with schools declining to be visited. As it was, the mention of 'sex' in the third pastoral care question meant in one school that I was asked not to give the questionnaire to girls below a certain age. A few schools were assured enough to allow discussions with the girls of the sort necessary to establish some confidence; it is from these conversations that some of the ideas in this chapter arise.

Personal Problems and Needs for Pastoral Care

What do girls worry about? Some worries are those of adolescents anywhere; others are connected with the reasons for which girls are at boarding school (families broken, or abroad, other sources of maladjustment); some worries arise from the circumstance of living in a close community. Here is what some girls say:

I worry . . that I'm a dreadful liar and whether I'll be able to break the habit . . .   (10)

I worry about mummy at home with only our dog for company.   (11)

I worry about maths, because our teacher is so strict.   (11)

I worrie about growing up 'cause I don't want to start periods. I also worrie about a pony I know because I might never see or ride him again.   (11)

This should be remembered when the relation of young girls to pets, especially horses, is discussed later on. Further worries arise specifically because of the boarding situation.

I trust no-one or no-body to talk to. I wont stand by anyone because at this school we are always having 'bust-ups'.   (11)

I have plenty of worries like people way they treat me and say mean things about me or my parents because my mother and father are devored.   (11)

A glimmer of existential *angst* sometimes shows at an early age:

I sometimes worry about weather people have the same feelings and worry's as I have and weather other people are people or just things. (12)

Despair is sometimes reached, and extreme possible solutions considered:

The worst thing I ever considered doing was committing suicide. I still do though *not* because I go to boarding school.   (13)

And further:

I deal with my worries by just swareing at everybody and losing my temper or trying to kill myself it may sound silly but I tried the other night I tried to jump off the window but I couldn't do it.   (14)

Other girls contemplate the lesser escape of merely getting away from the school, though the worry this would cause to parents seems to be one deterrent to those who would not go as far as suicide.

Often you feel as though you wanted to run away, but I always think of my mother worrying. My mother says if I really, truely hate it here I may leave, but I would never leave because it would cost her a lot of money to keep me at a day school.   (12)

Thus writes a girl who has an assisted place for reasons of family need. The desire to shield parents can show in other ways:

Letters never show any feelings, at least if one is miserable one tries to hide it in ones letters so one's parents arent unhappy.   (12)

This shows a burden not only of her own worries, but also that of shielding her parents. Some worries are associated with bizarre circumstances.

I have been afraid of going to the lavatory at night because a Yob climbed up the pipe and looked in.   (12)

This kind of visitation is rare. We do not know if this girl was intruded upon herself or whether she is reporting what happened to someone else. The category of 'Yob' is maintained by girls and even staff in several schools, denoting an uncouth and id-brandishing male; this conception is widely spoken of with distaste, sometimes fear, though some girls are possibly directed by this phobia to be more drawn to such young men than they might otherwise be.

Older girls may stage their worries in wider arenas.

Nowadays I begin to worry that Russia will let off a bomb.   (14)

Though this 'political' perspective appears rather rarely, horizons of worry are also extended by looking to the future.

Nowadays I have begun to worry that I'll fail my O levels, wont get married.   (14)
I am worried about how I am going to leave home. For this reason I am melancholy and can not properly control my feelings.   (15)
When you get into the VIth form your worries become very big and by that time the biggest worry is what I am going to do when I leave school because I dont know and nobody can give me any good suggestions.   (16)

This girl's trouble may hinge around her interpretation of what makes a 'good' suggestion. Her school made a point of explaining the care and efficiency of its concern for future careers; but she may have found the school's ideas unacceptable.

Sixth-formers' worries concern not only their own careers, but also other people's worries. In their seniority, they become approachable members of authority, not quite as remote as staff, and thus have to carry out 'pastoral care' as well as perhaps needing some themselves – as any human being does, whether child or adult.

Security is needed desperately!! Junior members of the house tend to trust their prefects more than the staff. Speaking for myself that is. Many girls have complained to me of their worries and yet would not dream of going to a member of staff about them.   (16)

In some schools, there may be less tendency to take troubles to seniors, though perhaps it may depend on the individuals, or on the house, as much as upon a general status level of seniors in the school. Two remarks follow, from the same school:

Turning to staff is not encouraged. Most juniors turn to their own contempraries rather than us (VI formers) as we seem distant. Anyway, most VI formers become rather hardened to most worries about school and therefore are of little use to juniors.   (17)

A colleague, however, disagrees:

If other people have problems, I feel they would be wise to come to me rather than our housemistress as she is an unfeeling spinster (*no* exaggeration) and also impractical, whereas I am more likely to understand girls' problems being one of them and also I'm logical, practical, sympathetic and understanding which many school staff are not.   (17)

This extract poses many fascinating problems. If this girl is as sympathetic as she says, has she judged staff with equal sympathy? Are they really as 'closed' as she suggests? Even if she has not had time enough to write as clearly as she might have wished, what is the overall atmosphere which gives rise to views of this type, and expressed in this way? Is this real sympathy that can be extended 'downwards' to junior girls, and can this exist without equally real sympathy extended 'upwards' to staff? It seemed to me as a visitor that many of the older spinster staff were particularly easy to understand and sympathize with. If girls do not see this, it may well be that their occupancy of a lower position in an authority structure obscures their view. The figures to be shown later will tell more clearly how extensive the difficulties in communication may be.

However, the self-confident charity above is more hopeful than the apologium provided by another girl at the same school:

... they are very reluctant to come to us. When they do, can cause awkward situations for people who have to keep some discipline. Everybody is I think rather selfish, they are very conscious of their own problems, not very interested in others. (17)

Seniors do, of course, have their own problems, some of which stem from their boy-friends outside school. *Vis-à-vis* these boys, many of whom are undergraduates, the girls live out roles as almost-adults, with the possibilities and responsibilities of stable relationships and of marriage very much in mind. Yet at school, the girls are sometimes placed in a world where these outside possibilities are not thought of as real (by the girls' interpretation of staff views). At a time, therefore, when girls are striving to clarify their ideas and perceptions of their own identity, they have to live out an important ambiguity. This they often report as a problem. Furthermore, it is one whose roots start surprisingly early.

I like being a girl because I think boys are super. (12)

This simple view at the launching of womanhood soon runs into complications.

Nowadays I have begun to worry that boys are too fresh, they always want to go to bed with you, or go on holiday together. I have a boy friend he is not very fresh, sometimes he is a bit but he does not go very far. He is just an ordinary nice boy. (13)

This consciousness of boys soon becomes a yearning for them, sometimes simply expressed, but by others translated into fantasy.

I wish boys would come for walks near our school. (13)

And:

If only this school had boys in it, but I supose you would have to use the san for a Maternity Hospital, and the people might think it were a brothol. I think girls + Boy who are seperated are sexually excited and I think Girls + boy should be together and if they were they wouldn't have it out with any old bloke. (14)

Such statements were not uncommon; they tended to come from particular schools. This may have meant that those schools had developed atmospheres producing that kind of thought; or that a particular form interviewed might have arrived through some chance combination of circumstances in this kind of mood, which might therefore occur at (in)opportune moments in any school. I incline to believe the first line of explanation. From the mass of writings in this area, it is worth noting four contributions, from different schools:

I miss very much, boys, not on a sex point of view, but I used to go to a mixed grammar school and now without boys this school is dull and monotoness. I find if I hitch my skirt up or put make up on, there is nobody to impress (and you can't impress girls!!).   (15)

Everyone else seems to have a good time when they are living at home, and I think my life is being wasted because you should be enjoying yourself when you are young and I am not enjoying myself at all.   (16)

You never know whether if you have a letter from a boy it will be opened or whether you will ever see it, problems arise out of this! (16)

Then there is the boy friend. I'm frightened and worried about him taking drugs while I'm away because he gets depressed a lot. I'm not worry though about him going with another girl because I know he's faithful (well after two years of waiting for me I believe he wont go off now) – he's great but I worry about him drinking, smoking, and becoming a drug addict.   (16)

We cannot know whether this girl's worries are well-founded, or perhaps based on a mixture of separation plus the alarms sounded by the press. But obviously her worries exist, and can cause unhappiness and impede her work. Another girl judges the situation at her school:

Personally I think the whole conception of a single sex community life is totally unrealistic. So – I can people my inner world with friends – through letters etc. but leads to some exaggeration of reality – especially in relationships with boys, unless can manage, during absence, to keep relationship on a smooth, fairly even level – not too emotional.   (17)

A final two examples by no means exhaust the range of types of problem, but show the individual ultimately at odds with the community she is in:

I have been forced to stay on an extra year by the headmistress and have nothing to do. I loathe the place and quite a few of the staff.   (17)

I hate the school; it batters too much the wings of my self-will.   (17)

At the age of these girls, 'pastoral care' may not be able to help adjust their own feelings towards accepting the community. Two questions then arise: will those carrying on pastoral care consider it as one of its functions that they should attempt to adjust the community in some way to fit it to the individual? This depends perhaps on how many individuals share the same types of problem. Organizations have a considerable momentum, and are less likely to change unless enough individuals are at odds and leave, fail exams or in some other way embarrass the school. The second question is, does pastoral care have as one of its functions the management of an individual so that her dissatisfaction is reduced, or so that it does not affect others? The answer here is probably Yes.

A Summary of Worries and Pastoral Problems

A few problems can now be drawn together (though many will be omitted from this list). Younger girls feel the impact and pains of physical adolescence. They worry about how other people notice their changing selves, and about bad behaviour they develop, about their families (especially if there is hardship); they worry about the social risks of community life (rumours, teasing, competition for and possible loss of friends) and they battle to find and keep some human haven of security in the quicksands of community life. This 'pastoral agent' must not only be acceptable to the self, but also to one's friends ('thou shalt not suck up to the staff or the seniors'). A few girls have existential doubts, and a few consider suicidal notions. Other girls think of absconding, and several actually do so; very few take up the burdens of political anxiety (H-bombs, Vietnam), though several become concerned with social service needs. The latter, however, seems to cause little vicarious suffering; rather it flatters by the opportunity occasionally afforded (or allowed) to make some small contribution.

Older girls begin to worry about exams, and of their chances of securing good futures (careers and marriage). They are themselves consulted by smaller girls with worries, which can be a burden and present difficulties in the exercise of authority. Seniors worry about increasingly mature sexual relationships, interrupted (also rendered more poignant – a few enjoy the romantic enhancement this can offer) and carried on by letter. Finally, some have reached a general distaste for the life of their school, and by the very definition of their 'problem' pastoral care from any school member is not likely to be found acceptable.

The Provision and Use of Pastoral Care

What do the girls do about their problems? To whom do they intend to go for consultation and solace, and for what sorts of problems? Statistical evidence is here available. We will also see comments about how problems are, and sometimes are not dealt with.

The question format has already been explained, posed thus, 'If you had X problems, is there anyone to whom you would go?' The answers have been categorized simply for tabulation. We will be interested in the answer that a girl will go to 'nobody'; also to staff, and thirdly to friends. Staff is the category necessary to include all the various sets of roles that occupy adults in different schools. Further subdivision would have resulted in false comparisons; thus people called 'housemistresses' in one school may have a very different job from 'housemistresses' in another school. 'Friends' has collected all girls, of same age, seniors, and sisters together.

First let us see the proportion of girls who specifically say (NB this is not merely indication by default, or omission of an answer) that they will go to nobody with a personal problem. This percentage I have called the NPF ('nobody-personal-factor'). It represents the most severe form of keeping to oneself at all costs. The percentages who would refuse to consult about work, or home problems, are smaller, and can be inferred by examining Table 7·4.

Table 7·1. NPF for boarders and day girls of different ages

	percentage of girls who do not want to take personal problems to anyone:					
number of girls	aged: 12	13	14	15	16	overall
1,036 boarders	0·0	29·2	35·1	37·3	35·5	34·1
255 day girls	—	79·5	55·3	40·0	62·7	58·0

This allows us to infer several things about school life. First-year boarders will not be reluctant to discuss intimate problems with staff or with friends. As they settle in, nearly one-third separate out and say they will not intend to discuss personal problems with anyone in the community. This is the overall pattern, though of course there are wide differences between schools, which will be discussed later. The reluctance to seek pastoral care seems to rise to a peak at the age of 15, then eases off slightly.

Simplified, it seems that about 340 out of 1,000 boarders would not want to seek help with a personal problem. This is not just a measure of self-confidence among the oldest girls; it applies similarly to 13- as to 16-year-olds. It does not mean that all these girls remain silent about their troubles. Some of them may surface in gossip, or kind staff may notice and inquire; or there may be dramatic behaviour disorders which signal clearly that there is trouble beneath. What we see here, though, is the extent of unwillingness to look for help.

The day girls show a very different pattern. They are much less concerned to deal with their personal problems through consultation in school; their readiness to consult, however, rises to a maximum at age 15. The oldest day girls are more likely to have not only family, but also boy-friends outside school, with whom they can discuss their troubles (unless these people are responsible for the problems!).

What do girls write about the way that their personal troubles get dealt with?

At school I get los of worries and my housemistress would take me in her room and talk to me and that would soon cheer me up.   (11)

This is the picture that is presented to visitors and, as we have seen, it is more likely to apply for the younger boarders. Thereafter, however, we see doubts and distance beginning to crystallize.

I sometimes might trust the matron, but I might be thought silly by her. I would also trust the housemistress, Headmistress, and my parents.   (12)

But elsewhere:

The teaching staff are O.K. It's just the housemistress that one has to live with and have as *mothers*! I quite frankly think this is an insult to our poor mothers!   (16)

Next there comes a problem in the path of the effort to relieve problems:

The people I trust to talk to are my friends. I would not tell a house-mistress or matron as people would call you a teachers pet.   (12)

Girls realize that pastoral needs can promote relationships of special closeness, and apparently function as a group to prevent any such relationships which they perhaps suspect could be used for 'unfair' advantage. Specific problem areas, such as that of sex, may be surrounded with a particular aura of inhibition.

I think we should be taught about growing up because all the prob-lems women and girls one that we never get talked about it to nuns we have to talk about it among our selfs.   (12)

It should not be thought that nuns are the only ones involved in an atmosphere of reluctance to raise sexual problems.

I'd never go to the school doctor for advice on a sexual problem as the whole aspect of sex is tabu in the school although they occasionally make efforts to give lectures on sex. Once a decade.   (16)

At one convent though – which it must be said was outside the research sample – not only was sexual advice in short supply but it was also inaccurate. A girl who asked was told that circumcision involved scratching a small circle at the top of a male's thigh.
Girls not only shun consultation when there is staff inhibition, but also if there is too much readiness to talk.

I would never go to any of the staff if I had worries because the teacher I told would broadcast it to all the other teachers, but you can trust prefects to keep things to themselves.   (13)

The issue of how and whether to share problem-knowledge is one of great delicacy, but it can be handled with intelligence. One head-mistress wrote as follows:

By the time the girls reach the VIth form pastoral care should be exercised, I am sure, on a basis of equality, discussing very freely and rather humbly with them the problems and difficulties, helping them if possible to see the difficulties of background and character in those under them. I have never found that any confidence of that kind has been abused by the Prefects and senior girls . . . [as to] the rest of the staff. I am sure that as far as possible they should know most of the details about the children in their care. Again and again we have saved trouble here by the fact that the staff do know most of what there is to be known about the children, and do not feel unable to ask me. . . . by taking the staff into my confidence on everything except the most confidential matters, there is far less gossip about the children in the staff room. I am sure that the thing which makes for gossip and kills the pastoral approach to the children is lack of confidence from the top.

That these are not idle views is attested by the fact that this school had a very low NPF (i.e. the girls were willing to communicate). For such a situation to exist, the school must not be so large that the head cannot know everybody. If it is, it is usually split into houses, and housemistresses have this responsibility. Many housemistresses in such large, 'federal' schools claimed an effective pastoral role, though this was not clearly supported in their girls' writings. The statistics do not show federal schools in general to be either at an advantage or a disadvantage with regard to pastoral responsiveness.

We come now to a comparative innovation:

I think it is a very good idea about having House-*Masters*, because a) I think they understand you much better than women do and b) they don't fly off the handle at you for no reason at all. (13)

Although masters are not rare in girls' boarding schools, housemasters are. One school not only had at least one housemaster, but also used a structural event (tea) not shared in all schools.

I am glad that some teachers are now beginning to ask girls out for coffee or tea now, which helps to eliminate the teacher–pupil line. One of the new house masters is very hospitable, and he and his wife let girls go to their private house one evening a week, and do what they like. (Read, watch television, play the gramaphone etc.) (14)

This contrasts with other schools which, having single staff living in staff houses or flats, expressly forbid girls from visiting staff accommodation. The other frequent point of contact between girls and staff is the 'drawing-room'. Whereas girl-country is usually spartanly furnished (common rooms, studies), drawing-rooms are adult territory. Their more comfortable furnishings, pictures and ornaments stand for some of the high points to which Western culture has striven. In these drawing-rooms of an evening, housemistresses read to girls, who sew; sometimes they come to shake

F

hands, even to curtsy, and to say goodnight. Drawing-rooms are suitable places in which to talk to parents, or visitors, and can remind girls that rooms of the kind they know at home exist and are accessible (at certain times) in school. Drawing-rooms can clearly matter deeply to some housemistresses. In one school, where several housemistresses had denied that inter-house rivalries or politics existed at staff level, when I casually mentioned that a carpet was identical with one seen in another house, there was a distinctly piqued response which suggested that there was more than appeared explicit in superficial conversation. Girls often built up an awareness that the drawing-room was an unrelaxed place, a training-ground for acquisition of social graces, an arena in which a new concept of adult non-relaxed relaxedness was to be learned.

On the other side of this 'Silence Room' is the housemistress's Drawing Room . . . one cannot expect miscreants to escape a row; and the house-mistress's voice is not the quietest in the world! (15)

Girls who say they will go to friends, but not staff, may not distrust all adults, but merely the ones at hand. A girl may have a choice from half-a-dozen girls of similar age to befriend in her house, or more in the school. But she has only one housemistress plus perhaps an assistant or matron. The choice of adult referent for the closest problems is therefore limited by house structure. Very grave or embarrassing problems may only heighten a reluctance to talk about them if and once such a reluctance exists already.

[To whom would you go with a personal problem . . . ?] A friend, if she were interested or able to help. But definitely not staff. (16)

The importance of this girl's estrangement became clear later, when she became pregnant. She hid this fact from staff though not from friends, as she had predicted; they, however, were reluctant to believe her. They chose friendship with her rather than some notion of social duty which might have led them to discuss with staff a matter of whose truth they were not certain, and the staff only got to know at an advanced stage of the pregnancy. Another girl wrote about referring 'home' problems:

– never a member of staff or headmistress, as they can never see one's point of view and problems. (16)

A chance encounter later showed that this girl had in fact discussed her problems with her housemistress, though I do not know who initiated the contact. This reminds us that the questions and statements we are examining concern intentions, and intentions are not always fulfilled. Intentions are a psychological reality though, and give some idea of the climate of life that prevails.

We sometimes hear that personal pastoral care is not essential for at least older girls, who generate maturity by coping themselves.

There is no one that I feel I can tell person, or home problems to, although problems of work are always readily catered for. I don't think, however, even if a teacher did set herself up as an Evelyn Home that it would help me, personally. There are problems that can not be discussed with other people.   (16)

It is arguable as to whether the last remark reveals strength or weakness; pastoral machinery must exist for those who need it, and these may include some of those who do not realize they need help. It must, of course, be sensitive enough to know when to let a person alone who wishes for some privacy at a troubled time, and who can cope in this way. Sometimes girls prefer to refer to friends, sometimes they keep to themselves.

Most worries about boys are discussed quite openly sometimes between the whole common room or if it is more personal between close friends.   (16)

And elsewhere:

The best way is to keep your worries to yourself, because if you tell other girls (not including best friends) they just gossip. This is very noticeable in our school, some girls just can not keep their mouths shut. Personal worries are best confided in your best friends. Home worries can be discussed with the Housemistress. I shouldn't think that that would do much good though.   (17)

Quotations carrying the same gist could be easily multiplied, while it is difficult to find those who are pleased to say that they would consult staff. This is not a result of biased reporting, as the following figures show.

Table 7·2. Percentage of boarders who would consult staff or friends about personal problems

would consult	ages: 12	13	14	15	16	overall
staff	20·0	26·1	17·5	11·9	18·6	16·9
friends	74·2	36·9	54·1	53·7	55·3	53·9

The basic trend is of less readiness to consult, the older the girls become. Girls are about three times as likely to want to consult friends, as staff. Some (we have already seen in Table 7·1) say that they intend to consult nobody, though others mention two or more referents, not all of whom are reflected in this table, which omits relatives, for example.

We have so far been concerned chiefly with care of personal problems. But girls were asked what they would do with three different sorts of trouble. If a girl names one referent for each kind of problem, she will have a total of three. This may represent three different people with whom to discuss her affairs, or the same person, or combinations of people. If a girl names two referents for each kind of problem, she will have a total of six referents. The average number of referents per girl has been called the Communication Index (ci) and has been worked out; this can be done for different schools, or for different ages.

Table 7·3. Communication index for girls at different ages

	ages: 12	13	14	15	16	overall	total number of girls
boarders	2·94	2·77	2·70	2·48	2·73	2·66	1,036
day girls	—	1·54	1·91	2·36	2·01	1·93	255

Obviously, the boarders are more likely overall to want to discuss their problems with someone inside the school than are day girls. While the boarders are least likely to communicate at the 15-year-old level, this is when day girls reach their greatest integration – by this yardstick – within the school community. Nowhere does the ci reach, let alone rise above, the figure 3·0. This means that throughout the schools there is a net reticence to have all problems dealt with by consultation. Not all schools had the same results; six schools out of the twenty-three had CI scores for boarders above 3·0. The highest was 3·39, at the school whose head has already been quoted as writing that pastoral care is helped by confidence and trust at the top. The school with the lowest CI for boarders scored 2·08, except one with 1·33 where there were less than twenty-five respondents, the head having declined permission to set these questions before younger girls.

How ready are girls to discuss the different types of problems? The next table puts together all types of referents, staff, friends, relatives, even pets.

Table 7·4. Percentage of boarders who will want to consult somebody, on three types of problem

| type of problem | ages: | | | | |
	12	13	14	15	16
work	100·0	92·3	85·1	80·3	79·3
home	88·6	91·8	89·7	81·0	85·8
personal	100·0	70·8	64·9	62·7	64·5

It must be pointed out that the questions we are dealing with here do not have the same degree of reality or immediacy for all girls. To someone who has, or has recently had, a problem, the questions are very pertinent; but to others whose lives are relatively trouble-free, it is easier to deal more lightly with such questions. Having said this, the figures still illustrate some solid points. Older girls are less ready to communicate on all types of problem though after age 15 there is some small return of communicativeness. The desire for silence is greatest with personal problems. Somehow 'home problems' seem to be reacted to as something that can be more readily discussed, more like work. This is not to say that families become seen as impersonal entities. A separate chapter deals with this question. The quotations throughout this chapter suggest that personal problems include many sexual matters, and staff are felt to be unsympathetic in this regard. Much of the reason for this is inherent in the situation; girls want to explore the world of sexual experience in one way or another, and staff are there to block off for the time being the avenue that the outside world heavily endorses. Even without the staff responsibility though, many girls find it hard to forgive unmarried staff their spinsterhood, not realizing that this was not what many staff chose. Perhaps it is surprising that there is as much readiness to communicate as we find.

How much of the 'pastoral readiness' shown in Table 7·4 is in response to the staff? And does readiness to communicate with staff vary in a similar way as the overall pattern?

Table 7·5. Percentage of boarders who will want to consult staff, on three types of problem

	ages:					
type of problem	12	13	14	15	16	overall
work	48·5	64·6	59·0	48·5	66·8	58·4
home	20·0	36·9	16·7	20·5	27·8	22·1
personal	20·0	26·1	17·5	11·9	18·6	16·7*
number of girls involved	35	65	388	268	280	1,036

* This line also appeared in Table 7.2.

The 15-year-olds are again at a nadir of communicativeness. This extends even to the sphere of work. At this time they are preparing for their O-levels, and making decisions about what to do thereafter, yet they are least ready to discuss even work problems with staff. Table 7·4 shows that home problems would be discussed with someone just as readily as work problems. Table 7·5 shows that this readiness to talk about home does not extend to staff. Clearly then, girls will want to talk about home problems and especially personal problems, to friends, relatives, or not at all. An overall conclusion is that boarders would appear to consider staff (except matrons and other obvious non-teachers) largely as teachers rather than as pastoral agents. One completely unverifiable, though interesting hypothesis, is that the limitations on the staff's pastoral role are connected in part with parents' attitudes. Parents who part with their daughters to boarding, though many do so after deep consideration, may incur even subconsciously an element of guilt; they may not feel they are paying other women to act the part of substitute mothers too gladly; thus parents may not place daughters in the care of housemistresses and other staff with the meticulous understanding and interpretation of the situation to the child that would be necessary for the girl to go to the housemistress with confidence and openness. This whole area was difficult to discuss except with a very few heads and housemistresses, and one has to proceed in interpretation chiefly by conjecture.

Now what have girls written about dealing with their problems?

In some schools an older girl is appointed to chaperone each newcomer. The pastoral relationship can be reciprocated by the younger girl doing chores and duties for the older; whatever evidence I have suggests that the relationships here lack the service and power aspects of fagging in boys' schools.

> I have a housemother and she is cold Vi. I chose her and she said she would be my housemother. I do not have to clean her shoes, but sometimes I have to do a few jobs for her. At night she tucks me up in bed and gives me a kiss. (12)
>
> My housemother was given to me by my housemistress she is very kind and conforts me when I feel homesick and if I have any problems she will tell me what to do. My mother is a 3rd year. (11)

Some girls start by wanting to confide in the staff.

> I think that if you have something worrying you, you ort to be able to speak freely to the headmistress about but your not so its just hard luck. (11)

This was at a small school where thirty-five per cent of those responding said they would consult nobody about personal problems; they were particularly reticent about consulting friends, though their overall response regarding staff was quite high. The role of friendship is acknowledged by staff, and one head writes:

> The girl who can talk about her problem will take it to the member of staff or older girl in whom she places most confidence. Many come to me direct or one or two friends come with 'can we talk to you about . . . she's unhappy'.

Here is an example:

> If I do not receive a letter from my home in two or three weeks I will tell my best friend, not our housemistress, for certain personal reasons, and she will comfort me and make me see that may be they have been very busy etc. (12)

This fending off of staff may not only be because her housemistress is not necessarily one whom the girl herself has chosen;

some girls also fear a staff grape-vine, and others harbour for a time a generalized antipathy to adults. A head writes:

Long hair and mini-skirts, for instance, have been the cause of a temporary ? break in communications between many a girl and her parents ... but when open war has developed in the holidays and angry letters follow the girl to school I must expect a period of unrest or downright defiance, for all the adults are now held suspect.

There may be yet more reasons why girls are shy of consulting staff. Several adults said they knew a direct inquiry might be felt by a girl as brusque, and it might be rejected; while if adult and girl were busy doing something together, confidences would flow.

I wish that teachers were nicer and I wish that they would mind their own bisness. (12)

On the other hand:

Matrons only communicate with girls at night, when they are putting them to bed, or when Matrons are telling girls that their skirts are too short. However, if you get a nice Matron, they let you talk to them at night if you have washed and are ready for bed. (12)

Several matrons told of the free flow of conversation and the confidences that could be gained while they were all busy on the domestic front, especially in the evening. Nobody spoke of tongues wagging in the morning before breakfast. Though plenty has been said about girls mistrusting staff, other girls are also sometimes mistrusted. One girl went so far as to acknowledge that 'there is an enemy wrapped up in your best friend' (because information is power, and if the friendship were to turn, the more intimate the information shared, the more threatening its misuse could be). There is one confidant, however, who can be completely trusted.

I don't trust anybody and never tell my secrets at all cause a lot of people spread things round. If I do tell anyone its my stuffed toy cause it cant tell anyone if it trys and all you really want to do is to tell somebody the trouble and a stuffed toy is as good as anything else. (12)

This girl has ushered in a topic which is of great importance to girls of all ages. All the ideas here come from the girls.

I think that some of the only people, or rather things, to trust or talk to are your toys. Some people are too old to talk to while others are

too young, and again, some talk about things that you dont know
about.   (11)

There is a hint here of a wary approach to the world of sexual
knowledge. This is evidently usually introduced in the dormitory,
after some hurdles of incomprehension and teasing. A girl has in
a short time to acquire a new sexual outlook and inlook, both as
regards herself, and concerning males. Pets and toys can provide
a comforting link across this divide to those who find that other
girls tease and to whom adults are unapproachable.

Sometimes you worry about when you have periods and you tell your
friend. We are told about these things when a sex teacher comes to our
school. She came about 2 terms ago. One thinks having a male gonk
can be a comfort because you can call it a boyfriend and play that
way.   (11)
I like a female pet better than a male pet because I have a female border
terrier and she is much cuddlier and you can talk to her and she seems
to understand more than our collie.   (11)
It is nice to have pets or teddy bears, it is nice because males seem to
understand everything about yourself.   (12)

The male toy is docile, patient and understanding. It can provide
'creature comfort' when it is needed, in a socially acceptable way.

If you have a teddy bear at school it comforts you and you cuddle it
at night instead of your mother.   (12)

At another school:

There is no one I would ask advice from, but I would go and pour out
my troubles to my hamster!   (14)

A distinction between pets and toys, and their several functions,
is introduced by an anthropologist aged 12.

It's nice to have female pets than male pets because females are so
motherly.
It's nice to have male gonks better than female because males are much
nicer and you feel the females will tell others.   (12)

Some girls who own pets find male dogs to be too boisterous and
energetic. This may be a projection, or a valid observation on their
part, nevertheless, that is what they suggest. Female dogs are
attributed with female virtues without the vices. They listen but

do not gossip. They bear young, with which drama in life girls can identify, at the start in a painless way. On the other hand, woolly toys which are often manufactured as a-sexual, are given male names and ascribed male characteristics. Some small pets may be ascribed a sex possibly regardless of the true facts.

It is nice to have a female pet because I think they are more sympathetic. My Guinea Pig still went on eating when I told him about dog which had died, but my dog liked* my face.   (12)

Several schools realize how important pets can be, and provide for a pets' corner. This is clearly appreciated. Two drawbacks have been mentioned though – one is that several girls in one school did not welcome a population of mice, because of its smells, its attacks on girls' tuck and because a minority retained the traditional fear of mice. Secondly, some schools fear that pets will get contagious disease or die in an epidemic leaving a distressed pupil population. However, many girls reported the deaths of guinea pigs and smaller pets without too much distress. The lives of dogs and especially ponies are held more dearly.

A headmistress who valued pets had several in the school and wrote:

I also agree that dogs are most helpful – we have three – and there is no doubt whatever that they have been the recipients of a large number of confidences. I do not think it matters in the least that the confidences go no further. I think that what does matter is that the child feels that she can take the dog for a walk and that the dog will understand.

Here is what one girl in that school says:

Talking to [naming the three dogs] is nice because I love dogs. . . . I find myself talking, especially to my own.   (13)

This observation was made without the girl having been asked how she got on with the pets. The presence of dogs in this school did not detract from the human pastoral care, as all the scores calculated (NPF, CI, SPI) show a higher level of readiness to communicate with people than in most other schools.

Sometimes there are fauna present which the girls find unwel-

---

* This probably means licked – i.e. showed sympathy, compared with the insensitive male guinea pig.

come! This undoubtedly illustrates the effect of context on perception.

This term I have seen three slugs in the salad and a beetle in the marmite and I have heard from someone who saw a frog jump out of the Sunday cabbage.   (12)

These animals might have been protected in other circumstances, but they had the misfortune to appear in food, which is traditionally a focus for complaint rather than comfort. Pets should be cuddly then, and not in the cabbage. They should not be a-social, and very little pastoral mileage was evidently got out of cats. Cats are aesthetic objects, except when they smell, when the girls will readily object. If the species of animal is repellent, it can be made coy and cuddly as a toy – witness the girl who kept a three-foot-long snake of stuffed cloth as a bed companion. This is curiously acceptable in a school where sexual manifestations of a less symbolic nature are not at all welcome.

Horses are a great love for girls. It is usually mares or geldings which are owned or ridden. In spite of their femaleness, it is possible that a horse represents a 'virile' and sensuous being with whom a girl can have a dominant and affectionate relationship, before she grows into the adult world, where the notion still survives that a woman surrenders dominance in affection. The relationship with the horse may be at once a girl's first taste of acting the male, and her swansong as such. The horse-loving culture seems to give way by about the age of 14, when communal noise ('music') and fashion take over. Not all girls give themselves over to these interests, and the individual who has awarely to cope with problems, increasingly devises lone methods.

I deal with my worries by going away somewhere by myself . . . also I like to have a good cry! I find it helps sometimes.   (13)

This is the age (see Table 7·4) at which the proportion of girls willing to discuss personal problems drops to seventy per cent, after having been 100 per cent for 12-year-olds. With increasing age, one of the signs of what we consider maturity is an ability to wait for one's satisfactions, and this begins to appear in girls' writings.

I deal with my worries by laying in or on my bed and thinking of all the things I can do when I get older.   (13)

I am longing for the day when I get married because then I feel as
though I have really got someone to tell my troubles to.   (13)

I deal with my worries by cry my eyes out and then fighting for my
life. Then I might go and tell my sister the tail.   (14)

There are signs that trouble brings an increased sensitivity to
what others say:

I deal with my worries by going for a long walk by myself or shouting
at anybody who says one wrong thing.   (14)

Undoubtedly many girls will by random chance (if not by intention) be saying 'wrong things', especially when some of them are
acting out their own worries. Where girls of an age are living within
a small space, the situation may develop into a chain reaction, or
a 'positive feedback' in which social disturbance at one's own behaviour intensifies one's worry.

Worries are greatly emphasised in a community. If a solution is not
found almost immediately, they become out of all proportion, and if
a solution is still not forthcoming the health of the individual may be
affected.   (17)

The burden to some of the presence of one's fellows can be lifted
if the school is fortunate enough in its setting, and if it allows girls
to make use of the space available.

A nice open view of land and hills – which makes me feel nice and free.
Lovely trees and animal life, when I'm unhappy I go out for a walk
in the grounds and it cheers me up.   (14)

Not all schools have agreeable grounds, and some that do have
them inhibit free movement in case the girls fall into bad company.
Another individual avenue which offers space in self-expression is
to develop a skill, especially if it offers room for the exercise of girls'
aesthetic sensibilities. Some choose a verbal art, in which one's
predicament can be held up for contemplation and the discovery
of something beautiful in it; others prefer non-verbal arts.

If things are going wrong the best way for me to cheer up is either by
playing the piano, going out for a walk or making a point of cheering
other people up. I hate roudiness but silence can make people very
unhappy.   (14)

If I had any worries about boy friends, etc. I wouldn't talk to relations, staff etc., but probably would go to one or two good friends, then go and write something to get the whole emotion out. Hence the vast amount of poetry I write at school and after some sort of intense relationship at home. My opinion is if one isn't a 'complete' person, one will need religion or help to get through the difficulty.   (17)

At one school, someone was on the staff to take people in English composition, and to give special encouragement and attention to developing creative writing partly for pastoral and therapeutic reasons. At another school, the art teacher was also in charge of a house; though this could emphasize the development of a pastoral role, other house staff sometimes resisted the advantageous pastoral position of this one staff member. Girls were abruptly summoned out of the art room to keep punctually to their appointed routines, instead of being able to relax and talk. Here is another example of the delicate predicament in which an individual staff–student relationship may find itself.

When I myself have trouble I go to my music teacher and she helps me with all my troubles personal and work and home troubles. I don't want you to get the wrong impression, but I am very fond of her, its nothing homosexual or anything like that, but she really is like a mother to me. But our headmistress disapproves of strong relationships, it is strictly forbidden to go to the teachers' own rooms.   (16)

There are schools where several avenues for gaining solace are not very fruitful – little privacy, perhaps restricted facilities for developing arts. Some girls then may find comfort in their routine duties:

If one is deeply upset, it is better to go on with trivial duties, rather than just sit and think about it, especially at school in a form where there are many responsibilities and one has to achieve a certain standard of outward calm and handling of the situation.   (16)

The shouldering of pastoral care by senior girls is sometimes part of what they see as their duties:

Housemistress . . . does not appear to try to understand ones feelings . . . when younger girls are homesick and worried . . . thinks they are stupid. Matron tries to be motherly . . . looks down on girls who obviously are more intelligent than her. I do get some girls pouring out their troubles . . . No one to go to when *I* feel worried . . . my own worries then mount up and send me nearly mad. Lots of frustration from minor stupid problems of the house, created by the housemistress. (17)

At one school, pastoral roles are not possible for senior girls:

No senior girls are allowed to talk to junior girls – they are accused of encouraging the juniors who are supposed to be a difficult age emotionally. If so they need someone to talk to and can't to teachers so why not us ???!!! The teachers are not the types you can easily talk to. They are mostly spinsters and fail in our eyes to truly understand girls in their school years. (16)

The NPF and CI for this school were among the three lowest of nineteen schools. Elsewhere another senior appeals for trust:

I think seniors should get more respect from staff as well as juniors in order to get their duties done. If staff do not respect the seniors, why should the juniors? The seniors are looked up to for guidance among the juniors, and the seniors are not likely to give it readily if they do not get respect and privileges. (17)

This trust is to be found in some schools and, in one of them, two seniors write as follows about pastoral care:

It is one of the responsibilities that a senior takes on and helps her to understand others problems and to help with them. . . . I think it helps in the exercise of authority and if you can help in problems can gain respect. (17)
At this school everything is very 'elastic' so whether younger girls confide in you . . . depends on your character.
The problems are normally of 2 kinds; if you know the girl well it might be home troubles . . . (a 12 year old tells me nearly every night . . . her mother has had a mental breakdown . . .). Others bring school problems . . . for instance a prefect or teacher may have been unknowingly unfair over giving a bad mark and we can tactfully enquire. (17)

The pastoral care indices at this school were all very good. Incidentally, the fact that one can very aptly match such writings with the statistical results lends confidence to the validity of the latter.

That there are needs for pastoral care should not now be in doubt, as also that ways of alleviating worry are often not too smooth and sometimes are cut off. One other possibility is to have outsiders visit. Girls might be able to 'pour their worries' into some sympathetic outside receptacle, who in human form would provide sympathetic listening, might not gossip within the community, and would remove troubles as did the ancient scapegoat. Only one girl actually suggested having an outsider visit:

My inner world never or very rarely gets a glimmer of light to the rest of the community only to very close trusted friends (few) . . . one is not able to show ones true emotions because if one does it is dramatic or it is never forgotten . . . any personal relationships developed in life i.e. male friends are almost frowned upon . . . one cannot talk external problems of this sort over with anyone older and often friends find sorting out your problems difficult, if not as confusing to them as it is to you. They should definitely have someone e.g. psychologist or someone like that one could confide in without the thought of that it could and probably will go straight to the staff room.   (17)

In a few schools examples were found of external agents who visited to consult with girls and listen to some of their problems. In one school, a monk came on a mission, and after preaching in church was free to talk to individuals. Much use was made of his presence. Whether he could make a bridge with school staff would be up to his discretion over the way each girl had trusted him with her confidences. In another school, a retired senior staff member continued to visit, and kept up the trust she had built up with the girls on the basis of sympathetic consultation and guaranteed confidence. It was a meticulous point with her that 'confidences' were understood by her as entrusted to her 'with faith' – that is, that she would guard their privacy.

At a third school, an outside preacher was introduced as a pastoral expert, and made a very explicit public appeal for confidences. Descriptions of this episode were given by several girls who felt that they had been collectively led into a state of heightened emotion and conscience and led to part with private information. Looking back on it, some felt that what they had divulged was perhaps not so important after all, though it included elicitations of their sexual experiences with boys. One residual feeling seemed to be of some embarrassment that they had partaken of a kind of communal wave of self-surrender. Another feeling was of indignation that the confidants had discussed some matters with the head.

This breached the trust that had been understood on the girls' side that their confidences would be kept private. Clearly, if they got the idea that no staff discussion of any sort would ensue, even though one case might be referred by the visitor to the head with that girl's full agreement, then this would place the other girls in doubt as to what might have been passed on of theirs. This shows that the role of an outside consulting visitor would have to be clearly managed and understood, in order to keep up trust in its value.

A Summary of Some Points on the Need for and Provision of Pastoral Care

Pastoral care is thought of here as being a human response to a human need. 'Pastoral agents' are as islands of security in what to some girls, at some times, are the quicksands of school life. Pastoral agents need to win girls' trust, and they can do this by easing distress (the Androcles situation); it may also help to win not only trust, but goodwill and enjoyment of each other's company for those interested to give pastoral help, to play and enjoy recreation with the children. For some girls this scene may be set with sewing or cooking; some may prefer the art room, and one head, for example, was seen helping girls to paint murals on the walls of the assembly hall.

Pastoral needs may occur at odd times in the school's routine. If the routine is very rigid, an atmosphere of trust that troubles can be attended to may be difficult to create and maintain. Several girls and some staff speak of boarding as promoting personal independence: 'makes you stand on your own feet'. The moderate provision of pastoral care can be seen as one way of forcing individuals to cope for themselves. For some this means that they develop the ability to convey that they have authority and self-reliance; but this may be a form of social exoskeleton which only hides a hollow within. The skill in maintaining these exterior forms is not unlike what may be needed in acting and certainly several boarding-school girls have been attracted to, and have done well in the theatre. It is not implied, of course, that schools which provide generous pastoral care thereby fail to develop self-reliance. It is likely that the opposite is true, though it would need a different kind of study to show this.

Pastoral care is concerned with the successful management of privacy, of those parts of people's lives which are most 'confidential'.* There is a problem then as to what the staff should do with confidential information. Evidence suggests that if girls think their information is secure, but then find that other people know of it, they lose trust. There can develop a dread of an omniscient staff room, whose teachers carry intimate knowledge that can render their casual glance loaded with access to the very inner recesses of privacy, and which makes life in school an existential threat, a risk of unpredictable and silent exposure. Girls in such a situation are like Adam after his misdemeanours, with nowhere to hide their privacy. For this kind of reason, one girl thought an external pastoral agent might be helpful, though at least three examples of where this is done show that it is a delicate matter to arrange. The evidence from one school shows also that it is possible for staff to share confidential knowledge among themselves, and even with senior girls, and yet to maintain an atmosphere of trust and care. Such a situation can only be built up gradually, and depends for its maintenance on staff never abusing, or dealing indelicately with, their trust.

Statistical evidence shows that the youngest boarders are quite ready to discuss their problems with someone or other in school. Soon this changes, and by the age of 15 girls are least ready to discuss, especially personal problems, in school. Thereafter there is some small resurgence of trust. The least inclination is to discuss personal affairs with staff; most of this trouble-sharing is destined for girl-friends. Staff are chiefly there, according to the girls' response, to deal with work problems. Several causes may produce this relation-estrangement from staff. Staff have to personify the idea that sexual adventure has to be surrounded with care, and postponed, opposite to what the mass media have in mind for their fans. Staff carry out extensive organizational and authority roles, girls being unwilling to take these over to the same extent as it is said boys do. Many staff are unmarried, which condition the girls find unwelcome, perhaps even threatening as an example, and this does not help in building trust. The introduction of housemasters has helped in some schools to produce more pastoral confidence.

* It is worth pointing out that the word confide means 'to trust with', and implies here the shared privacy of some information that it is trusted will go no further.

Day girls are understandably less concerned, overall, to discuss their problems in school. However, in their case, we find trust increasing to the age of 15, after which it reduces. This is opposite to the trend for boarders. The fact that day girls will bring up problems for discussion in school (at 15, sixty-six per cent of day girls are willing to consult in school on personal worries, compared with sixty-eight per cent of boarders, as shown in Table 7·4) reminds us that boarding does not just in itself create problems. Boarding can provide an outside-the-family source of pastoral care, or of counselling on home problems. How far schools can, or do, satisfy this kind of function depends on the individual institutions.

Inter-School Differences in Pastoral Care

Out of the twenty-three schools visited, four yielded pastoral care answers from less than twenty-five girls each. This was made the criterion for leaving their scores out of the present analysis. These four schools were not all 'typical' small boarding schools, and it is difficult to know how they may cause a bias in the sample. At each of the other nineteen schools, an average score was calculated for each of the three pastoral care indices explained already – CI, NPF and SPI. The girls from each school were drawn from more than one form, and thus represent various age levels.

Schools differed widely as to their pastoral care scores. The range of these differences is shown below.

Table 7·6. Ranges of schools' scores on indices of pastoral care

	NPF(%)	CI	SPI(%)
top school's value	17·4	3·39	39·2
middle school's value	30·0	2·73	15·8
lowest school's value	60·0	2·08	0·0

There is one school at which as many as sixty per cent of the girls answering (thirty-five in all) said they would not want to consult anybody on a personal problem. The next in rank is not so extreme, with forty-eight per cent (out of fifty-six girls) being reluctant to communicate in this way. Even at the most communicative school, seventeen per cent (out of sixty-nine asked) would not want to discuss their private worries at all. At this latter school, twenty-four per cent were willing to take problems to staff – the school conveyed a very friendly atmosphere and the head was very aware of pastoral care needs. At other schools, up to thirty-nine per cent of girls would be ready to talk to staff about personal problems. The top five schools on this index each had a head conspicuously and alertly at the centre of life. At the other end of the scale was a very large school, at which not one out of seventy girls answering said she would take a personal problem to discuss with staff members.

The communication index shows six schools with scores over 3·0 which, as has been explained, shows a willingness to discuss each type of problem with at least one other person. Six other schools had CI scores less than 2·5, which means that half the girls are reluctant to discuss one of their three types of problem asked about.

Rank orderings have been prepared for the nineteen schools on their pastoral care scores, and also twenty-two other types of score. By the statistical technique of rank order correlation, we can see what sort of phenomena tend to occur together. Another technique helps us to judge how pastoral care qualities occur in each of two groups of schools, when schools are divided by some relatively crude criterion into two groups.

For example, schools were visited either in summer (s) or in one of two winter (w) seasons. Were the s schools different in pastoral care scores from the w schools? Yes;[1] schools visited in summer certainly tended to have girls more ready to communicate than schools seen in winter. This is understandable. In winter girls are more cooped up and can get more irritated with each other; they may wish for less communication about their problems. In summer girls may have exam problems and be more ready to discuss these especially; this would raise the CI, though it would not affect the NPF or SPI. This kind of finding raises a serious possibility. If we find that some other phenomenon relates to pastoral care, does it do so independently – or did it happen that this other phenomenon was linked to summer or winter visiting? We shall have to check for this kind of hidden effect quite carefully.

I mentioned earlier that the severity of regime may inhibit pastoral care relationships. We have an institutional control score that reflects this, and indeed institutional control correlates quite highly with all three indices of pastoral care in the expected direction. The more lenient schools show more readiness among the girls to come for care.[2] Now, has this anything to do with summer and winter? Perhaps the more lenient schools were all visited in summer, and the effect is really due to sun rather than social structure? This is not shown in the statistics. There was no sign that summer visits were systematically to more lenient schools. The feeling is therefore strengthened that tightness of social structure, as reflected in the institutional control score, is linked with the level of pastoral care that comes about. Interpretation is strongly tempted to the conclusion, of course, that there is a causal link, and I for one believe there is.

Does pastoral care have any link with happiness in the school? It does;[3] a happier school is likely to have more communicative girls, and they are less likely to keep personal problems in particular to themselves. They are not particularly more ready to consult staff, however, though the figures do actually lean in this direction. Unfortunately, there are some complications. High satisfaction was also found more often in summer visits. So it may be either the satisfaction, or the summer, which somehow increases the pastoral care level. Common sense suggests that all three are linked up. Expert interpretation of the statistics suggests that in summer girls are happier and more ready to discuss work with staff (also they need to do so more), and personal problems among themselves. These effects occur both in severe and in lenient schools, though a separate effect links severity of regime with pastoral reticence.

Perhaps schools with greater number of staff may show higher levels of pastoral care? Two staff–pupil ratios were calculated and correlated with pastoral care scores.[4] The outcome is that for the overall staff–pupil ratio, there is no significant relation with any pastoral care index;[5] however, for the staff–sixth-formers ratio, where there were schools with more staff per sixth-former, there tended to be more communication;[6] this did not mean increased discussion of personal problems, so we may infer that the extra communication concerned work, or less likely, home affairs.

So far we have not found any conditions which particularly associate with readiness to discuss personal affairs with staff. There are, however, several points on which we can distinguish schools where there is a readiness to talk to staff, from those where there is not. Two brief tests were given to girls; the first 'convergent' one involved unequivocal problem-solving, on which the answers were either correct or not; the second 'divergent' one taxed the imagination, girls having to produce as many different sorts of answer to one question as their knowledge and ingenuity allowed. Schools with low overall scores on convergence tended to have girls who were more ready to talk with staff about personal problems.[7] We cannot say that these were 'stupid' schools, compared to 'clever' schools where people do not talk to staff; for on the second test, of divergence, there was no relationship at all with this readiness to talk to staff. 'Imaginative' or 'unimaginative' school populations were no more or less likely to discuss personal problems with staff. On the other hand, divergence implies an outwardness with ideas, and one would expect the imaginative school population to have a higher general tendency to communicate. This is indeed found,[8] but it applies to communications other than with staff.

It is rare for girls to aspire to be prefects (see Chapter Three). However, schools with a high level of aspiration to be a prefect also tend to have a high level of readiness to communicate with staff.[9] One would be tempted to theorize that the latter phenomenon causes the first. This aspiration to take up authority positions does not relate significantly to other indices of pastoral care. If we were very pessimistic, we might suppose that staff-oriented 'goody-goody' schools would be particularly low on desire to discuss problems with other girls, with some competition to rise in status, producing barriers between the girls. This could lead to a negative correlation between prefectorial aspiration and general communication. There is no sign of this. We should tentatively conclude that in some schools there exists, more than in others, a sizeable body of girls who would like to have the responsibility of being prefects; these schools show greater readiness to confer with staff; at the same time there seems to be no particular loss of trust among the girls who are equally ready to confer among themselves as they are at other schools, where nobody wants to be a prefect.[9]

Interestingly, where there is a high aspiration for art, there is also a tendency for girls to find someone with whom to discuss their personal problems – but not among the staff, rather from among themselves.[10] So 'arty' schools tend to have girls who will be ready to discuss troubles with other girls; 'responsible' schools tend to have girls who will discuss problems with the staff.

We have seen in Chapter Two that certain goals were considered particularly important for schools to tackle. We had a score for each school of the success it achieved on the 'top five goals'. Schools with girls who give a good rating on this criterion tend to have high levels of discussion of problems in general, and in particular with staff.[11] These were also schools with lower institutional control, which is not surprising in view of what we have already seen. The picture emerges then that there are schools in which girls think well of their school, tend to want to become prefects, are happier than average, distinctly less good at verbal problem-solving (though no more or less imaginative) and are more ready to discuss personal problems with staff. These schools tend to be more lenient in structure. The converse picture is also likely to be true.

One thing that these statistics suggest is that the separate questionnaire measures are valid, and deal with truthful and relevant responses. These are answers to quite different types of question (for example, on personal aspirations, convergent test items, readiness to consult staff), and sometimes they have been elicited from different classes in a school. Thus I may be ranking a school on its aspirations by answers from two classes; and on happiness by answers from three classes. Yet these generalizations about schools as a whole hang together in a logical way. The demonstrations are not trite, either. Detailed interpretation shows how pastoral consultation focuses on staff in some situations, on girls in others. Furthermore, there are cases where we might expect to find a significant relationship between two factors, but where we have not found any such thing. This rules out certain lines of reasoning in interpreting what girls have written. For example, staff–pupil ratios did not relate significantly with pastoral care, except in one case out of six. This suggested that more staff did not imply more consultation on personal problems, though there was probably more readiness to use staff's presence to discuss work.

Where else was no statistical relationship found, where we might have expected to have done so? One variable examined was cost of fees. The schools were divided into the most expensive and least expensive halves of their range of cost. The more expensive ones might have had a mixture of better staff ratios, better staff or better facilities, leading to greater pastoral care response. This was not found in the statistical tests. Another category looked at was the difference between 'federal' and 'central' organization. A federal structure was said to exist when there were two or more distinct 'vertical' houses (containing girls of all ages) with different house-mistresses; the remainder were classed as 'central'. Over the nineteen schools, there was no clear trend proving that pastoral care may be better in either sort of school. By judiciously removing two extreme 'exceptions' from the list, we would have seventeen schools showing clearly that girls are readier to communicate in centralized schools. But the two glaring exceptions cannot be ignored, and they effectively nullify what was an incipient trend in the figures.

Thirdly, I categorized schools according to what the heads told me about their selectivity of pupil intake. Thus there was a 'grammar' group, which used 'common entrance' as an entry standard and rejected applicants; the 'comprehensive' group either dispensed with exams at entry or used common entrance 'as a guide to allocating the girl to the right form', and turned away very few applicants. There was no sign that readiness to discuss problems was any different in either type of school.

We are now dealing with the realm of tentative causal relationships; one in which it is easier to make firm statements than to defend them rigorously. One other variable may be worth mentioning here. This is the number of boarders in the school community. There is slight evidence[12] that in smaller schools there may be more readiness to discuss personal problems. Now the smaller schools are the more centralized ones;[13] and the one 'centralized' school whose results were obscuring an incipient link between pastoral care and social structure is also atypical here. Furthermore, it happened to have been visited at a winter season, which may have caught it at a particularly poor moment. However, these speculations must remain as conjecture, though they are offered here to try to show how complex the situation always is, and how difficult it is to tie up cause and effect precisely in social science. We should say that it is not proven that centralized schools, with smaller numbers of boarders, are much more likely to have good pastoral care; rather it is something that we may strongly suspect, and try to re-examine in a larger investigation.

A most important factor in the pastoral scene has not yet been tackled. This concerns the personality of staff. It was unfortunately not easy to get a majority of staffs to cooperate with a questionnaire; possibly a more searching inquiry would have been complied with, but the risk of refusal was not taken. This study therefore did not go further than subjective impressions, gained from talks with many staff and listening to, and noticing, what was going on.

It is now a commonplace in anthropology that language is not only a verbal matter. All manners of behaviour (and who would agree with this more than those who understand the 'public school ethos') convey their message. What is not in question here about staff is their outer manners (usually impeccable), but that which lies behind. One tries to sense whether 'manners' are a means to clothe a distaste or something unpleasant that candour might reveal; or whether manners are an expression of gentility and welcome within.

These considerations suggest that pastoral willingness among the girls depended not just on institutional control, or possibly on the size or type of organization structure; but clearly the personality of staffs had a great influence. One federal-type school had the fourth highest SPI score – readiness to consult staff; another federal school had the bottom SPI score. The first was not so large, and the head had a very close relationship with both staff and children. The other school was too large for the head to make a realistic attempt at widespread close relationships, but the personalities of some of the housemistresses seemed not to be able to take over pastoral credibility. Institutional control was very high and it appeared that in many ways the staff collectively expressed a rigidity that helped it stay so. More than one housemistress might have wished things to be otherwise, but the staff norms seemed to have an inertia that would have needed very vigorous and widespread efforts to produce a change. The housemistress in a federal system must to some extent move in parallel with the others, and cannot radically innovate. The pastoral response of the girls therefore adjusts to the prevailing climate, rather than to one or two covert (staff) points of greater potential contact.

A second example of staff personalities possibly affecting pastoral response came from two medium-sized schools. Both centralized in structure, they appeared, however, at opposite ends of the scale on all three pastoral care indices. Though the one with the lower scores was visited at a difficult season, this would seem unlikely to account for all of its difference from the other. The heads of both schools were pleasant, interesting, experienced and convincing exponents of their educational ideas. However, the one showed fluidity in the ability to 'ingest' a stranger for a week into the body of the school – while yet allowing him considerable freedom of action – and a continuing interest shown by further correspondence. The staff also showed a welcoming interest and an intelligent desire to help in an inquiry without compromising their values of privacy. The other school showed a different picture – I was accommodated and fed separately and there were fewer signs of a flexible and in-quiring attitude. The fact that the institutional control score of the latter school was the higher of the two would seem to be as much a result of the personalities of important staff who maintained the *status quo*, as of some inescapable factors of tradition, geographical setting or other impediment to change. In other words, some schools are severe partly because the staff like it that way.

Concluding Remarks on Pastoral Care

We are indebted to Royston Lambert for crystallizing the concept of pastoral care with regard to English boarding schools. He studied the pastoral circumstances in boys' and co-educational schools. This chapter shows, I believe, that what we are talking about is an important matter in boarding education. Boarders have a wide variety of problems, some of them acute; for several (and their number might increase) their presence at boarding school is pre-cisely because of their problems, whether economic, social or of individual adjustment at home.

These problems have to be dealt with in a humane system. A few may thrive by being forced to cope for themselves; others will manage without help, but some will suffer damage without sym-pathetic help and understanding. By and large, we have seen that trust in staff reduces as boarders get older; they will want to consult staff to a large extent about work problems, but not much about home worries and rather little about intimate personal matters. Not all schools are the same. It seems that institutional control level may influence pastoral confidence, which is also related to the different atmosphere arising in different seasons. Many other factors are bound up with readiness to consult about problems, and I hope that this chapter has pointed out some of the things that may be looked for. No observer will reliably be able to judge a pastoral care situation in a school, either by asking several insiders one question or by asking one person several questions.

Finally, I would like to think that in a school community, although most pastoral care would presumably flow 'downwards' from more mature staff to less mature pupils, at least some care might go the other way. This is neither likely nor often met with, as girls who encounter immature staff, or old people who do not much understand the young, do not react with sympathy or understanding, but with indignation and occasional unkindness. This may be partly because girls feel they do not pay to go to school to give to, but to get solace and support from staff. Yet if the matter was discussed openly, girls might show more sympathy in some situations, and in doing so release goodwill and some of the wisdom of older experience from staff, which it seems is not at present always forthcoming.

Notes

1. Mann-Whitney U test shows $U = 12$; $p < 0.005$ (for CI and $s-w$ dichotomy).
2. Rank order correlations between institutional control and NPF, CI and SPI are -0.57, -0.70 and -0.49 respectively.
3. Rank order correlations between satisfaction and NPF and CI are 0.43 and 0.63 respectively; with SPI the correlation is 0.36 which for $N = 19$ is not quite significant at the 0.05 level.
4. One took the number of full-time, plus half the part-time staff and divided by the total number of day and boarding pupils: the second balanced a sixth-form index (one point for each O-level candidate and two points for each A-level candidate) against the number of staff as calculated above.
5. Rank order correlations between teacher–pupil ratio and NPF, CI and SPI respectively are 0.31, 0.32 and 0.33, none of which reaches significance at the 0.05 level.
6. Rank order correlations between teacher–sixth-form pupil ratio and NPF, CI and SPI respectively are 0.37, 0.45 and 0.17 of which only the second reaches significance at the 0.05 level. ($N = 17$ schools here.)
7. Rank order correlations between convergence scores and NPF, CI and SPI respectively are -0.41, -0.25 and -0.75, which for $N = 16$ are significant at the 0.05 level, except the second value.
8. Rank order correlations between divergence scores and NPF, CI and SPI

respectively are 0·34, 0·43 and 0·09 of which for N = 16, only the second value is significant at the 0·05 level.

9. Rank order correlations between aspiration to be prefect and NPF, CI and SPI respectively are 0·35, 0·37 and 0·69 of which, for N = 18, only the last is significant at the 0·01 level.

10. Rank order correlations between aspiration to do well at art and NPF, CI and SPI respectively are 0·40, 0·34 and 0·11 of which, for N = 18, only the first is significant, at the 0·05 level.

11. Rank order correlations between rated success on top five goals and NPF, CI and SPI respectively are 0·26, 0·46 and 0·53, which for N = 18 leaves only the first failing to reach significance at the 0·05 level.

12. Rank order correlations between boarding community size and NPF, CI and SPI respectively are − 0·43, 0·01 and − 0·31, of which for N = 19, the first reaches significance at the 0·05 level.

13. Mann-Whitney U test shows U = 7 which for N = 19 reaches significance at 0·002 level.

Eight: The Individual and the Community

The question I shall try to examine here is how, and to what extent, have individuals been brought to fit in to their communities? How far have they adjusted or formed their outlooks and their ways according to the patterns set or prevailing in their respective schools?

One way of setting about this is to suppose that schools have certain *goals*, and certain *means* of obtaining these goals. Then we can suppose that girls might theoretically support goals, and means, or reject them; for example, according to the following plan:

What we can call a girl's adaptation:	*What a girl thinks of the school's:*	
	goals	*means*
conformity	accepts	accepts
innovation	accepts	sets aside, for own
ritualism	rejects	accepts
retreatism	rejects	rejects
rebellion	substitutes her own	rejects

Let us look at some points of view which might be said to exemplify some of these adaptations:

This school really makes you think for yourself, really we have complete freedom of speech and can do what we like. Our decisions are our own not the ones that are drummed into us. . . . I particularly approve of the way we can think things out for ourselves and make independent ideas, knowing they will be listened to and probably accepted. (16)

This girl is fortunate in being able to feel that what the school wants is what she wants, and that school and pupils can come to agree on how their goals are to be met. We can see at once that this is a special sort of 'conformity', a 'creative' rather than a passive conformity. Many further distinctions could be made to complicate the scheme above; we should remain aware of these possible distinctions – but continue to examine the other adaptations:

Schools can be terrible. Here a mistress has taken an intense dislike to me and does everything she can to make me feel uncomfortable. Consequently, I give as good as I get and I'm labelled as being rude – they can make life miserable for the individualist. All this talk about bringing out one's character but lets face it all they do is to suppress any eccentricity, especially uniformed schools. But also others too.   (16)

So speaks the rebel. This girl's unfortunate experience also suggests that things are more complicated than our scheme would have them seem. The girl focuses on one particular relationship, and interprets the school's goals in the darkness of this experience. This illustrates that the 'school's goals' are not some objective reality, open and equal for all to see; they are subjectively experienced. We shall look and see whether many girls feel the same way; for if they do, then we can speak of the school's goals as having some consistent nature, and of adaptation forming according to some pattern.

As a monitor I am expected to enforce rules I do not believe in. I enforce these PETTY rules as I do not want a bad reference for university. But when asked my candid opinion of school constitutions by any of the lower house, I tell them. . . . I have been told by my housemistress that as a monitor I must not speak my mind and as I know that I am undermining the authority of the other monitors, I SOMETIMES keep quiet.   (17)

This girl rejects some, if not all of the school's goals. She reluctantly acquiesces in the required forms of behaviour; we would call this a 'ritualistic' position. However, there are clear signs that the girl is sometimes so fed up that she diverges from behaviour expected by the school of monitors. This would place her in the category of retreatism; further, she has not disclosed particular ideals of her own, different from those of the school, but she may well have them. So it may be that in some respects she is a rebel.

All this shows that we cannot label or identify a person as simply conformist or retreatist, or whatever. There may be times when different responses are adopted to the same situation, or to different situations. There may be distinct trends whereby at various ages people are more conformist, or rebellious. Such adaptations may also be dependent on the type of school regime, and on numerous other factors.

To investigate these matters, we must have an 'instrument' in the form of a questionnaire. One was drawn up first by Roger Bullock and Spencer Millham, who were studying boys' boarding schools, and it was they who used the scheme explained above, which is due originally to the American sociologist, R. K. Merton. I kept very closely to the questionnaire for boys, as the data to be shown here can then be usefully compared with that obtained from boys. All I changed, in fact, was a few words, like master for mistress.

The questionnaire considers in turn six different situations, for example: 'Imagine you have been made a prefect'. There follow for each situation a choice of responses. These responses are supposed each to exemplify one of the five different types of adaptation. So if a girl chooses as her response: 'do your best', we may infer that she is a conformist; she could have chosen: 'don't worry much about the rules, and get what advantages you can from being a prefect', which we have designated as a rebellious choice. Unfortunately, I found that it is not easy even among sociologists to find perfect agreement on which of the sentences provided really indicates the ritual, retreatist or rebellious responses.* So we will rely chiefly on conformist and rebellious items, on each of which most readers can be agreed.

Even though we must remember that a girl might be conformist about one part of school life, and ritualist or something else about some other aspect, it might nevertheless be that some people are more generally conformist to all things, while others are distinctly less so to all things. I therefore gave a score of 5 to each conformist choice, 4 to each innovatory one, and so on, until 1 for each rebellious choice. As there were six separate parts to the questionnaire, a girl could have a score ranging from 30 (if she chose conformist

---

* The method adopted here was to get seven sociologists involved in boarding-school research to identify which sentence stood for which type of adaptation. Their answers were given numerical value and averaged. The average scores for each sentence were ranked, and this ranking in order was used to identify which sentences we would consider as conformist . . . to rebellious.

responses throughout) to 6 (if she consistently took the rebel line). In fact, fairly large numbers of girls scored 30, while the lowest score found was 11, recorded by only one girl out of over 750 who did this questionnaire altogether. This total score is referred to here as 'the Merton score'.

Part of how questionnaires of this sort are answered does not depend on a girl's true views alone – even if she is clear about these. Responses partly depend on the mood of the moment, the turn of recent events and how the girl feels about the person giving the questionnaire; thus in item four, 'Imagine you are selected for a school first team . . . would you?' – one possible response is 'Don't play, do something more important instead'. Choice of such item would depend on the note of conspiratorial furtiveness set by the questionnaire administrator, or upon the likeliness or absurdity of a particular person ever being chosen for a school team, or on the jocular or frivolous mood into which one could be thrown by imagining how these questions might apply to one's friends. We must remember all these and other difficulties when reviewing the results; these points were very much borne in mind when I was giving out the questionnaires and trying to control the manner in which I explained them. I estimate that this will have reduced the chance of any retreatist or rebellious responses being given flip-pantly; it should not have deterred true rebels from showing their feelings. It may conceivably have increased the number of con-formist responses. So with all these cautions, let us look at the results on the following page.

Many points stand out in this table. First it is clear that on most separate questions, and overall, the conformist choices were in a majority. I have already said that this may represent an over-estimate; but it is not likely, if there was some systematic tendency for such an error, for it to have been both consistent and great. We must conclude that, except in unusual forms or schools, half or more of the girls at least are conformers.

There was a dearth of support for what were intended to be the 'innovatory' items. The case in which most support for 'innova-tion' was found, that of being invited to meet v.i.p.s at a party, does not fit into a picture of an original solution in coping with a situation; although technically it shows some signs of suiting the definition for which it was intended, it was an item on which the seven sociologists did not agree fully that it represents innovation. A girl who says she will 'go, but keep in the background' may be accepting the implied goal of the enterprise while setting aside its methods for her own; but this is not in a colloquial sense innovatory behaviour. The response 'suggest they [the v.i.p.s] have tea with the girls alone which would be more valuable' seems more original, but only eight per cent chose this.

Table 8·1. Responses to different situations, suggested by boarders and by day girls

type of adaptation	situations, and percentages of girls choosing each type of adaptation					
	prefect	exam	chapel	games	play	party
753 boarders						
conformity	45	48	47	63	53	61
innovation	18	7	11	5	3	24
ritualism	29	10	22	26	7	8
retreatism	3	34	9	5	36	3
rebellion	4	1	11	2	2	4
	(99)			(101)	(101)	
235 day girls						
conformity	58	48	44	73	45	50
innovation	19	6	7	3	3	33
ritualism	20	7	30	16	11	6
retreatism	0	38	7	6	38	6
rebellion	2	1	12	3	3	5
	(99)			(101)		

On balance it seems that, at least through this questionnaire, we find a scarcity of original or innovative behaviour which still lies within the general aims of the school. This would agree with the relative dearth of a developed 'underlife' (compared to what was reported for boys' schools) discussed in Chapter Six. Was this perhaps because the researcher did not strike the 'right' conspiratorial note in meeting the girls, and thereby failed to unlock the doors of their reserve? There is not enough reason to suppose that the answer is 'yes'. One of the boys' schools research team came on a visit to one girls' school, and though he tried to detect a rich seam of 'underlife', he did not find one. As one girl wrote (at another school) when I asked about covert activities: 'all we can do is go and eat ice creams on the beach' (15).

ritualist positions. Here we infer that the girl has lost faith in what she sees as the school's goals, but continues to comply with required forms of behaviour, for whatever reason. It is not uncommon to hear some such position 'officially' advocated: 'even if you don't like it, you must go through with it; you've got to take the rough with the smooth; learning to do things even though you may not want to is part of growing up'. Such statements appear to advocate settling for what we are calling here a 'ritualistic' position, at least in some situations. If any staff do take this line, then the definition we are using leads us into paradox; for we can say that 'the organization' (in the person of its staff) is advocating this for girls, in which case we cannot say that, if the girl acts accordingly, she has rejected *all* the organization's goals. What may be happening is that she rejects one or another particular goal. However, the organization which tolerates or even encourages ritualistic (in this special sense) behaviour, has accommodated, and in a sense absorbed by tolerating it, a minor sign of rebellion.

Few girls indeed identified themselves with rebellion. What are the examples? Should one be made a prefect: 'do as little as possible'. Imagine one is egged on to work harder for an exam: 'don't give a damn either for the exam or for the teacher'. Both these situations do not find a rebellious echo in many girls. The second item especially is not likely to appeal to many girls, which fits in with what we have seen in the other chapters, that a dominant view of what school is about, concerns exam passing and work.

What is given as a rebellious response to the next situation, being urged to go to an extra chapel service: 'refuse to go, you don't believe in it anyway', earns a noticeable amount of support. Eleven per cent of boarders choose this item. However, the questionnaire may even at this point fail to tap true rebellion, as it refers to a 'voluntary chapel service'. In that it is voluntary, it is not rebellious to refuse. The overall impression therefore, is that outright rebellion is not a common response. The girls were assured their answers would be confidential, and many showed openly that they were going to use this opportunity to write down their grumbles with glee. Here, for example, is one:

In this school one is either a God-botherer or one is not. There is no acceptance of the people who are neither confirmed atheists or confirmed Christians. Even if one is a confirmed Christian, the staff will

G

only accept this if you go to bible study and fit in with their denomination. Personally, I dislike this attitude as I consider that Christianity should destroy barriers, not create them, and that no one should be forced to conform to a certain opinion merely to get a good reference on leaving. If a person has a religious doubt, she is encouraged to go to a member of staff about it, but she is then thoroughly converted and told to attend bible studies etc.   (16)

In this school, according to this girl, a 'ritualist' adaptation is not encouraged by the staff; one is forced to conform or to take up a retreatist or rebellious response. Once, for example, the girls rebelled by refusing to get down on their knees at prayers; this, however, was not repeated or generalized into an outright rebellion, and should be construed therefore as merely a significant sign of unrest. Now while one could quote more instances like this, one also has to acknowledge that in the questionnaire, answered massively by 750 boarders and 230 day girls, only about twenty per cent chose retreatist and rebel responses to the chapel item; and the item was so worded that it was probably not truly rebellious to choose these supposedly extreme reactions.

For the day girls, the patterns of response were similar to the boarders'. There was mostly conformity, little innovation, and substantial ritualist or retreatist choices, depending on the question. There was also scanty rebellion; and the only appreciable sign of this came, as with the boarders, with the chapel item. It is remarkable in fact that day girls did not reject this more strongly, as it would require them to give their own free time. But though the patterns of response were similar, the strengths by which day girls favoured certain items were different than for boarders. So it seems that boarders were significantly less conformist (or willing to serve the school!) on the question of becoming a prefect;[1] it was the day girls' turn to be less conformist over willingness to go to extra chapel;[2] day girls were also significantly less keen on coming in to a party in school,[3] though they were more enthusiastic than boarders to take part in a games match.[4]

First let us examine the extent of conformity which is shown at different ages:

Table 8·2. Percentage of conformist answers for boarders at different ages

	ages:				
	13	14	15	16	17
number of girls (= 100 per cent)	80	198	231	179	64
percentage of girls conforming to:					
become a prefect	64	40	42	49	41
work for an exam	68	48	41	47	40
go to voluntary chapel	54	49	43	48	46
play for a games team	75	62	53	66	63
attend a school play	56	53	50	53	54
come to a V.I.P.s party	55	54	62	70	70
average percentage for each age	62	51	48	55	52

The youngest girls on an overall basis show the greatest level of conformity. This falls off, in a way that not surprisingly parallels what happens to satisfaction, until we see that it is the 15-year-olds who are least likely to want to conform. They are also at the least happy age; this supports what we have found in other ways, that the 15-year-old stage in boarding seems to represent the lowest ebb at which the girls feel personally, and at which they feel like responding loyally towards the official regime. The position 'improves' somewhat among the sixth-formers. (There is doubt about describing this as improvement, as this is to assume that schools would like to find conformist responses from their older girls. Some probably would like this; others would not – though this does not mean they would like to find rebellion in the sixth!)

For the exam situation, the older girls are least conformist; one might interpret this as possibly because they have clarified their own academic goals, so that some new exam or new effort that the questionnaire asks them to imagine is superfluous to what they are already busy doing. Some girls at this age, though they have accepted the academic load, also wish for a break, and so might not respond conformingly so easily to this item.

Rather too much emphasis laid on academic work. I am much more interested in Art, Music and Drama which are *v.* cramped.   (17)

Age produces an opposite trend with regard to the V.I.P. party item. Here we have supposed that to agree to come to the party is to conform to the 'organization's goals'. However, one could also see it from a girl's point of view, that an adult party is of more interest to the older girls who might react to it as an item, however minor, of adventure or social exploration. For them it might be adventurous or innovatory in the normal sense of the word and it is merely an accident of circumstance that this fits our definition of 'conformist' to the school. This illustrates how it is that one does not relate to the organization in a blanket way, either conforming or rebelling or taking positions in between, but that the adaptation and its personal meaning depend on the topic at issue. It will also probably depend on time – on a long perspective as we have seen with changes associated with age, and on a short perspective depending on the quality or impact of current or recent incidents.

Even though the nature of adaptation depends on topic and on time, there may nevertheless be some underlying consistency of response depending on the individual. The 'Merton score' was therefore added up for each girl, and used for a variety of statistical comparisons. This might even be used to indicate the level of conformity or unrest in a school. We should be very careful about how the sampling was done if we are to make comparisons between schools; for example, if the test was given in one school mostly to B-stream 15-year-olds, but in another school to A-stream 13-year-olds, we might suppose that the second school had an enthusiastically conformist pupil society, compared with the first which might seem sick at the core with rebellion. Such a result might be a very false interpretation. We must be careful, therefore, to make sure that in all schools the Merton scores are derived from girls at similar ages and academic levels. This precaution was ensured as much as possible; however, it was not possible to fulfil such an intention perfectly. Fortunately, we shall be able to see from some of the statistical results that both the Merton scores for individuals and the average Merton scores for schools were recording something that was valid.

First we can notice that there is a modest, but very significant correlation (i.e. we can be very sure this did not occur by chance) between a girl's Merton score, and the head's ratings of the social contribution made by that girl.[5] So the conformist girl (by her own indication) is likely to be the one whom the head thinks is useful to the school or a pillar of society; she is also likely to be well rated for the use she is making of the academic facilities, though this overlap is not as strong as the first. Another set of correlations[6] shows that the conformist girl is more likely to want to excel by becoming a prefect, and less likely to want to excel at art, music or drama. These correlations are not large, but they are exceedingly unlikely to have happened by chance.

The above four relationships are very trite; and this is the whole point of them. Since we may choose to rely on the validity of heads' ratings and of girls' aspirations, the fact that these link up reasonably with our index of conformity shows that this index is reflecting something real and is not just a statistical oddity. To be sure, the correlation figures are not high; but this is doubtless because of the numerous other factors which also interact, making each girl's predicament a special one, with regularities and consistencies hard to detect.

When we work out the average Merton score for schools, we find that the top score is 26·9 and the lowest one 22·9. The differences between schools must therefore be considered relatively small (four points on this scale represent about sixteen per cent difference on the available range). This suggests that the sampling of girls within each school for this test was likely to have been over fairly wide a range, and that the presence of conformists as well as rebels (and those in between) in each school has 'flattened out' the averages. In spite of this small range, it is likely that there is a real and meaningful difference between the most and the least conformist schools. We can rely on this, as there are again effective correlations which show that the conformity score for a school is relatable to other known facts. For example, schools with high conformity levels tended also to be the schools wherein the aspiration to excel by becoming a prefect was relatively common.[7] I did not calculate average heads' ratings at enough schools (where the head rated twenty-five girls or over) partly because in some schools I only asked for ratings on a smaller number of girls, partly because in a very few schools heads omitted to complete the ratings; so we cannot validate the schools' average Merton score by comparison with average heads' ratings. However, I propose to treat the average Merton score obtained for each school as indicating something valid about that school; we will see that this 'conformity score' for a school compares interestingly with other facts.

We have now two classes of information to deal with. One deals with girls, and let us examine (as regards background) *who* are the ones that fit in (conform) as against rebelling; we can also look for other factors which characterize conformers in school. The second class of information deals with schools, and let us examine *which* schools are the ones where there may be a high level of conformity, or of rebellion.

There is no good reason to suppose that if an individual girl has previously been to a preparatory (independent) school, or to a prep boarding school, she will be more conformist in her secondary boarding role. Such a link with past experience may indeed apply in the cases of some particular girls; but the effect is not sufficiently general to be detectable by finding a significant correlation. On the other hand, it is clear that girls who say they have a good relationship with their parents (mother and father separately) are likely to be more conformist in school.[8] Conformity in school is by no means (if at all) so reliably relatable to girls' feelings towards brothers and sisters.[9] Now we have seen (in Chapter Four) that satisfaction in school, or happiness there, is interrelated with conformity,[10] as it is also with relationships to parents and to brothers and sisters. What we might infer from the finding that conformity is not conspicuously relatable to the quality of sibling relationships, is that the latter have the component of love (as does the relationship with parents) but not the aspect of successfully working out one's position with an authority figure. Girls who have sorted out their relations with authority well so that they conform in school, are also likely to relate well with their parents.

This explanation above is hypothetical, though it fits the facts; if it is false, some other explanation is needed, and I cannot offer one. The situation can be diagrammed as in the table on the following page (the figures refer to statistical correlations which are significant):

These associations between family relationships and conformity are derived from large populations of girls, spread over nearly all the twenty-three schools visited. They transcend questions of age, of ability or of schools' characteristics. The finding is relevant if one contemplates the plan to place pupils with 'need for boarding' (defined in some cases by unsatisfactory family relationships) into boarding places. We would expect such girls, if they follow present trends, to be less conformist, more rebellious. Whether schools could cope, and how, is another matter. We shall see presently whether it can be said that one kind of school, rather than another, integrates its pupils better.

Happiness, conformity and relationship with the family

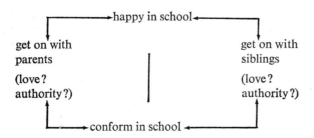

Once they are in school, we have already seen that conformists can be characterized to some extent by their different types of aspiration, and by their social and academic performance as rated by heads. There is no good reason to suppose that individual conformist girls aspire more or less strongly to excel at games, work or domestic science. Further, two tests of abilities were given, one requiring exact problem-solving, the other requiring a 'divergent' or imaginative performance. There is no strong reason to state that conformist girls were individually better or worse at these tests than, for example, were rebellious girls. This is in spite of the fact that conformist girls were somewhat likelier to be found in lower forms,[11] and these younger girls were much more likely to have lower scores on both tests.

Only if we compare girls who show extreme types of adaptation can we find any test differences. On the one hand, we have those who chose the conformist item in every part of the Merton test; we compare these with girls who chose at least one clear rebellious answer, perhaps more. There is some suggestion then that it is the rebels who include a higher proportion of the more able girls, especially on the imaginative side.

As the conformists are likely to be younger than the rebels, it is not surprising that they should score lower on tests. What is worth noting is that the test difference is more significant for divergence than for problem-solving. We shall see how these two tests link up in different ways with social factors below.

Table 8·3. Performance of consistent conformists and of part rebels on two tests

	problem-solving test[12]		divergent/imaginative test[13]	
	conformists (45)	rebels (144)	conformists (45)	rebels (144)
test score	7·58	8·03	15·04	15·70

Now we turn to the data about schools to see how characteristics there depend on conformity or not. We can see first of all how test scores related to conformity. Schools with the more able girls on the problem-solving ('convergence') test tended to be the ones which showed less conformism, more rebellion.[14] There is no evidence that divergence is related in any way to the prevalence of conformity. This means that, although we might have expected highly divergent, imaginative pupil bodies to have included more rebels, other factors probably have swamped any such effect. Thus we can have a school with very imaginative girls, among whom there may be many inclined to rebel; but it is just as likely that in a school without imaginative girls there will be several rebels too. What we know more certainly is that, where problem-solving ability is collectively low, there will be less rebellion. It is possible that the divergent mind dissipates its ideas, while it takes a collection of more acute and focused minds to marshal critical attention and develop a climate questioning conformity.

The mental abilities prevalent in a school are linked in a complex but notable way to another social factor, that is the attitude regarding pastoral care. Where schools have more imaginative girls, they are more likely to harbour a readiness to discuss problems in general with somebody;[15] this does not mean that readiness to take personal problems to staff members in particular is any more prevalent in the more imaginative pupil bodies; so we see that divergence is related significantly only to readiness to communicate in general. With convergence, there is a complementary pattern of relationships. In the less able schools, one cannot detect any more or less readiness to discuss problems in general,[16] but there is a very strong likelihood that, in the less able schools, girls will be more willing to discuss personal problems with the staff (and hence probably the overlapping circumstance that they are not so likely to be entirely secretive about personal problems). This bears on what has been said before – that many girls see school as primarily concerned with work, and that they can presumably discuss work problems with staff; the present evidence suggests that greater ability, and hence presumably greater academic contact with the staff, by no means necessarily brings a greater level of pastoral relationships with staff. Individual girls may get to know staff more closely through their working contacts and this may happen in a few schools, but it does not happen consistently enough to appear as statistically significant.

As regards Merton-registered conformity, it seems safe to say that it is the more conformist pupil bodies which show more desire to discuss personal problems, including with the staff.[17] We saw that it was the less clever groups (as indicated by the test for convergence) who were more ready to accept pastoral care; now we see that it is also the more conformist groups who will accept pastoral care. This reminds us of the link discovered just before, that the more conformist groups will be less clever on the convergence test. This can be diagrammed to make it more clear.

Links between problem-solving ability (convergence), pastoral care and conformity

some schools tend to show these characteristics together	→ conformity (Merton scale)	—ready to discuss pastoral problems	—less ability (convergence)
	→ rebellion	—unready to disclose problems, especially to staff	—greater ability (convergence)

I must emphasize in all this that we cannot be sure we are dealing with 'intelligence', whatever this is thought to be. We are dealing with ability to do a certain test, and what this associates with. If anything, we can see that the notion of 'intelligence' may not be unitary. The tests of convergence and of divergence, which probably tap different aspects of intelligent (i.e. discriminative) behaviour, relate differently to conformity and to social communication as manifest in the pastoral care scales. There is another measure which relates to conformity, and to ability, which is the 'sixth-form prominence' (calculated as the relative size of the sixth forms to the whole school). This shows[18] that schools with smaller, or no sixth forms, tend to have a greater measure of conformity; this squares both with the fact that such schools are more weighted with younger girls, who are more conformist, and that such schools are likely to be less academically advanced – thus their girls would score lower on the convergence test. It is not merely the size of the sixth form that relates to conformity; if we calculate the staff-to-senior (all those doing A- and O-levels) ratio, we see[19] that greater conformity is found in schools where a greater number of staff exist to cope with the seniors. This may come about because the schools with few seniors obviously have a very favourable staff–seniors ratio, but are less academically advanced than schools with huge sixth forms – even if these have adequate staff. Nevertheless, it indicates the possibility that if one compared only schools with large sixths, those with more staff might have more conformity (throughout the school, not just in the sixth).

It might be thought that we are only occupied in establishing fairly trite observations as true. So it might also be thought that institutional control would be reflected in the level of conformity among the pupils; perhaps in the more severe schools there would be more rebelliousness. This may indeed have been so in some severe schools. Yet in other equally severe schools the girls were obviously more conformist, as there is virtually a zero correlation between institutional control and Merton scores.[20] This suggests that it would be useful not to treat institutional control as a single entity, but to subdivide it into physical (size of dormitories, access to free time and space, etc.) and emotional parts (for example, compulsion to go to chapel, to cheer at school matches, etc.). These parts were all ingredients of the scale used here, but their separate statistical effects have not been calculated. The scale has substantial correlations with pastoral care response, but not with conformity or rebelliousness levels. This reminds us that pupils might relate well or poorly to staff, but that though this can be predicted to some extent from knowing the institutional control, or the conformity level, these last two are not associated together. This can be diagrammed as follows:

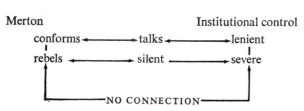

Pastoral care

I shall now turn to consider a few special aspects of the question of 'fitting in', and deal with the limited evidence I have of those who have been called 'integrants' – that is, girls from classes or families which would not 'normally' have sent them to boarding school. We saw before that, if we looked for possible links at the level of individuals, no connection exists between type of preparatory schooling and conformity in school; nor with regard to parental boarding experience. We might reasonably infer that these two measures indicate whether girls are 'integrants' or not. Girls neither of whose parents boarded are first generation boarders; while if both parents boarded we may suppose that their families may have instilled attitudes towards boarding, possibly leading to better adaptation to the system. These two circumstances, incidentally, are closely linked;[21] schools where parents had been boarders were distinctly schools where girls had previously been to independent preparatory schools. Now, spanning the whole group of schools, there is no effective trend linking independent or boarding background with conformity within schools. As this is an important question it deserves further attention; not to have found a link by one statistical method does not mean that it does not exist. Therefore I have compared the schools with most, and least independent and parental boarding backgrounds. As these schools represent extremes, they are labelled 'traditional' and 'integrant' schools respectively.

Table 8·4.
'Traditional' and 'integrant' schools and Merton conformity

	range of parental boarding experience	average rank of Merton score
five schools most 'traditional'	65·6–81·7 per cent	10·2
five schools most 'integrant'	1·9–26·0 per cent	15·6

	pupils without independent prep school experience	average rank of Merton score
five schools most 'traditional'	8·3–12·4 per cent	9·2
five schools most 'integrant'	45·7–92·1 per cent	14·6

The 'rank of Merton score' is found by arranging all the schools in order of Merton score from the first (greatest level of conformity) to the last (lowest conformity – most rebellion). So a smaller average rank shows more conformity and a greater average shows rebellion. These figures are not substantial enough to convince a statistician that a real link between circumstances is most likely to exist. However, they are in the direction that gives a lead to whoever seeks to describe real situations which may not be quite so clear-cut as to lead to statistically significant conclusions.

We need now to examine what happens in particular schools to see how the complexities of their situations affect their performance in getting girls to 'fit in'. In the school with the greatest integrant proportion – girls placed by local authorities – there was a very high degree of (Merton) conformity. There was a negligible proportion of older girls, which though it gave greater weight to the conformist adaptation of the younger ones, also placed the 15-year-olds in relatively senior status, getting them to some extent out of the rut in which they find themselves at other schools. Institutional control was strict but this did not prevent rated success on ideal goals and satisfaction from being high. The school was relatively small, and the head kept a high degree of personal contact with everybody. It is possible that both staff and many of the students having relations with the local authorities could perceive the latter as 'them'; this reference to an outgroup could provide some cohesion within the school. All this is not to say that there were not also extremely dedicated and effective staff. In this school, regional accents were to be found, and they were accepted, which might also help in not creating a gulf between staff and pupils.

Another school with a high integrant proportion had a (relatively) high degree of rebellion. This was a large school, broken up into houses. The central staff could not have effective personal knowledge of all the pupils in the same way as in a small school. The deputy head said, 'we try to get rid of accents; they are a lazy way of speaking'. The school was seen as outmoded in its occupational ideas by the girls, and the satisfaction and rated success on ideal goals was low. Here is what one girl says:

Girls with different accents get teased and taken-off. They feel sad and want to go home. (13)

This does not apply only to younger girls.

I come from Yorkshire and suffered from frequent reprimands in my junior forms about my accent. Now everyone has accepted it – I hope. (17)

In this larger school there is a greater mixture of social class background than in the smaller one first described and one girl says of this:

Girls who come from higher class familys are revolting think they are higher than the middle, and lower, tend to boast. Generally throw their weight about. Girls from the middle class seem to be the best friendlier you feel more able to confide in them. Lower class are OK. (14)

So we see that two of the more 'integrant' schools differ in the conformity they evoke, and in many other respects. Obviously also, the conformity in the one school is to a different set of official goals from the second.

At the opposite extreme, the traditional schools (purely as regards the origin of the clientele, not necessarily in their own structures) also include those with high conformity as well as others with rebelliousness (though not quite so strong). At one such school with high conformity, one housemistress spoke of her belief in maintaining social stratification. She was happy to know that there was someone 'above' her (e.g. the landed gentry) and considered that those below would feel awkward if brought in to public schools. Further, she considered one should be Christian about it, respecting the other for what he is and not wanting to change him. The question of regional accents did not arise in this school (except perhaps for distinctions between Oxford and Chelsea, which I am not qualified to tease out). At another school, this time with some small but noticeable proportion of integrants, there was a low level of conformism. This was probably linked with low institutional control and high aspirations (encouraged by facilities) to excel at arts, and other factors all interacting. Here, a very trusted and senior girl wrote a white-hot account of how nothing prevented most of the Registrar General's Social Class D, whom she considered (and showed, to her satisfaction) could afford it, from sending their children to private boarding schools, but the lack of suitable intentions. As this girl herself came from a family background where a dedicated effort had been made, she has some power to her argument. Such attitudes, however, may lead to some disdain of those who do not choose to make this kind of educational effort. Another girl in this school shows some such views:

I have found at boarding school that people from even slightly different backgrounds – say a book-shop (trashy mags etc.) owners daughter do not fit in with the others. Some are not willing to conform to rules which they consider petty and pointless.

Others have different moral standards, & think nothing of going to bed with any boy they meet. I have met these people and, although I tried to like them, I found I couldn't get on with them.   (15)

This girl's views suggest, and several others could be similarly quoted, that attitudes are perceived as determinants of social class. The 'uppers' may consider the 'lowers' to have 'lower' moral standards. Flirtatious episodes among uppers will be seen as an aberration rather than as a mark of class; from lowers it will be seen as a mark of class and help establish social distance.

The 'lowers' may consider 'uppers' to have poor moral standards, a lack of tolerance expressed as snobbery. Intolerance among lowers will be seen as an aberration rather than a mark of class, while from uppers it will be construed so as to establish distance. Eventually, in the view of one girl, integration depends on the numbers involved.

In independent schools with equal proportions of girls from every class, it is no problem. However if 95% came from one exclusive class, then the other 5% whether in a higher or lower class would find life difficult. The tendency to think that the problem of rejection would only arise when the supposed 'intruder' is in a lower class than the majority, is wrong. A minority in a higher class would suffer just as badly.   (17)

This is presumably one of the reasons why parents who can afford it pay for independent education in which they hope their children will encounter others like themselves. This girl suggests that, if proportions were evenly balanced by class, there would be no problem. If we examine four schools at which experience of independent preparatory schooling involves half the girls (the other half having been at state schools) we find these four schools have rankings rather low on Merton conformity (i.e. towards rebelliousness) and on average pupil satisfaction. Again, there is not enough evidence to use for statistical calculations here, but it lies in the direction opposed to the girl's argument.

Some schools also consider that aspects of social homogeneity are to be desired. At the first school I mentioned, full of girls new to boarding, the head emphasized the value of uniform. It made girls look equal; those with good clothes to flaunt would not be able to do so to the misery of those without. Even the Christmas dance was attended by girls in uniform; the only males present were adults connected with the school and girls complained of 'having to go and politely ask those fat old bald men to dance'. At the other extreme, in the school with the housemistress approving of stratification, although uniform was worn, girls could do their best for dances, and I heard several complaints that to manage only a modest finery made some girls unhappy. Among girls it is often not enough evidently to compare one's dress against some absolute aesthetic standard (the commerce of dresswear has made sure this does not exist) but they must compare their own against others'. The matter of uniform and dress is clearly not superficial to girls or of small relevance compared to the male money- and occupation-oriented criteria of class. Dress and make-up affect how girls feel and also denote information about class, and hence attitudes and compatibility.

All classes of girls are mixed together. Usually the upper class are snobby to other people and some girls pretend they are above the rest, it is always the catty ones. The nicest people are the ones not bothered about classes but some are tarts and they are proud of it. We usually get on OK because the uniform hides everything. (13)

The last sentence is belied by the preceding ones. It may be the purpose of uniform to 'hide everything' but clearly it has not hidden it from this girl! In one of the schools where integrants and girls of more traditional background are evenly mixed, we have these two opinions:

I am not sure whether this is intentional but when I first came to this school recently I felt inferior. In fact the reason for this I think maybe is because I am . . . not fee paying. . . . People of one background tend to stay together and a certain amount of snobbery emerges. (16)

Yet

. . . differences in social background don't have any effect on . . . school life at all. I think this is helped by the fact that we all wear school uniforms, which makes each one the same. I don't think that girls worry whether or not their friend lives in the poorest part of town, and if her father is a dustman, its just the girl, and whether she is friendly or not. (16)

The second girl clearly does not consider herself in the dustman class; the point about uniform is repeated – though it seems not to have affected the experience of the previous girl. Friendship is said to depend on outlook, values or interests rather than on parents' occupation in itself. However, outlook is often connected with parents' occupational class; the implication is that if working-class values (if such things do in fact exist for girls) do not conflict with, or are changed to meet, middle-class values, then integration will occur. This school has a high level of pupil satisfaction, in spite of pupils coming from difficult homes and families (by their own ratings), but a low level of conformity. It is possible that this relative prevalence of rebellious attitudes is linked with the heterodox population which cannot easily crystallize a conformist body of opinion.

A new girl shows some uncertainty about identifying others, and also implies that differences in attitudes are a possible sign of class membership.

Girls from both upper and working-class families are here together.

We don't know who is from upper class and working class and so don't find much difference. If I find someone has a funny view I change the subject for another.   (12)

The girl notices that attitudes differ, but has not (yet) aligned a typology of outlook and class; further, she chooses to act tactfully. Many of those in this girl's form were daughters of widows, and it might be that absence of fathers with their easily recognizable class status due to jobs, was what led to this perception of class anonymity. However, other girls in the same form showed clear awareness of the social class of their fellows. Rebelliousness and pupil dissatisfaction were relatively quite high in this school, and it seems an example of where attitudes have not coalesced harmoniously. However, an older girl suggests that an attitudinal *modus vivendi* can be sought by a convergence upon a middle way – provided that this really is a middle way and not an outspoken majority.

Girls from the middle class very seldom find class a problem. Partly because most girls at boarding school are middle class partly because the middle class is less identifiable. There is always the tendency to place oneself in the middle class through fear of being thought inferior or superior.   (17)

This presents the classic rationale of the compromise solution. It may prosper if there really is an element of communication or exchange by both sides – rather than, for example, one side having to give up its accent, or other distinctive characteristic. Further, if there is a sizeable minority which is itself coherent – for example, of day girls in a predominantly boarding school – then either organizational factors or aspects of shared attitudes or experiences can make this minority characteristic something that they will choose to emphasize, because this is the nucleus around which identity and self-esteem is organized.

If the minority is a small one, the devices for maintaining the difference may become very unostentatious – as, for example, of a Muslim girl who whispered '*per Jesum Christum Dominum vestrum*' when the others said '*nostrum*'. Many minority girls were foreigners such as Arabs, Persians, Thais, Chinese, Africans or South Americans. Few of these appeared to be miserable because of their difference. On the contrary, they appeared to get on well, if not exactly being at the centres of groups. Many of them, in spite of requests to the contrary (and sometimes because of language difficulties), did not take the opportunity of joining in the research and illuminating it with the benefit of their outsiders' points of view; instead, they appeared to consider the research 'an English thing' to do with the English school, and thus for the English girls to be concerned about. What views were collected from them tended to include the same views as from their English peers, but together with an unmistakable respect for things English that most English girls would feel too modest to assert.

One source of social difference which girls might notice concerns their families. Their outlook, behaviour, nationality might all be integrated, and this might occur without anything being known about families. Yet some girls may fear what will be thought if their parents appear at school, possibly arriving by bus or in a trades-man's van, or appearing 'common' in their ways. Friends might not mind such surprises, but not everybody feels they can trust all their friends. One area of doubt concerns brothers and boy-friends.

At several schools, there is a nocturnal buzz of young men who cycle around in a more or less dishevelled state; girls sometimes acknowledge their presence by waving from windows, sometimes clad with a carefully carefree lightness, and occasionally even come out to rendezvous. Youths have also climbed in. Elsewhere, they peer at girls swimming during the day. Frequently girls, and even staff, refer to these youths as 'yobs'. It is likely that some integrant boarders, for all their uniform and possible desire to integrate, might identify in part with these young men; if this is so, they are liable to be alienated by their companions' attitudes to 'yobs'.

At this school there is quite a large range in social background. Per-sonally, I think this is a good quality of the school . . . but although the pupils are indeed quite a mixed bunch, we are not allowed to associate with those who come to visit us if they are below a certain standard. This, I suppose, is acceptable as the headmistress' duty is to preserve us, but to me it seems quite a demonstration of class distinction contra-dicting the way in which we are asked to mix with our pupils 'below the standard' . . . in the staff, when a person who is at all different in any way is employed, it takes quite a time to overcome the mocks, nick-names and giggles of a girls' school like ours.   (16)

I asked in several schools about how the scanty numbers of working-class girls might feel towards the derogatory attitude to 'yobs'. It was difficult to find any comments on this; possibly this is an area in which otherwise articulate girls become reticent. On the other hand, it also seems possible (based on conversational impressions only) that, while working-class girls might feel uncomfortable about themselves, or their parents, they may aspire to make boy-friends and marry those who are 'superior to yobs'. Thus they may not mind joining in digs at yobs, as this contributes to putting themselves out of that category.

The next comment will be the last on this question, and seems to summarize several of the points (and uncertainties) raised. The school is one where the parental boarding background is about fifty per cent, though the girls themselves (over eighty-five per cent) have been to private preparatory schools. Nevertheless, a point is made of admitting 'need cases' sent by local authorities, and considerable efforts are made on behalf of these girls. The girls rate their school most highly on attaining ideal goals, show a high level of conformity, and a medium average level of happiness in school. The headmistress is a popular idiosyncrasarch.

One cannot generalise about social class and boarding schools; whether a child from the lower classes will fit into boarding school with girls from the middle and upper classes depends entirely on the girls and the atmosphere of the school itself. . . . Two girls have been sent here away from the bad influence of their home environment but have settled in very well even though they have accents. The only difficulty they find is to accept authority but this is due perhaps to the circumstances under which they came.

I think in many schools girls can be very hurtful about parents, occupations. . . . The two girls . . . find it difficult to re-adapt themselves from home to school and vice-versa.

As far as teachers are concerned social class doesn't really affect the relationship between teacher–pupil, but I think that if a member of staff had an accent this would make a difference – girls from backgrounds where parents speak well etc. may feel put off by an accent.   (17)

The point that accepting the authority of the school system is linked with having satisfactory relationships with parents is made; adapting to school is also not the only problem. This may entail growing away from home, and trouble with adjusting during the holidays. A double adjustment problem of this sort needs to be wisely handled or it could otherwise lead to maladjustment on both fronts. Reactions to staff partly depend on their social class, which is signified by accent. One teacher told me, in a school with more integrant pupils than most, that he had his own problems of not rejecting the middle-class girls with their more languid accents and ways. In another school a clearly non-middle-class judo teacher was trying to put some snap into the performance of upper-middle-class girls to whom such attitudes were apparently alien, and did not match with their concept of the lady. The instructor might have won them over eventually, but the scene strongly suggested that an officer-type wearing paramilitary (preferably cavalry) garb would have more easily conveyed the desired mixture of deadly earnest and *élan*. We can begin to see then that an exhaustive analysis (which would also be exhausting) of how the individual comes to adapt to or integrate into a community would depend on its authorities as well as on the individuals. The focus of attention has, however, lain with the pupils.

In all this so far I have dealt with aspects of 'fitting in', and adaptation. But what about 'fitting out'? Is there some process parallel in time with the school career, during which girls somehow do, or do not, adjust better to 'outside society'?

In Chapter One (Table 1·12) we saw that there is some tendency for older boarders to say they make fewer of their holiday friends from within the boarding-school system. This effect is noticeable among the 17-year-olds, though not before. There is more evidence to show how friendships (during the holidays) diversify as girls get older.

Table 8·5. Extent to which boarders say they make holiday friendships (percentages)

| | ages: | | | | |
	13	14	15	16	17
'I make friends':					
many, easily	34	35	43	38	41
few at a time	42	47	47	50	51
one friend or so	24	18	10	12	8
total girls	186	306	289	276	183

Clearly, the older girls are less inclined[22] to describe themselves as lonely or friendless. In these terms it could be said that their wider social integration, apart from the conformity at school, is proceeding. Furthermore, friendship-making becomes more diversified by sex.

Table 8·6.
Sex of friends made by boarders of different ages (percentages)

friends made	ages: 13	14	15	16	17
mostly girls	33	17	9	7	9
mixed	63	78	81	81	80
mostly boys	4	6	10	12	11
total girls	180	276	276	266	171

Some have not answered this question who did deal with the previous one. Others may have ticked two spaces, or made some other response that one cannot interpret. The burden of the findings[23] is that, after 13, girls report mostly mixed friendship-making (in the holidays); between 14 and 15 there is a slight increase in those who claim to make friends with mostly boys. However, after 13 there is a distinct and steady reduction of those who say they make friends with mostly girls. Perhaps they have had enough of girls during the term. There is not enough evidence on which to conclude that immersion in a female society has made many girls 'boy mad' during the holidays. The general comment of very many girls is that they want to dissolve the differences between the 'school society' as something different from 'outside society'. Two comments, both from large schools with high institutional controls that apply also to seniors, exemplify this:

This school promotes frustration to the umpteenth degree. This place is soul destroying. It turns out cookie-cutter people all very nice, sweet etc. but they're bores!! We have no contact with people 'outside' at all. I think it is an extremely artificial existence. We have a completely different life here than that which we lead during the holidays.   (17)
... should mix with other schools. Does not hardly at all. Too cloistered seriously. Favourite phrase of teachers living in 'when you go out into the world' – surely we should be part of it now?   (17)

Not all schools are like this. One smaller school, whose institutional control is not heavy for juniors and even less so for seniors, produces this comment:

Being allowed in the town over the weekends and having bicycles is a very good idea, because you dont loose contact with outdoor world. It also gives you responsibility apart from the 'usual' school responsibility which we (at our age) and may be younger should have.   (16)

So older girls are clearly occupied with and concerned about adjusting to the 'outer world'. This affects how they propose to deal with demands of school conformity, either living it or even enforcing it. They become very articulate in writing about their dissatisfaction, and it may be a surprise that the Merton responses (see Table 8·2) do not show a much lower level of conformity among the oldest girls. Possibly for them it is a question of fulfilling academic goals, and being patient.

Summary

A school is a community with many purposes. These purposes may differ in the minds of any person who experiences or tries to describe them. Many would agree that a general purpose is to bring young individuals towards an integrated membership of the wider society which they join on leaving school. If the school is so structured that it resembles a lock on a waterway, with its upper end open to the 'outer world', then one would hope to see conformity, or even innovation to the organization among the older girls. If the school is so structured that it resembles a lock closed at both ends, then even the school might claim that it looked to cultivate a certain amount of restiveness, preferably like the 'innovation' Merton adaptation among the seniors.

In any case, there is a very widespread assumption (and this is shared by others in educational establishments in diverse cultures around the world) that the school is a body in which staff do the teaching, help to bring about integration into society, and the pupils receive knowledge and become integrated. This view is paradoxically enhanced as well as contradicted by one organizational factor. While the average time for which staff belong to a school might be less than that of pupils, the latter come in order to leave in due course. The staff do not come in order to leave; further, a few may stay for many years. Thus, on the one hand, pupils are being passed on into the wider society, for which school is presumably somehow preparing them; yet it is the staff who can become thought of as the stable members – not of the wider society but of the separate microcosm, the boarding school.

It therefore has to be judged separately in the case of each school, by each observer, whether they think conformity, innovation or even rebellion are the states of adaptation to the school which they would consider desirable to find among senior girls. I am presuming here that ritualism or retreatism would not often be approved adaptations; yet this is not to be assumed without question. Each reader must therefore judge the material in this chapter individually.

The most common adaptation is in fact conformity. Further, this does not seem to increase among the senior girls; instead, it is commonest among the new girls, then decreases to a minimum for the 15-year-olds. Though this overall statement can be made about 'conformity', it is also true that a girl may reply conformingly with regard to one topic but not to another. Thus it is that conformity to the questionnaire item dealing with a party increases among older girls, while conformity as regards a school exam decreases with age. I have pointed out that the items were carried over almost unchanged from the questionnaire used in boys' schools, so the interpretation of what appears to be 'conformist' choices regarding the party is really in the personal context more innovative.

What were defined here as innovative choices, or outright rebellious ideas, were distinctly rare. These are the items embodying some element of personal initiative, of the girl 'substituting her own' ideas for the supposed goals or methods of the school. Instead, there was a certain amount of choice of ritualist or retreatist adaptations. To an extent, the definition as implied at the beginning of the chapter of the retreatist position is either logically inadequate or absurd. Faced with a situation a girl cannot just reject goals and methods. She must do something. The choices are of some displacement action – which will involve either acceptance or rejection of some other set of goals and means, or bodily disappearance, which is not possible. It is also possible to interpret 'rejecting the organization's means' as implying by default the substitution of one's own. I prefer to treat the retreative position as logically inadequate. It has merely served here to generate some items on a questionnaire which have not often been chosen.

In spite of the snags in design of the Merton questionnaire, scores from it have shown significant agreement with ratings made by heads. Girls who tend to conformist answers tend to get better ratings from heads for 'fitting in socially'; they also tend, though to a rather weak extent, to get better ratings for the advantage they are thought to be taking of the existing academic facilities. Conformist choosers also tend individually to say they want to excel by becoming prefects. This particular association remains true at the schools level; schools in which there are many conformists tend to be the schools where it is commoner to want to become a prefect. One should note that this type of parallel finding on an individual and on a school level is not a logically, or sociologically (especially) necessary event. For example, it appears that there is some slight sign that people who decline conformist choices with the Merton questionnaire are the ones who prefer to excel at arts; we cannot say, however, that less conformist schools are the ones which have a higher general desire to excel at arts. Clearly if such individual links occur, at the school level they are obscured by the workings of other factors.

As regards finding which girls are more likely to choose conformity, there is no sign that either girls whose parents were boarders, or those who had been to independent primary schools, were more conformist. That is to say, there is no sign that, by these criteria, 'integrant' girls were less conformist. But as regards quality of family relationships, the picture is different. Girls whose descriptions implied they got on well with their families, tended to show more conformity. Perhaps this was due to some general disposition among affectionate or easy-going girls to answer compliantly with both such questions. In that case one would expect a similar effect to be observed with the question on relationships with brothers and sisters. But no such thing was found. Relationships described as good with brothers and sisters did not necessarily imply a conformist adaptation in school. I interpreted this as follows: that with parents, not only love but also an adjustment with an authority source is involved; the adaptation with the school also involves adjustment to an authority source. It may be this aspect of being able to accept or relate to those in authority which causes the correlation mentioned. With brothers and sisters, plain love (or jealousy) but no bargain with authority is systematically involved; so that there is no correlation with Merton adaptation scores. This possible aspect of adjustment to authority is of great importance if legislation brings pupils with disturbed family relationships into boarding schools as many of them now are.

We turn now to examine whether different types of abilities are linked with conformity. Time only allowed two short tests to be given. One test, of divergence, was not relatable to the level of conformity found in schools. High divergence levels were related slightly to desire to excel at arts. The test with convergent problems was related to conformity. Schools with the more able girls on this test were more rebellious in general. This finding can be explained by supposing that divergent-minded girls may not focus on grievances as convergent-minded ones might. Several other factors, of institutional control, sixth-form size and staff ratios, all interact in determining the coincidence of levels of ability and conformity.

Another sign we can use of adaptation is the extent of pastoral care communication in which girls say they are ready to take part. In the more divergent school populations there was more chance of finding a greater readiness to communicate – in general, and not with any greater valency towards staff. The more convergent-minded schools (disregarding for the moment how they stood as to divergence) showed pupils who were less ready to discuss personal problems with staff. One might expect to find on intuitive grounds some connection between high institutional control ('tyranny') and low conformity ('rebellion'). In fact, though individual case studies could back up this idea, it was not supported on a statistical basis. Other factors complicate the situation and swamp any systematic link between oppression and revolt.

Turning to examine the predicaments of individuals, and of separate schools, and paying special attention to the position of 'integrants', I suggested that integrants are much more likely to be found among those whose parents were not at boarding school, and who had not been at private preparatory schools (these two factors are strongly correlated together). Looking at five schools containing the greatest number of integrants, we find a lower level of conformity than at the five schools with fewest integrants. There was no evidence that integrants personally were more likely to be rebellious; but some slight evidence that schools containing greater numbers of integrants might be more rebellious. As some girls pointed out, it may be a question of relative proportions of integrants and others.

Many girls observe how numerous factors, including for instance the use of uniform and the treatment of accents, interact with how a girl feels as an integrant. Moreover, not only is there a problem of how to integrate a girl with the ways of a school or of the majority of its population; but by doing so one may be developing a problem between a girl and her family. In this study it is not possible to tell whether poor family relationships coexist with, and cause, poor adaptation in school. We can only examine the question of co-existence; but inferring which causes what, must remain a matter for interpretation.

There seems to be no doubt, however, that older girls, whatever their intentions about fitting in to the school, want to adjust to the wider world outside school. In fact, if they are to be believed, they are doing this. Older girls tend to make more friends, and are less likely to make friends with girls only. They cannot be said to be 'boy mad'. Also, they are busier making friends from outside the boarding-school system. The figures are not given in this chapter, but day girls show exactly the same proportions of those who say they make many or few friends in the holidays, as boarders. To a small extent, more day girls say they have mostly girl-friends, than boarders. Boarders are perhaps sated with girl-friendships during the term, while day girls are not. But a sign of day girls' greater parochialism is the clear fact[24] that more of them say they make their holiday friends from the same or similar schools; while more boarders say they find holiday friends from non-boarding schools, from colleges, or anywhere.

If we accept that what these girls say is true, and not influenced to a great extent by what they would like to think is their pattern of holiday friendships, then it seems that boarding has certainly not impeded boarders' ability to mix in outside company during the holidays. In fact, boarding seems to have enhanced such sociability.

The total picture then is very complex, and we can hardly expect it to be otherwise. We must presume that what has been mentioned here is a considerable simplification, and possibly even (unwittingly) a distortion. The only proper way to approach the data is with caution; there is much then that deserves attention.

Notes

1. Chi Sq. $= 19 \cdot 39$; for $df = 4\,p < 0 \cdot 01$.
2. Chi Sq. $= 9 \cdot 89$; for $df = 4\,p < 0 \cdot 05$.
3. Chi Sq. $= 13 \cdot 11$; for $df = 4\,p < 0 \cdot 05$.
4. Chi Sq. $= 12 \cdot 46$; for $df = 4\,p < 0 \cdot 05$.
5. With Merton score, r for head's rating of social contribution $= 0 \cdot 24$; r for rating of academic advantage taken $= 0 \cdot 13$, in both cases $N = 495$.
6. With Merton score, r for aspiration to be prefect $= 0 \cdot 12$; for aspiration to excel at arts $= -0 \cdot 13$, in both cases $N = 694$.
7. For rank orders of Merton score and aspirations to be prefect, rho $= 0 \cdot 39$ $(N = 22)$.
8. For Merton score, r with relationship to mother $= 0 \cdot 22$ $(N = 645)$; r with relationship to father $= 0 \cdot 21$ $(N = 727)$.
9. For Merton score, r with relationship to brother $= 0 \cdot 08$ $(N = 513)$; r with relationship to sister $= 0 \cdot 07$ $(N = 437)$.
10. $r = 0 \cdot 28$ $(N = 761)$.
11. $r = -0 \cdot 12$ $(N = 761)$.
12. Student's $t = 0 \cdot 565$; for $df = 187$, not significant.
13. Student's $t = 2 \cdot 07$; for $df = 187$, $p < 0 \cdot 05$.
14. For Merton v convergence ranked scores, rho $= -0 \cdot 51$; v divergence, rho $= -0 \cdot 14$, in both cases $N = 20$.
15. rho for communication index v divergence $= 0 \cdot 43$ $(N = 16)$; for staff personal index rho $= 0 \cdot 09$ $(N = 16)$.
16. rho for convergence v NPF $= -0 \cdot 42$; v CI $= 0 \cdot 25$; v SPI $= -0 \cdot 75$; $(N = 16$ in all three).
17. rho for conformity (Merton) v NPF $= 0 \cdot 57$; v CI $= 0 \cdot 16$; v SPI $= 0 \cdot 47$ $(N = 18$ in all three).
18. rho for conformity v sixth-form prominence $= -0 \cdot 60$ $(N = 22)$.
19. rho for conformity v staff–seniors ratio $= 0 \cdot 52$ $(N = 20)$.
20. rho for conformity v institutional control $= 0 \cdot 05$ $(N = 22)$.
21. rho for parental boarding experience v independent prep school background $= 0 \cdot 80$ $(N = 22)$; v preparatory boarding experience $= 0 \cdot 36$ $(N = 22)$.
22. Chi Sq. $= 100 \cdot 7$, for $df = 18$, significant at $0 \cdot 01$ level; this table is condensed from a 7×4 contingency table.
23. Chi Sq. $= 43 \cdot 9$, for $df = 18$, significant at $0 \cdot 01$ level; this table is condensed from a 7×4 contingency table.
24. Sixty-two per cent of boarders make friends outside the system, fifty-two per cent of day girls. Chi Sq. $= 10 \cdot 07$, for $df = 1$ significant at the $0 \cdot 001$ level.

Nine: Effects of Boarding on Family Relationships

Many people have firm views on the question of boarding. Some consider it 'unnatural'; others see it as coming within the 'normal' order of things. Some consider that separation from parental homes causes harm; others see advantages in this step. How are we to introduce any useful comment into what can be an emotionally loaded controversy?

To ask staff in schools what they think boarding does is only partly useful. If they support the view that boarding is beneficial to family relationships, it could be answered that they have to take this position to support their jobs. Yet if they deny benefits in boarding there follows an implied question of how well-adjusted such staff are, and consequently how sound their judgement may be, seeing that they work in a system to which they ascribe a major defect. Some staff recognize this, and say that they provide a necessary service, for example, for orphans, girls whose parents travel abroad or who stay at home but have not enough time for their daughters. Sometimes staff deprecate boarding, do not want to serve the system which they see as helping to perpetuate the social and family divisions which they oppose, but continue in their work because they like the pupils personally and because the job is convenient. So it can be seen that a staff view, while likely in some cases to be caring and insightful, is also fraught with complications stemming from their own involvement in the system.

It remains to ask the obvious people their views – the girls. They, too, might have axes to grind; but in their case, if they do have a partisan view, then this is the stuff of the answer we are looking for. If a girl hates her school, she is most unlikely to say boarding improves her family relationships; if she says it worsens them, and if we believe that, we have both a cause and an effect of boarding as far as one person is concerned. If we do not believe her, then it follows that her family relationships are not being harmed, so the balance of error in interpreting the results may be that things are judged as worse than they in fact are. If a girl loves her school, she may say boarding improves the relations with her family – which statement we would have to accept; she may like school, but still feel that family relationships are harmed by separation, and this we would also have to accept. There seems little reason therefore to doubt the validity of what the girls say; they may lack insight into some of the causal factors of their feelings, but they are the ones who experience the emotions and situations we are asking about. It would have been much more useful if I could have put questions to parents also, to cross-check on girls' replies; also, one could study families which have one child in boarding, one at day school. However, this was a boarding schools' study, and so these other possibilities were out of the question.

The information in this chapter comes largely from three sources. One is from general written information that girls provided; the second source is a highly structured scale. In this, girls were asked to 'put a tick, one for each person at home, to show how you get on with that person . . .'. Ticks could be put in any one of six positions indicating a situation varying from 'we get on very well together' to 'we get on not so well at all'. Where there were several brothers or sisters, one tick was put for each. It was pointed out that, if one left out a tick, this would indicate that there was no person there now, no brother, or mother, or father, etc. For step-relatives, the tick was placed in brackets. This question dealt with potentially a very sensitive area. For many girls with happy homes, there would be no difficulty; but for those who had lost close family members, or for whom there was dissension, a response could be a painful and reluctant admission. I tried to give great consideration in the way this question was put. There were no complaints except at one school, where parents objected to such questions having been asked. Their daughters' responses showed that they were not within the lower half of the group of twenty schools (from which I calculated averages provided answers had been collected from at least twenty girls); the school which showed the greatest proportion of family relationships marked as difficult was one of the easiest to get on with. The girls there also showed the second highest group average score about the effect that boarding has on relationships. I will now explain how this last, third source of information here was organized.

After the rating scale just mentioned, girls were asked, 'Has being at boarding school affected your relationship with your family at all? Please answer fully.' No hints were given, but most girls wrote busily on this question. Usually only day girls complained that they had nothing to say. To mark the results of all this, everything written (by 1,393 boarders) was read; any girl who unequivocally mentioned a deterioration in perception or feelings towards family members, was marked 3. Examples of such views follow.

I've become detached from them, see through them as they are and couldn't care what they think of what I do.   (16)
. . . boarding . . . has affected my relationship with my family, as now I am totally indifferent to whether I am at home with my parents, or away from them. Also school has taught me independence and my parents resent this to a certain extent. I am now so used to [in term time] keeping my feelings and thoughts to myself that I find it hard to confide in my parents, and they find it hard to listen, so consequently I think there is no basic understanding between us.   (16)

All remarks which showed that the girl felt that boarding has produced some improvement in how she saw or felt about her family were marked 1. For example, one girl writes:

Being here has affected our relationship, we have grown much closer and now appreciate the luxuries of home life and the love and freedom our parents give us. They have made it clear that I am not here to be 'out of the way', but that they are doing what is best for me in their opinion.   (15)

Also:

. . . boarding has made me respect my parents more. I think it makes you understand their feelings. My Mother didn't have much choice about sending me here, and now I would never blame her for sending me here as I think it has done me good. I get on famously with all my family.   (16)

Here boarding is implied as not being happy. Nevertheless (and against the overall trends shown in the figures below) boarding can be seen as part of an improvement in family relationships.

Remarks which were mixed, equivocal or in any way not clearly committed positively or negatively were marked 2. For example:

... now I find I don't know my parents. When the holidays are on, mum and dad are usually tired from working about the house etc. and we're happy to be free, so everyone gets irritated.   (15)

It is not clear from this whether boarding has been detrimental to relationships. It could well have been that without it there would have been more friction. We are not in a position to decide unequivocally about this statement, so it is marked 2. The same applies to the next statement:

I feel that I have become farther away from them and they [my parents] are no longer my parents but people I know very well.   (14)

The writer may have intended to show that she feels an improvement has taken place; but she refers to feeling further away from her parents and it is not clear in what way one could infer that things were better or not. A third equivocal statement:

Parents should not come and see their children every week. Being at boarding has affected my relationship with my family I have grown up and I am not so 'rowdy'! but otherwise I feel more for them when I miss them which is not often!
On the whole I enjoy school very much. Yes.   (13)

It is customary in researches to have this kind of marking done by at least two judges, whose results are then tested to show they are mutually consistent before one proceeds further. However, in this case there were not enough resources to cover a methodological refinement in such a large study, so we must accept what we have.

For each school (or for each age, or for any other defined group) an average score could be found showing how it stood on the effect of boarding (as judged by the girls) on family relationships. The school with the best record scored 1·22 (the maximum is 1·00); the worst score was 2·00, which means that as many boarders consider that boarding is having a poor effect as think it is helping their relationships; it could also be that every single girl was non-committal, but we know that this is not so from a technical statistical detail.[1] A colloquial way of expressing this difference would be to say that at the first school opinion was 88·9 per cent leaning in favour of the view that boarding benefited family relationships, while at the other, opinions divided equally for and against. The average for 1,393 girls in twenty schools was 1·46, which can also be expressed as a 76·7 per cent inclination towards the view that boarding affects family relationships beneficially.

Before looking at further statistics on the alleged effects of boarding on relationships, let us examine more basic information about the condition of family relationships. In Chapter Four I showed that the day girls say that they are happier in school than the boarders say. Further tables (which I will not give here) show that the day girls were not drawn from significantly different age levels from the boarders; they were of similar levels of ability or reacted similarly on two verbal tests; boarders did, however, come in greater numbers from the milder schools (i.e. those which had lower institutional control scores). More of our day girl sample was drawn from schools with high institutional control; not all of these disciplinary or physical regulations would affect the day girls though. Nevertheless, the ethos of high institutional control may be felt also by day girls, and as we know (also from Chapter Four) that high control is associated with lower happiness or satisfaction, we might expect day girls to be less happy than boarders. But this was not so. So we can argue that day girls tended to include more happy ones because of their ages, their abilities or their type of schools. The reason for their greater happiness must remain unexplained – unless we put it down to their not being boarders, and being able to go home.

Since day girls are happier in school, and go home daily, what might we find them saying about their family relationships? Let us see.

Table 9·1. Family relationships of day girls and of boarders

| girls | relationship with | number | percentage giving relationships thus: | | |
			get on very well	get on fairly well	less well to not so well
boarders	mother[2]	1,304	65	21	14
day	mother[2]	408	61	24	15
boarders	father[3]	1,272	69	19	13
day	father[3]	389	60	24	16
boarders	brother[4]	902	59	28	13
day	brother[4]	258	51	34	15
boarders	sister[5]	779	61	26	12
day	sister[5]	222	45	40	15

In all cases it is the boarders, rather than day girls, who are more inclined to say they get on very well with the people at home. These differences are statistically significant, except in the case of relationships with brothers. So what have we to explain? Boarders are less likely to say they are happy in school, but they are more likely than day girls to say they get on well with the family at home.

This makes it unlikely that the population of boarders should be seen as loaded with 'emotional need cases' any more than the day girls. It could be said by advocates of boarding that it helps in regulating, explaining and raising the value of family relationships; this would be one possibility, though it is by no means proven. Opponents of boarding might interpret this finding by saying that boarders are driven to making a pleasant fantasy of their home relationships, which unreality is not shared by day girls. Such a view is also by no means proven, nor is it clear what the meaning and implications might be of making a fantasy about relationships, if that fantasy is benign. At any rate, it cannot be said that boarders overall acknowledge worse relationships than day girls, because the reverse is the case, quite significantly so. Furthermore, they do so even though they (the boarders) say they are less happy than day girls, and we know that happiness is related to the condition of family relationships.

The quality of family relationships appears to vary with age. The connection is a curvilinear one, starting with best relationships reported among the youngest girls, dropping to a minimum at age 16 and then improving somewhat. The general pattern is parallel to what happens with satisfaction, though in this case the low point comes a year later. These facts pertain to feelings regarding parents. In the case of relationships with brothers and sisters, the minimum point comes at age 14.[6] It is possible that a general malaise over relationships at home and adjustment at schools arrives at about 15; however, feelings about brothers and sisters pertain to 'the younger generation' and may pick up sooner than feelings about adults. The details are on the following page.

The ages at which good relationships are at a minimum are underlined. One might note that the disposition towards fathers fares slightly better than that towards mothers; the statistical significance of this difference has not been tested. The main point

H

is that there is a substantial drop in good relationships rated. It might be thought that what we have here is not a real index of the condition of family relationships, but merely a reflection of happiness in school. This may be partly true, but this does not explain why feelings towards parents change at different ages from feelings towards brothers and sisters. It seems highly likely that there is something valid in these ratings, truly reflecting feelings in the family.

Table 9·2. Age and quality of family relationships among boarders

	age: 12	13	14	15	16	17	18
relationship with *mother*, number of girls	45	184	299	281	268	182	37
percentage answering: 'get on very well'	82	79	68	59	58	61	65
relationship with *father*, number of girls	44	178	291	277	261	174	38
percentage answering: 'get on very well'	82	82	69	65	62	68	71
relationship with *brother*, number of girls	32	123	210	195	181	126	28
percentage answering: 'get on very well'	59	64	54	56	63	57	61
relationship with *sister*, number of girls	29	112	162	178	173	90	27
percentage answering: 'get on very well'	72	65	57	61	62	59	52

Some correlations have been worked out relating aspects of the experience of individual girls. The chief of these[7] shows that there is a connection between the quality of family relationships and the effect the girl thinks that boarding is having. The fact that this is a tautology, or vicious circle, does not prevent it from being understandable. Girls who feel happy with their families say that boarding is having a good effect. There is probably a good reason for this; happy families will know what boarding entails, will prepare their daughters for what to expect, and will take an interest in the girl's new boarding experiences which she relates during the holidays.

Girls have written about all of these things, as we have seen and shall see again presently. If a family is using boarding unwillingly, or as an aspect of rejection or insufficient effort, time or ability to care for their daughter, she will feel this and record that boarding is part of an unwelcome set of family relationships and behaviour. Both the quality of existing family relationships,[8] and the alleged effects of boarding on relationships,[9] are related to satisfaction in school. The correlations are small, but highly significant.

These three statistics form an interlocking triad which suggest that there is likely to be an overall condition of well-being, or its opposite. This shows the possible dangers of any plan to place girls from unhappy families ('need cases') in boarding schools. Unless the school is exceptionally understanding, the girl is likely to be unhappy – partly due to her difficulties at home – and this unhappiness may in turn alienate her further from gaining a happy place back at home. Too definite an interpretation should not be placed on these statistics, though their burden should certainly not be ignored.

I have dealt so far with what can be said about girls as individuals. Now I shall deal with schools as units. By making average scores for each school, we can list which are the happier and less happy schools (bearing in mind the problem of sampling which has been mentioned in other chapters), which schools produce the conclusion that boarding has a good effect and which show that it has a mixed effect, and so on. Some of the correlations bring together factors which may help us to understand (if not incontrovertibly to explain) the effects of boarding on family relationships, and vice-versa.

Parents' own education in boarding school has been treated in a previous chapter as an index of family integration with the boarding system. Now I shall examine this as possibly having something to do with a healthy state of family relationships during boarding. Statistics show that schools for which more parents had been boarders are also the happier schools.[10] They are also the schools in which girls are more likely to say that boarding has a good effect on relationships.[11] It is important to note that these schools where parents had more boarding experience were not any more or less likely to show a good level of family relationships.[12] This enables us to isolate the two factors which have so far gone hand-in-hand –

quality of relationships and the rated effect of boarding on relationships. What we have now is that parental experience of boarding is connected not with quality but with effects of boarding on relationships,

Some quotations may clarify these issues. We start with the way parents prepare their daughters for the separation:

My mother was here and told me all I had to know. (11)

Another girl says:

... the housemistress took my parents and I up to my dormitory and we talked awhile. Then my parents went home, I was not homesick then. (11)

So parents link up with the school. Homesickness is not necessarily staved off, and is often described as sudden and caught unawares. Often as well, it passes. This comes from a different school:

... our dormy head was in there ... all chatting away merrily. All of a sudden they left the room, and for the first time ever in my whole life I felt homesick. I wrote a desperate letter card home, telling my parents how desperately unhappy I was. Unfortunately I forgot to post it! (Thank goodness!) (11)

This note of concern for the parents, and an implied acceptance and sharing of their goals in choosing boarding is shown by another girl:

... the first few days draged away so slowly and unhappily. I felt dreadfully homesick and wrote to my parents telling them of my miserable feelings. The second week past quicker than the first and I felt I was settling in more. Now the third and fourth week the days flew by. . . . I from then on wrote cheerful and amusing letters to my parents which I feel made them happy at the thought of me settling in. (12)

So far there is nothing to show directly that parental experience of boarding is connected with their daughter finding it a fruitful experience; we have seen evidence of a crisis and one around which it is possible both for parents and daughter to show consideration for each other. Other girls make the connections more explicit.

I am much closer to my parents as they have had the same kind of education and understand the problems it presents. I regard them, mother especially, as friends on whom I can rely. (14)

When we are interpreting statistical correlations there is also a negative side of things to look for. Not only are good conditions found together but unfavourable circumstances also are linked. Here is something from a girl who evidently feels jaundiced both about home and school:

I feel my mother is rather jealous of my youth and sometimes makes me feel awful, in public . . . I get terribly irritated and if we are to get on at home I think my whole outlook here should be altered.   (14)

Another girl is also troubled by a malaise linking circumstances at home and at school:

My mother's ideas on boarding-school life, as she has never been to school [sic], are completely based on things she reads in books. She tries to force these ideas on me and make me behave according to these ideas. . . . Boarding school life has also, I think, affected me as a person, making me less polite, less inclined to accept authority and I find this affects my relationship with my family.   (16)

Although it is rare, it can also be heard that some malaise might have occurred if the girl had not been to boarding school.

. . . my aunts and uncles would have been rather shocked if I hadn't been to boarding school. If anything I get on better with them now I see them less frequently.   (14)

This illustrates the problem of what one is to understand as being good relationships. It can certainly be supported that 'absence makes the heart grow fonder'. There are at least two aspects to this matter. One concerns perceptions, how girls think about their family, though the distinction between thoughts and feelings may be less clear than the overlap between them. Several different girls will be quoted.

Not until I first went away to boarding did I realise how attached I was to my family.   (13)

Not only the parents but the whole *ménage* may be included in the glow of a distant view.

My parents now mean much more to me, and so do my horses and other pets.   (13)

We can see how contemplation of one's family in a better light

is supplemented for some by what they claim are improved relationships.

> ... it has affected me, it has made me realise what my parents are, and
> who they are, and made me more effeconate to them and them to me. (14)
> Being at a boarding school has made me realise the love of my family.
> I respect and love them more. Before I came here I took advantage of
> my mother e.g. asking her for money etc. now I wouldn't dream of
> it.   (14)

Some improvements, like the one above, may be said to be due
to the added insight which comes with growing older rather than
being at school. However, where improvement is ascribed to the
parents who are presumably mature, this may well stem from the
boarding situation.

> Being at boarding school has made me appreciate home more. It has
> also made my parents realise how much they have missed my brother
> and I.   (15)

Sometimes a girl's remarks about family relationships are embedded in what might seem to an outsider to be trivia, but might
well be considered as of great importance to the writer, who sees
her family relationships and boarding education as closely interconnected.

> I got sent here to keep me away from the friend I used to go with (I
> don't go with her any more). She was a bit common I suppose, I see
> it now. Very scruffy. Glad Dad had the decency to send me here. My
> parents are great. I mean it! Mum's a bit soft with us but she's marvel-
> lous. I don't know where I'd be without her. She gives me advice, helps
> me to choose clothes etc. Dad's more strict. He's great though, wouldn't
> change him for anything. He's witty too. ... Dad won't let me wear
> *too* mini skirts, but he'll let about 3½–4″ above the knee.   (15)

Very often it is considered that boarding involves a psychological
as well as a physical separation of the daughter from her parents.
This girl implies that this is not necessarily true. She writes as
though she is still linked in a real way to her parents. In fact in
the boarding school year about thirty per cent of the time is
spent at home, in spaced intervals, so when it is psychologically
dealt with in a certain way by the parents a feeling of continuity and
involvement with the family can remain with the boarder. A

sophisticated view of an advantage in boarding is shown by an older girl, who shows that relationships are not carried on purely via face-to-face contact. She has realized that privacy and intimacy can be imparted to impersonal paper via the written word. This can mediate a relationship where sometimes the routines of life nominally 'together' may be obscuring communication.

If anything we have a better relationship. . . . I find by writing letters to my parents I establish more contact with them than when I am actually there – mostly because I go out a great deal and do not see a lot of them. (17)

Now while the statistics show that most boarders feel they can get on well with their families as well as being boarders, and illustrations have confirmed this, it is not the whole story. The negative side exists and must be shown.

I think parents are a drag. They always agree with pointless school rules and agree with the headmistress. (14)

Such expressions may occur when people are going through 'stages' out of which both school and parents hope and expect they will emerge. Mid-adolescence is one such stage, where difficulties of communication can arise. One daughter may need to discuss her current problems (while other girls might accept a convention of conversational continence with a wider range of topics considered 'delicate' or taboo), and a strangeness can be brought about by discontinuities in family life. When the reunions happen at the end of term the girl may be a slightly changed person, who may need to get to know her mother again. Some parents may look forward to exploring the changes, and helping to mould them; yet other parents want to find again their daughter as she was before. Several girls complain that their mothers do not expect them to change during the term.

I sometimes, when I first get home find that things are slightly strained. My brother . . . goes to a boarding school and things are often difficult between us. Also, I find myself getting terribly embarassed about talking to my mother about personal things. (15)

The whole field of inter-sex relations offers several stumbling blocks to understanding between parents and daughters.

I wish my parents were dead they drive me sick they think we are still in their stay and age they think that girls of 14 should not go out with Boys of about 20–25 just go out with Boys of about 15 or 16 they are hopeless.   (14)

Though this girl claims a right and a need to go out with 'mature men' she does not write about her mature (?) parents in an adult way. There seems to be a mis-match between galloping needs (whipped on by efficient modern methods of communication) and dawdling capabilities which struggle to accommodate them within life's major circumstances.

My parents do not like me to mix with the local boys but they do not stop me. I feel they are trying to make me a snob, but I try to mix with them otherwise I will lose many of my friends.   (15)

The social class-consciousness reflected in the phrase 'I try to mix with them' already builds up the social distance that the girl feels that her parents want to create between her and her friends. From another school one writes:

I think there are still parents who would consider it an insult for their children to go to the same school at the butcher's children.   (15)

Similarly:

Daughters are mostly sent away to Boarding schools because they think their daughter will be taught to be a young lady. Also to keep them out of getting too friendly with the male sex.   (14)

These thoughts are clearly expressed by other girls:

Most parents send their daughters to boarding school I suppose to escape the evils of life. . . . Parents are a bit off – they don't want their daughters to grow up.   (14)
Parents these days don't realise that their daughters are growing up quicker.   (14)

The finding we are still discussing is that there may be either a generalized good feeling which informs both life at school and at home, or its opposite, a malaise which is sometimes expressed more pungently than the rather more vaguely described states of happiness.

I find my parents immature, suburban, narrow-minded, 'safe', too concerned about me, restricting me, self-contained, self-absorbed, pathetically anxious to please (they rarely succeed). Holidays are a strain – the only outlet is sex and poetry (reading and writing). Life is unbearable at times. I adore my cat. I now can see my family objectively. (15)

From this wealth of material to interpret just one point can be selected; it seems that the practice of poetry is often a sure sign of the individual in stress with the community. It should be clear by now that parents' attitudes, at least in so far as they are interpreted by their daughters, have an effect on whether boarding is going to enhance or impede family relationships. Wisdom can be heard from the young, about whether entry to boarding is the start of a vicious or benign circle of events.

I wish parents would think more carefully about our lives. (14)

The findings to which I want to relate some of this are (see notes 10 and 11) that happiness at school and the chance that boarding will be seen as beneficial to relationships are linked to parents' own experience as boarders. It seems possible that they will have an understanding of the system, as well as there being an expectancy of boarding education in the family, that will help a girl to accept this type of school and make the best of it.

I have been dealing with statistics that pertain to schools as units. Previously I dealt with figures about girls as individuals. There we saw that, overall, if a girl said she had a happy family she would be likely to be happy in school and also say that boarding had a good effect on relationships. Now if we look at the figures about schools do we see, as one might expect, that schools which had happier families tended to have more satisfied girls?[13] Did schools with happier families tend to get good marks on the score that boarding helped family relationships (and vice-versa)?[14] The answer to both these questions is No. Take schools with girls from happier families and compare them with schools with girls from less happy families first. The former do not necessarily contain the happier girls – because it is not only the family, but also the school which determines happiness. Sufficient special circumstances pertaining to individual schools blot out a statistical correlation we might otherwise have expected. For example, one school had girls from unhappy families to a greater extent than all the other schools I visited. One might have expected the girls to be equally unhappy, and the school to score last on that list. But this school paid special attention to girls in trouble. The result is that it ranked halfway on the list of average satisfaction, and second to top on the point that boarding has a good effect on family relationships.

This statistical distinction about results concerning individuals being different from the results concerning schools may seem complex, but it is important. For it shows in what respects differences between schools can obscure generalizations we may expect to find true about individual behaviour and feelings. We see that if a girl comes to boarding from an unhappy family situation, and one where there is little previous experience of the boarding system, we must be concerned about her chances of happiness at school; she is likely to be unhappy, and this may well rebound unfavourably on an already difficult home situation. However, the case of the school cited above shows that unhappiness does not necessarily follow. This school had a head with unusually close knowledge of most people in it (it was just not too big to make this too difficult); its pastoral care (judged by scores on the three indices measured in Chapter Seven) put it among the top two schools regarding this item. Senior girls acknowledged and understood their pastoral care roles, and institutional control was relatively low. It is true that the research visit was made during the summer, which is known to show schools somewhat to an advantage on those measures, but I do not think that this can account for all of the good atmosphere at the school.

Are there any other generalizations one can draw about the social constitution of schools and their position as regards family relationships? There are some positive findings, and also instances where the statistics show that we are not entitled to make a generalization we might have expected from studying one or a few cases.

For example, the level of institutional control in schools has no significant correlation, either with the quality of family relationships[15] or with the rated effects of boarding on relationships.[16] Perhaps one might have expected 'traditional boarding' families to send daughters to 'traditional schools' which maintain more rigorous regimes. In fact there is no reason to support such a supposition. Also, though good pastoral care was mentioned above as associated with a good effect of boarding on relationships, this was not a sufficiently conspicuous factor to produce a significant correlation. Probably we should regard pastoral care as an effect, like girls' feelings about the role of boarding in their family life, of personality and organizational factors which underlie both.

Some schools are academically more high-powered than others. We can make a distinction here. Two verbal tests were given to girls, but there is no evidence that schools with more able pupils have better or worse effects on family relationships.[17] However, an index of the relative size of sixth forms compared with the size of the whole school shows that schools with bigger sixth forms have worse rated effects of boarding on relationships.[18] Fitting in with this is the fact that, where girls have a higher aspiration to excel at work, there will be a poorer effect judged by them on family relationships.[19] We should remember that these aspiration scores are not only collected from sixth forms, but through several ages at each school. So we see that, if there is an organization geared to greater academic performance, and if this is mirrored by girls' own desires to excel in this area, there is likely to be a less beneficial evaluation of the school's part in promoting family relationships. The converse follows also; in schools with smaller sixth forms, or where girls aspire to excel at other things than work, there will be better feelings about the part school plays in family relationships. This does not mean that schools with duller girls are better for the family; we have seen that abilities (as measured) are independent of these organizational and aspirational factors.

Schools with which girls are willing to be more compliant (that is judged by their scores on the Merton test explained in Chapter Eight) are also those where they will judge a good effect is being had on their home relationships.[20]

So let me summarize some of the properties of schools that tend to occur together. Schools which girls feel are acting well on their family relationships tend to show happier, more satisfied girls who are more willing to comply with the regime (there is nothing, incidentally, to indicate that these regimes tend to be more, or less, strict); such schools will tend to be those without particularly large sixth forms, and where there is not a strong desire among girls to excel at exams and work. Schools in which girls say they come from happy families are not necessarily those which record any particular good or adverse effect of boarding on these relationships.

Where parents have themselves had boarding experience to a greater extent, daughters are more likely to feel happy together in school and to say that their schools have good effects on family relationships.

For individual girls (unlike for schools as social units) happy family backgrounds are very significantly related to a feeling that boarding is helping the relationship. This finding, somewhat difficult to grasp in the context of all the others, illustrates two distinctions. One is between generalizations that can be made about people and those which can be made about schools; the other is between the quality or level of family relationships and the effect which boarding is felt to be having on these relationships.

It remains to state two types of caution about coming to conclusions about the material in this chapter. The first is one that has been pointed out by many experienced staff; this is that girls who grumble deeply about their school predicament and who see their relationships and everything pertaining to them in the gloomy light of their attitudes towards school, may when they leave develop different evaluations; they may look back with nostalgia, revisit their old school, renew pleasant memories they hadn't realized were being established. Against this it must be remembered that several girls leave school feeling badly about it, and continue to do so. Others may move in circles which deprecate boarding and, though they once liked it, come to see it in a poor light. Overall, then, this point must be observed, about when is it best to ask a girl to evaluate her boarding experience – during, or after it? However, on balance, a strong case can be made for examining present feelings for what they are worth, and leaving later developments to some other study or inquiry.

The second caution is that effects attributed to boarding might also have occurred if a girl had been to day school; more, they might have occurred even without any school – like growing taller; perhaps a cycle of attitudes towards parents would be experienced in a similar way whether a girl went to one or another kind of school, or to none at all. About this it must be said that the chapter does not set out to distinguish boarding from day education; it primarily describes what happens in boarding. No matter what happens in day school, what is recorded here as being true for boarding must be judged on those terms. Further, it is not as though statistics only have been shown. Many quotations explaining and suggesting reasons for the findings have also been given. From these (and from some limited data from day girls), it should be possible to see to what extent conclusions drawn here stem from the special conditions of boarding, or to what extent (by comparison with other books or studies) the situations may be duplicated in day schools. It seems probable that many similar effects take place in boarding as in day schooling, but that separation can act in some ways like the lens of an eye: for some, it puts things in greater focus; for some it magnifies and for others it diminishes perceived relations; finally, for others it is like a lens with cataract which dims communication. For understanding when and how these circumstances apply, we can study what girls have written, above. And for deciding about which effects preponderate we must look at the statistics which have been given.

Notes

1. This mean of 2·00 has a standard deviation of 0·84, indicating that the responses were not uniform.
2. Chi Sq. $= 13·89$, for $df = 5$ (table condensed) $p = 0·02$.
3. Chi Sq. $= 19·89$, for $df = 5$ (table condensed) $p = 0·01$.
4. Chi Sq. $= 6·4$, for $df = 5$ (table condensed) NS.
5. Chi Sq. $= 24·18$, for $df = 5$ (table condensed) $p = 0·001$.
6. Discounting the category of 18-year-olds, which is too small to generalize from.
7. $r = 0·29$, which for $N = 1,391$ is significant at 0·001 level.
8. $r = 0·13$, which for $N = 1,391$ is significant at 0·01 level.
9. $r = 0·17$, which for $N = 1,391$ is significant at 0·01 level.
10. rho $= 0·63$, which for $N = 20$ is significant at 0·01 level.
11. rho $= 0·40$, which for $N = 20$ is significant at 0·05 level.
12. rho $= 0·07$, which for $N = 20$ is not significant. In this, relationships towards mothers and fathers have been combined, as there is a substantial correlation ($r = 0·37$ with $N = 1,247$) between the two.
13. rho $= 0·16$, which for $N = 20$ is not significant.
14. rho $= 0·16$, which for $N = 20$ is not significant.
15. rho $= 0·34$, which for $N = 20$ is not significant.
16. rho $= 0·06$, which for $N = 20$ is not significant.
17. rho $= -0·29$ and $-0·11$, which for $N = 19$ are not significant.
18. rho $= -0·40$, which for $N = 20$ is significant at 0·05 level.
19. rho $= -0·51$, which for $N = 20$ is significant at 0·05 level.
20. rho $= -0·40$, which for $N = 20$ is significant at 0·05 level.

Ten: Religion in the School Community

This chapter will provide information and set it against a background of some points culled from Chapter Two, on goals. In some schools, religion may not loom large as an aspect of communal life, but in others it does. Dr Kathleen Ollerenshaw in her book on girls' schools (of all types) has this to say about religion in boarding schools:

Time spent on religious worship varies greatly; those schools which have a charter or other instrument of foundation which prescribes a particular denomination tend to spend most time. Some give a bare ten minutes each weekday to a usually undenominational religious assembly service with an hour spent in religious observance on Sundays; others of specific denominations spend up to twenty one hours a week in religious observance with two Church services on Sundays. Special arrangements are made for girls whose faith is different from that of the school.

Though this is the sum of the attention she devotes to this topic, it suggests that in many cases religious forms and ideas are central to a boarding school's life. Although there is not universal agreement about what is meant by the term 'religion', and a short chapter will not settle this point nor adequately expound the place of religion in the lives of boarders, we clearly need to venture a little into this area. I will make a starting assumption that 'religion' refers to Christian worship and guiding principles for life, and later examine a few extensions of the idea, seeing how it may relate to aspects of personality development, aesthetic sensibility and group behaviour. In this, I shall depart somewhat from the style of the rest of the book; there will have to be less reliance on intricate figures and consequently what I say will be more open to challenge and to a different interpretation and analysis. There are some statistics, however, from which one cannot escape.

Chapter Two has shown that a few schools make an overt point of saying that they intend to instil Christian principles in their pupils' minds and lives. A quarter are demonstrably Christian in this way; but over a half make a point of describing the kinds of ordered behaviour and social morality which they intend to instil, and clearly Christian precepts and tradition are both a means and an end by which schools hope to promote such a morality and which they would like to continue into the future.

Prospectuses usually mention the religious denomination of the school, though some do not. One of the latter sort says: 'girls should be educated as individuals . . . their potential spiritual . . . qualities may be awakened . . .'. No further religious avowal is made in this prospectus, which makes it clear (by implication) to non-Christian parents that the institutions of the school will allow some flexibility in religious education. Another way in which a school may consciously or unwittingly show that its institutions can accommodate a varied population, is by having among the governors one at least who is conspicuously known as a non-Christian. A third school among those visited says that its aims 'depend on a general acceptance of Christian values and principles which affect the whole of education. This gives a fundamental unity to the school although it is undenominational. . . .' There were some girls at this school whose comments implicitly questioned this notion of fundamental unity. This suggests that the word 'un-denominational' may have been used by the school to refer to the various denominations of Christianity; yet when it is read, some girls will expect it to refer to all religions.

It's supposed to be undenominational – but we're always read in prayers about Christ or how good the people are who are Christians. (15)

This girl's name suggests that she came from a nominally (at least) Christian family; yet the school contained more pupils of other faiths than several other schools visited. It even experimented with inter-faith services, and undoubtedly made an impression of religious understanding and tolerance. However, it becomes apparent that the question of being denominational or not depends on institutions rather than on the make-up of the population; even inter-faith services may be seen as a concession or an experiment by one dominant denomination. Probably there is no question of a school being able to 'achieve' non-denominationality so long as there are even a minority of people present who avow some religion; for secularity then itself may assume the characteristics of a denomination.

Some schools can be just as tolerant, though they define their own religious position quite clearly. They intend to run a community life based on a Christian consciousness, and say so.

[this school] . . . aims at providing a thorough modern education combined with definite Church teaching. [prospectus]

Another school says:

. . . a religious attitude is the starting point of a real and deep understanding of life and even of all knowledge . . . with [religion] . . . a girl is better equipped to face conflicts and to give love and service in her own time and generation.

Though we realise that what a school can do is no substitute for early home training, we believe in the Christian ideas as our inspiration and goal.

The last sentence reminds one that it would make for greater harmony between home and school if parents back the school's religious stance. They presumably read the prospectus and where considerable fees are involved are not likely to send their daughters to schools which are substantially at odds with the religious orientation of the home. This is an important selection mechanism which influences the homogeneity of school populations with regard to religion.

Some schools belong to or are associated with the Woodard corporation, which is a body which makes a point of the centrality of Christian life in education. Others need not belong to such an organization to have very similar ideals:

[X] . . . is a Church of England School and much thought is given to religious training and instruction.   [prospectus]

Another school intends to:

. . . develop character, to cultivate responsibility and the right sense of values founded on the Christian interpretation of life.   [prospectus]

Nowhere is it suggested that the right sense of values, or the ensuing social system that is designed to inculcate these values must necessarily be Christian; in fact, the implication of the less denominational schools is that similar values and methods can arise otherwise. However, no a-religious school was visited, and all had a framework of religious observance and instruction.

The institutions (i.e. the social framework) in schools, which had to do with religion were these: chapels or assembly halls (the physical apparatus); religious classes, confirmation, worship (human activities); chaplain (or special staff); and the times when religion becomes the focus of attention; these all served as a structure intended to bring attention back from any distance or distraction to which it might wander.

The physical apparatus varied considerably from one school to another. The convent schools had chapels or the use of adjacent convent chapels; other schools had chapels also. One was the domestic chapel of the landed family who had owned the estate; others were built for the schools on Victorian or Edwardian lines. Consciousness of these chapels was not neglected; at one school new girls were taken to be shown the buildings, to be immersed in their history and atmosphere (there was no ritual aspect of introduction that was heard of). At another school church vestments and accessories were explained so that the girls would know of their functions and meaning. The orientations of girls to such introduction appear to range as follows: they could accept the spirit and methods of the religion being shown them; they could show various degrees of lack of interest or disenchantment (which would seem unlikely when a school has advertised its style of life and chosen its new girls by exam and interview); or they could disagree with spirit and methods. This last would be more likely with members of other denominations. As sometimes the school in the person of the chaplain then makes clear to newcomers that religion in a certain form is central to the school's idea of life, this would formally be placing out-denominational girls as outsiders to the society. This may be another reason why, at least nominally, homogeneous religious populations are found in most schools.

Several schools, including the most overtly Christian ones, made a point of illustrating their universality by saying that they had foreign girls; these included Thais (one Thai, non-Christian girl suggested that there were over 500 Thai pupils in British boarding schools), and Muslims of African or Asian origin. These are likely to feel, for reasons suggested, a keen sense of difference from others, a difference to which religion is probably more central than colour. To the Muslim girl who said '. . . *per Jesum Christum Dominum vestrum*' at grace after meals, this small alteration, noticeable to nobody else but herself, was a daily symbol of individual independence. This kind of independence, which links the individual with a substantial reference group elsewhere, is open to the non-Christian, whereas lapsed Christians tend not to search for these devices nor to have them to hand, as the community of lapsed Christians as an external reference group is rather less distinct than, for example, Islam.

The majority of the schools, therefore, try to function as Christian communities, and the formal outsiders are few. The Christian life is sometimes led by an internal chaplain, but this was uncommon, and only something the larger schools could (or wished to ?) afford. In one case, the chaplain carried a substantial teaching load, and also lived in a boarding house of which his wife was housemistress; this arrangement meant that he was available for a good deal of pastoral care activity and, compared with elsewhere, was highly integrated into school life. In another case, the chaplain had fallen foul of the kitchen department (a powerful faction) over the matter of chapel times; the ensuing developments had reduced his freedom of action in pastoral care, though he maintained good relations with senior girls. In this case the practice of girls meeting the chaplain socially over dinner in a homely setting, however infrequently, could mean that they had personal access to the Christian leader, which would presumably affect their experience of services when they would be able to see and feel the person behind the ritual role adopted by him, and thus in a sense be joined to the proceedings.

More often, schools relied on local vicars. They would treat the school as peripatetic parishioners; they took scripture classes, usually sharing these with full-time women staff. The girls would go out of grounds to the church on Sundays, and for many younger ones this was the only trip out of the school precincts in many weeks. The excursion would be made formally, with uniforms, hats, often gloves, and could hardly be experienced as a stepping out of the body of the school. Schoolgirls reported different reactions from local parishioners; there were those who were glad of the extra congregation to fill the church and sing; others were felt to be disturbed by the take-over of the church which swamped the local worshippers with a group which were in no sense true members of the local society. Some schools in fact arranged to have their services at the local church, but as a school service apart from other service times.

In many of the schools working with local clergy, arrangements were made for girls of other Christian denominations to go with relevant staff to their own church services. Women staff took a number of internal services, particularly morning assemblies, which rarely had the single religious function, but were also used for communal administration, reading notices or making announcements. These lay officiants sometimes showed more faith than the clergy. In one instance, a girl had seen what she described as a vision of the Virgin Mary. She was placed in the sick room, and the vicar went to see her. After the interview, he was describing how he had exhausted all possibilities of secular explanation including lighting effects through glass doors, digestive disorders and worries about home, and it was left to the lay person to suggest that the vision *was* perhaps the Virgin, a prospect which suddenly enlivened the vicar. He was presumably faced with the modern problem of the credibility gap, which would most likely have been invoked in his disfavour if he had been the first to consider the vision valid.

At this stage it may be opportune to return to statistics, to stabilize the direction of interpretation and analysis. In Chapter Two, I explained how girls indicated what they thought schools *should* be doing (out of fourteen different goals set down in a questionnaire); they also indicated what they thought schools *actually were trying* to do, and yet again what they thought schools *succeeded* in attaining. I have chosen to examine the results on four particular goals here; three are directly or otherwise connected to the topic of religion; the fourth is put in for sake of comparison. I have devised a scoring scheme[1] which gives figures as percentages; these percentages combine two measures; they refer to the force with which a viewpoint is held collectively.

It is important first of all to see to what extent girls (and some staff) supported religious goals. It will be remembered that the sample of staff includes not only teachers but boarding staff and matrons; response was very uneven from staff in different schools and in general represents a minority sample. This does not mean necessarily that the results will be different from what would have accrued from a good sample, merely that one must be cautious in interpretation.

Table 10·1. Strength of opinions as to what goals *should* be pursued

goal	strength of opinions expressed by: girls in twenty-two schools (per cent)	186 staff (per cent)
enable girls to decide for themselves what is right and wrong ('moral sense')	85·1	83·0
put into practice Christian principles	49·5	77·5
teach people to live happily together	80·2	84·0
get good exam results	80·5	68·2

In some respects staff views and girls' views agree. They agree on giving high importance to inculcating what I shall refer to as 'moral sense', and on the high importance of learning to live together, which implies either loving one's neighbour or at least tolerating or not provoking her. Girls appear keener about exams, which may reflect their evaluation of what they can see most clearly as being a possible 'payoff' of their schooling, whereas staff included many non-academic matrons and house staff – who nevertheless also support the idea quite strongly. Clearly, however, girls do not react enthusiastically to the item on Christian principles. The fact that they favour the 'moral' item which leaves out mention of religion, together with impressionistic evidence from writings collected and from discussions, suggests to me strongly that the word 'Christian' evoked to many the institutional apparatus of services, divinity lessons and prayers; it was these phenomena, which presumably are intended as the means of propagating religious principles, to which there is some negative reaction.

At some schools, a distinction is clearly made between the function of church attendance and worship as a means to attaining moral goals, and of these as an end in themselves. Some schools appear neither to realize, nor make the distinction, but questionnaire results show that there are large differences between schools on the item referring to Christian principles. At one school, a convent, the strength of support was seventy-five per cent for this item, while at the other extreme the support was twenty-five per cent. There is some reason to think that at the convent where the nuns got across the idea that worship was of value in itself, partly because it directed human attention in awe at a mystery, this played a part in the girls quite strongly approving the item on Christian principles. Elsewhere:

Chapel is a bluddy waist of time and a bore and should be given up. (12)

It might be thought that this is an immature view, not to be relied upon from so young a girl. But an older one, at another school, says:

This school puts a lot on religion, its all right in small parts but being forced to go to Chapel twice every Sunday is a bit too much, the service becomes automatic and nobody really thinks about what they are doing. (16)

We do face the need to explain the finding of the relatively low level of enthusiasm about overtly stated Christian principles. Now if girls do not feel strongly that a goal should be pursued, and if they see that the schools' efforts in that direction are of a suitably limited degree, then one might consider that the girls should be well adjusted to what is going on. What in fact are the results?

Table 10·2. Differences in strength of opinion about what *should* happen and what schools actually *try to do*

| goal | differences of opinion expressed by: | |
	girls in twenty-two schools (per cent)	186 staff (per cent)
moral sense	—28·2	—4·6
Christian principles	+18·3	+5·2
living together	—17·1	—1·2
exam success	— 2·5	+9·9

Here there are wide differences of opinion between girls and staff. Staff consider that there is little gap between what schools should do and what they actually try to do. Staff think a small excess of effort is spent on exams, and even on inculcating Christian principles. Staff also admit a slight leeway on efforts towards promoting moral sense. Girls think that a wide gap exists between what should be done and what they consider schools are trying to do as regards promoting moral sense and the ability to live together happily. However, they think considerably more effort is being spent on 'Christian principles' than ought to be. If they had been asked to identify what they understood by Christian principles, they might well have included these 'moral' goals. Clearly, they cannot be approving one moment what they disapprove the next; we must infer that girls reacted in the 'Christian principles' item to the routines of worship and of religious instruction with which so many of them feel at odds.

So much for what they think schools are actually striving to do. What do people think is being achieved, compared with what they think ought to be achieved?

Table 10·3. Differences in strength of opinion about what *should* happen, and what schools *actually succeed* in bringing about

	differences of opinion expressed by:	
goal	*girls in twenty-two schools* (*per cent*)	*186 staff* (*per cent*)
moral sense	− 37·7	− 21·3
Christian principles	− 14·3	− 16·4
living together	− 28·8	− 10·4
exam success	− 24·4	− 4·5

Apparently everybody is agreed that they do not believe that goals are being attained as much as they think they should be. Girls are particularly severe (or disappointed) in their view that moral sense and the arts of living together are not successfully inculcated as much as they should be. Girls even think that Christian principles should be inculcated more than actually happens. Staff follow a broadly similar view, except that they think exam success is not far from the ideal and the learning of how to live together not far behind. On this question one is unsure how to interpret the result from girls about Christian principles. If we follow the previous interpretation, it might seem that girls feel that not enough worship and religious instruction takes place. I am inclined not to advocate this interpretation in this case. I think the negative result comes from these reasons: a general parsimony about saying that schools succeed to a high degree on any goals; and some feeling that moral values are implied in the Christian principles (as well as the routines).

There is probably an element of feeling that too much worship occurs overall, and this serves to make the score on this item (minus fourteen per cent) nearer to the positive levels of success[2] than is seen for the item on moral sense (minus thirty-eight per cent). For this item, there may be an overall parsimony about perceiving success as well as the negative feeling about efforts in the sphere of moral leadership, which gives the very serious result that we see.

How true are these interpretations? Where is more evidence about what girls feel about the routines of worship and what they signify? First of all, in one of the more formally religious schools, one girl made the following calculation:

1,008 days at school over 4 years
$\times$ 10 minutes on knees each day
10,080 $\div$ 60 = 168 hours on knees!! = 7 days exactly
            In which time we could have:–
        (a) 336 meals of $\frac{1}{2}$ an hour
    or (b) 504 baths of 20 minutes
    or (c) 67 exams of $2\frac{1}{2}$ hours
    or (d) 126 letters of $\frac{3}{4}$ hour
    or (e) 112 lessons of 40 minutes   (15)

All this time spent on the knees is not to mention the rest of the time involved in services, let alone religious instruction. However, such an intensive programme is not always unsuccessful. A great deal obviously depends on how the services and instruction are put over, and this will depend on the sincerity, the perceived sincerity and the talent of the staff. In the above school there were several expressions on the following lines:

I believe in the Christian religion most strongly. There is too much disbelief particularly among the young people. The Church tends to be rather 'stuffy' in its service, particularly the Church of England.   (15)

However, it is easier to find remarks showing disaffection with routine forms. At another school, we hear:

Chapel is the most boring thing on earth the priest* thinks he takes ten minutes with his sermon but it normally takes half an hour.   (14)

And elsewhere:

---

* He was not actually a (Catholic) priest at this school.

Sometimes we are told to pray too much! Sometimes on Sundays we have to take communion in the morning, then go to church (school service) and then have Evensong in the evening plus two silence times in the morning and at night.   (13)

Why should there be antipathy towards forms of Christian communal worship or boredom with it among so many girls? Some reasons may suggest themselves with the aid of an examination of what may be the nature of worship in communities like convents. In one convent a nun said, when asked, that the life of nuns in her order was dedicated first and foremost to worship. The best form of human activity was to turn towards God, and worship expressed this. Service to mankind was also an expression of devotion to God, and teaching was a case in point; however, no nun joined the community in order to provide herself with material security while freeing herself to teach as a form of service to God. Nuns joined, and were admitted, after a stringent period of selection and training, to lead a life of prayerful worship. The resulting community of the convent is one where there is a high degree of shared orientation, thought and feelings. In particular, there is a widely shared belief in a religious philosophy which explains the origin and nature of man, his relations with God, and so on. This religious philosophy and the epic stories connected with it I shall refer to as a myth – not because it is untrue; the truth or otherwise is not in question. If this analysis is true, or approximately true, about a convent community, we can see that when the group joins in worship there can develop a powerful sense of intercommunication between the membership and with an outer divine being. Group worship is therefore likely to be a very suitable form for prayer in a convent.

A school differs from a convent in many ways. Particularly, the members are of varying maturity, and have been sent there, rather than having made a mature decision to join. They have not undergone a long training in the techniques and feelings for joint worship. The intention of some schools, therefore, to make corporate worship a central nucleus of the community's life, is not likely to meet with the same favourable circumstances as it does in a convent (where, in any case, perfect homogeneity is not always reached). The point is that group worship is a procedure that essentially is relevant to a body where there already is a strong group consciousness; this is clearly seen in tribal conditions in pre-literate societies, or in low-literacy societies where personal discreteness and individuality is not so highly developed (frequently because of economic pressures); furthermore, group worship is described as showing most cohesion, and most correctly reflecting the beliefs of the members, when these beliefs include a high degree of faith in supernatural beings and powers, because these are thought of as being eternal or long-lasting rather than ephemeral.

Girls who enter boarding school (aged 11 to 13) probably do enter a section of society where individuality is relatively subservient to the group-expressed norms. In no school visited, however, did the group norms of the younger girls appear to include a dedicated orientation to divine worship. (Quite seriously they often 'worship' idols on the pop scene, and a formal religion which sought to capitalize on these feelings at this time would have some chance of success.) The society of juniors is therefore not fertile ground on which the school might base a sound community of worship. Some points of common feeling towards supernatural life are there among them (e.g. worship of the pop stars), but commercial interests ensure a competition among different idols and so even this area for the possible growth of a consensus group consciousness is therefore fractured.

People like pop music (at least I do) because it kind of numbs your brain . . . you can forget everything and absorb the music. (14)
I like Pop Music especially the Kinks, the Who, the Monkees, but not the Rolling Stones because they are naughty boys. . . . There are more boys in pop because girls like pop much more and of course girls like boys – I do at any rate!! (13)

Where group worship grows out of voluntary devotions which coincide in a shared belief in a myth, it can provide a valid group experience over and above the individual contributions to it. This is what we can say is happening in convent worship. We can say it happens at a pop concert when the whole audience subscribes to the myth (however meagre) of the present pop star; it might also be said to occur at a football match where a crowd adores its team – especially when it validates their belief by winning. Where group worship is an unasked for institution, the participants are diverted in their attentions. Their minds wander over the topics of vital concern to themselves. They have also had training in this technique of internal mental adventure, prompted by their adaptation to group life in conditions of low privacy in which they have lived. This may start slowly; at first, many younger girls shun individual space, space in which they can make their own moves expressing individuality, personal discreteness, freedom.

What do I mean by 'individual space'? It is not only geographic space, as some understand it, but space in time or in responsibility on which an individual takes up a degree of liberty in which to think, decide or act.

. . . space. . . . People here are inhibited by it. There's the fear of being alone (unpopular) even if one hates the crowd.

This later gives way to the confidence with which one looks for personal space, or creates it for the individuality which needs it:

But you forget that one can create space in a crowded room. The most spacious place I know is a library full of people – or not. In our library one can sit, to all intents and purposes a normal hearty beast and go away somewhere quite different. This feeling of being alone yet with people is reassuring in a way.   (15)

While schools are continuing with their practice of group worship as an expression of the goal of instilling Christian principles, they are also trying to encourage individuality and self-reliance (among other things), and social responsibility expressed as authority or junior leadership, all being functions of increasing personal discreteness. This discreteness does not stop such people from being able to join in true group worship; but it will allow this only when worship is voluntarily joined in. This statement is not a manifesto on some partisan behalf (it may coincide with similar statements and be misunderstood as such), but it is a conclusion drawn from social psychological theory. Furthermore, high literacy (also promoted in many schools) is one of the techniques for reaching a higher degree of individuality, of personal discreteness, of being able to organize, devise and occupy a personal space; thus the more a girl advances academically, the more she is familiar with the world of books and of abstract mental processes. It is not an accident that the girl who wrote the above statement set it in a library.

As we see then, the mind wanders during communal worship to

which it is not dedicated. There are a very large number of writings on this, which may well be left to speak for themselves.

My thoughts usually wander during prayers. But if everybody else did not look about and distract you I should think I would not think of as many things . . . we are being taught mostly by teachers who either never bother about religion or cram it down your throat.   (12)

At one school during morning prayers, prefects' duty was to look down the lines and call to attention, by surname, any girl whose eyes were wandering. The mind evidently, however, can wander equally or more efficiently when the eyes are shut.

While saying prayers events that have happened run through my head. Such as, if I have been playing hockey I think why couldn't I have tackled that girl and prevented that goal.   (13)
During prayers, I may be watching the pianist's bandy legs.   (13)
During the Lord's prayer I nearly always think about home. I think about the awful supper we have just had and what I would have had for supper at home.   (14)
. . . I think of when I was caught smoking. . . . I often wonder what the heads schooling was like whether she was bossed and bellowed at . . . three girls last week were caught smoking! Three in one toilet, I mean it's so stupid if one has to resort to do it somewhere like that!   (14)

It appears from the above very small sample of what people think about during prayers, that the range of thought and experience is wide. It is not always for want of effort to pray:

. . . if I feel that I ought to say the prayers I do and I also say my own prayers. I don't feel that I should say the prayers because God wants me to, I say them because I want to.   (13)

The element of personal direction of devout emotion is seen here. It sometimes tries to channel itself in the way the organization wishes in the forms of collective worship but falters:[3]

My thoughts during prayers: '. . . Father . . . Amen. I've got a lot of Maths. Haven't finished my English either. Only half an hour. . . . Now . . . hour of our death Amen. O my God I am sorry and beg pardon for all . . . wonder what the time is ? . . . sins. . . . She's looking at me . . . BECAUSE THEY DESERVE THY DREADFUL. . . . I don't like saying prayers parrot fashion. I prefer them in my own, thanking God for today and asking for a good day tomorrow.

Tomorrow never comes . . . I'm tired. Ow! I'm kneeling on salt! I'll bear the pain for Jesus' sake. I wonder what Daddy's doing. In the name of the Father and of the Son and of the Holy Ghost Amen. (13)

For some, the devout emotions, the searching for the motives, if any, in nature, for knowledge for man's place in the world, and the feeling of personal dedication in these thoughts, are found and expressed in poetry. Those who find this *métier* have found an activity in some ways resembling worship, though one as intimately personal as communal worship is collective (ideally). It is by no means an idolatry, but a momentary glimpse we are given of a continuing devotion (devoutness) that leads a girl when tired of writing late to end:

I must stop, pray to Dylan Thomas, and then sleep. (15)

The lone individual in appreciating poetry is living a lyrical experience, which is the antithesis of the personally subjugated, collectively oriented experience necessary in real group worship.

. . . lyrical poetry has to be read by someone with the same training or understanding as the poet, so that the more frequent, more personal emotive touches are shared. Thus group-prayer is less personal; there is 'no room for lyricism' as there are but a few communication points. This is why lyricism is easier for a clique and harder for general circulation as it is harder to avoid unfortunate and find many emotive words. (16)

What this girl seems to mean is that the complexity of emotions that it is necessary to achieve or to sense and share with another in order to experience a lyrical poetical appreciation, determines that only a few readers will get themselves in touch with the message; in the same way it is probably most unlikely that a congregation will share the same complex experience. A congregation of schoolgirls is likely to have a less complex common experience at any one time; the way to transmute an audience with mixed feelings and thoughts into a coherent congregation capable of real group worship is to have them all believe in a complex myth, which is re-enacted in a ritually agreed manner during one or a series of services. This is possible in a modern Greek village, or in a convent or monastery, but is exceedingly unlikely in an English girls' boarding school, where the necessary beliefs just are not deeply enough held (if at all). The questioning process, which disperses any chance of a wide range of beliefs held in common, begins early:

I can't understand the . . . way of teaching religion. We have marvellous discussions on how the world begun and if there really is a God, but of course we are always overruled by how did such and such a thing exist if there wasn't a God. (13)

This girl shows signs of interest in religion that could, in favourable circumstances, develop in accord with the religion the school wants to teach; but she seems irritated by having assumptions made for her and the possibility then must develop that her attitudes might become antagonized. If the inquiries of the more able girls need careful guidance if the school is successfully to transmit its religious ideas, the minds of the less able pupils may be difficult to interest in 'higher' pursuits and the outcome may be determined by default.

It is very rearly I say my paris. In the morning befor brafast every one go's to top corowdoor and neils in the hall . . . what we do . . . pinch each other. our do our home work. pres after Brick We would read our letters. At night to tird. (13)

If this girl, or others like her, develop habits of religious observance and even profess faith in its philosophy, they would illustrate the distinction I made in Chapter Eight between two possible kinds of conformist. These would be 'passive' conformists agreeing with the 'goals' and 'means' of their religion; they would be different from 'active' conformists, who agree with goals and means, but try to refine the rationale behind them, to improve the 'official' rationale and justification.

The more romantic minds, preparing their journey to the aesthetic world of lyricism which sees the individual liberated in outer or inner space, can find more in the 'divergent' contexts than in the 'convergent' formulae of prayers:

I look at the priest's vestments and think – oh what a pretty colour, just like the crags. . . . I remember that day we went into the crags. . . . I come to my senses and feel very ashamed and start to think about what I'm saying. But more often than not I listen to readings. Readings convey more to me than prayers, I think its because I'm more a thinker than anything else. (13)

But the needs of daily life – one of which is prayer – also affect the response to worship:

During prayers I start off being very pious and thinking about what I have done wrong. In prayers before breakfast I am usually . . . hoping it isn't tomatoes. . . . Then at prayers at night I again start off being pious, however it doesn't last. I think to myself 'I've eaten too much again. I really must cut down'. I think the reason why my thoughts wander is because I prefer to pray when I feel the need.   (14)

Here is a connection in feeling between piety and guilt. It does not occur frequently in the girls' writings, and much oftener seen is the search for meaning in prayer, a personal meaning that is not apparently to be easily found in prayers designed for everybody.

Occasionally I say my prayers with the others, but not often. In the morning . . . I constantly think how horrible it is . . . to be saying words which may mean nothing to me . . . when I say prayers in a group it means nothing to me everyone is babbling away as hard as they can, how they concentrate I don't know.   (14)

Personal meaning is found through the medium of private prayer, at times suitable to the needs of the individual.

I myself hate the ritual of Church service yet have a firm belief in the Christian Faith. I can be closer to God by sitting and thinking for an hour in a bathroom than by singing hymns and saying long prayers in Church.   (15)

The feelings described as experienced during group prayer often suggest an innocent impiety. The girls sense that it is through no fault of their intention that the feelings in the group do not converge on devotion.

In prayers I think of . . . how boring life is in school and how stupid it is reciting the words of the 'Lord's Prayers' with no sign of meaning in my voice.   (14)

Girls know each others' performance in devotions and there may come about a superficial group norm of bravura disbelief. This could reinforce inner religious neglect and doubt, though some may see their way past the surface of the acted roles of their friends.

Most people in their hearts believe in God and enjoy the services excluding the serman. But most girls make out their athiasts when every-

one knows there not. Many religious discussions go on after lights out
where one's true beliefs come to the surface. (14)

Here again is a key to the door to inner space, the closing of the
eyes or the talking aloud of inner thoughts in the dark. At about the
age of this girl, inner questioning seems to go on and there are
signs in written material of the need to know more about religion
vis-à-vis other knowledge; there is a search among the more intelligent for criteria on which either to base or to accept a religious
belief. Not many reports suggest that schools successfully meet
these needs.

If we could have perhaps discussion lessons on other religions, of the
basis of religion, not just the Christian religion. One day we'll have to
make our own decision as to whether we believe, or in what we believe.
Why don't they make this clear to everyone. (14)

There are further suggestions which clearly more than one girl feels
are constructive, and which some schools do indeed anticipate and
provide for:

Lessons on 'religion' here are lessons in which we are taught unsuccess-
fully about God, the Israelites, Jesus, the New Testament. We ought
to have moral lessons, about the way we ought to live etc. At one
boarding boys public school, they (the boys) read books containing the
facts of life, and discuss sex frankly. Here, they avoid sex like the
plague. (14)

This girl takes the discussion out of the realm of worship. The
school appears to be trying to inculcate the basal emotive story on
which a community might agree to construct its collective worship;
but this meets with a feeling that its relevance is needed not as a
basis for group prayer, but as a moral guide. The areas of moral
curiosity are, however, those on which many school staff feel, or
are seen as being, out of touch with the electric pace of modern
moral change. The individualist moral curiosity begins to be strong,
and sometimes to lead to consideration of other religions, with
what appears to be a (remarkable?) degree of impartiality.

They cram us with religion here – I think its wrong and we're not
allowed to think for ourselves, which I also think is wrong. (14)
Religion is very forced on us and it is assumed that we are very religious . . . and though, possibly I may decide to be C. of E. I'm sure
I won't know until I've tried all other religions. (14)

This catholicity of attitude may only have as its spectrum the Christian denominations for this girl, but others look to atheism, and to non-Christian religions:

I am an atheist; when I was 11 I was confirmed into the C. of E., that was mainly because . . . it was the 'done' thing. Enforced religion broke down my feelings and after great thought I have become what I am. I give no explanations for anything to do with this subject (athesisum – which I can't spell) but I know that it is right.   (15)
Religion is in many ways crammed down your throat. I used to be more religious when I was younger. . . . The more I learn about other people's beliefs and ideas the more I wonder about the ones I have and am taught.   (15)
. . . I have an occasional spasm of believing and when I see someone else, mistress or something, being very devout I am sometimes influenced. But I'm sure lots of the staff are very hypocritical. . . . I expect if I was very worried about something I would fall back on God.   (15)

This girl raises the issue of staff as exemplars. It was clear from visiting, that in evaluating inter-school differences in putting Christian principles into practice, the school marked as having best success achieved this largely by virtue of the staff. The staff allowed a close relationship of respect though retaining a balance of reserve; but the emotion of staff in worship appeared to be conspicuously sincere to many of the girls. The difference in the staff position between here and elsewhere was marked.

However, the point being pursued here is not just the tentative, but the effective divergence in many schools of individual religious intentions from the formally expected standards with increasing age. Finally:

In the sixth form religious belief falls into three categories, strong, muddled, absent. Those who have been brought up to Christianity remain staunch, practising Church-goers, but the majority don't really know what they believe and either don't think about it or else develop their own philosophies of life, drawn from various religions such as Buddhism and Islam as a result of Scripture lessons.   (17)

Here is evidence of inter-denominational instruction or discussion; which evidently has some effect. But for the most part schools do not intend to encourage, or even condone, conversion or even movement towards non-Christian religions or atheism.

The prospectuses suggest the reverse, that Christianity will be positively encouraged. How then do girls see schools reacting to those who formally belong to other religions, or those who even show informal moves in other directions? It is possible to distinguish in replies from the above school, and also in others, the categories of people to whom religious tolerance is extended.

... there is a want of tolerance on the part of the authorities for other religious beliefs. There is much religious discussion among the students, the outcome of which seems to be a general belief in God though a dislike for conventional religion. (17)

... Religious doubts are soon quelled here, because it is a question of being religious or being thoroughly psycho-analysed until the subject submits to undergo the rituals even if quite unconvinced. (17)

The pressure to conform may apply to members of the same denomination as the school (which is in the above case carrying out the intentions stated in its prospectus). Girls of different Christian denomination sometimes report unfavourable treatment.

This school is high church and I don't like it maybe because I'm a Presbyterian I don't know. They drum it into us and if we don't think their way they say we're wrong and I loathe them for it. (15)
Because of the forced religion the non-Catholics are prejudiced about religion. (15)

The atheists may fall foul not only of the organization's attempts to induct them, but also of the pupil society's reaction to one who takes an overt 'abnormal' standpoint:

I asked the form in general, in a Divinity class whether Man had a soul. I was informed we had. I asked whether a dog had a soul. The majority said yes. I asked whether a goldfish had a soul. There were howls of laughter and an emphatic no. None of them could explain their reasoning (I do not believe in God). (15)

There is some reason then to think that not only schools formally, but sometimes also the pupil society, consider Christians of whatever denomination as fair game for coercion of a more or less intense kind. This has sometimes also been accompanied by allegations of material pressures being brought to bear. Such allegations were more often verbal than written, though there is written evidence:

I

Even if one is a confirmed Christian, the staff will only accept this if you . . . fit in with their denomination. I dislike this attitude as I consider that Christianity should destroy barriers, not create them, and that no one should be forced to conform to a certain opinion merely to get a good reference on leaving.   (16)

This type of feeling was encountered in at least two schools. Clearly, what matters is not whether one side feels it is being fair, but whether the pupil feels she is being coerced. Some clearly do. There were no reports from the (admittedly very few) girls of non-Christian religion, of any such coercion, or anything but a kind of formalized liberty.

I am Jewish, and am Orthodox and believe fully in my religion. I and my family keep all the festivities, and if a festival is celebrated and it is important, I am usually allowed home for it.   (15)

This girl's presence, as an Orthodox Jewess with requirements to be absent at unpredictable times, is most unusual for any of the boarding schools or departments visited, and depends on the peculiar circumstances at her school. As explained already, Muslims and Buddhists were also met in schools (though not making these demands for extra-organizational facilities), and when asked they reported no coercion. In one school, services had been conducted by locatable ministers of other religions, including a Rabbi, which had evidently been well received, and there were less complaints of cramming at this school than at some others.

Religion, it must be said, was in many schools not just a matter of occupying time or of staff transmitting their feelings for worship. One of the more successful devices for integrating pupil interest and dedication was for religion and music to overlap. Many schools have good music departments; and the most convenient form of collective musical expression is in choirs (orchestras are expensive in instruments, and practice cannot be done in the bath). Choirs are of course used in church, and lead the singing in daily prayers. Choirs sometimes share with boys' schools in performing major works in local cathedrals, and thus there are several reasons why girls are attracted to choir membership. Moreover, in a musical work, there exists the emotive material that individuals can share, and in sharing in it can compound their experience of an action which is dedicated and outgoing, that resembles worship. Listening to an orchestral work allows the individual mind to find its own response, the free inner wandering of lyrical experience; playing in an orchestra or singing in a choir is to concert one's actions with others', to pool one's feelings towards a group experience. This is the condition for which religion ideally aims, in corporate worship. Whether schools realize all this overtly or not, they operate choirs which lead the singing in worship; in these choirs, girls who wish to give themselves up to enjoying the music will find it difficult to distinguish between that and the dedication of the music to the sacred purpose. It will be easier for them to distinguish if the words of hymns appear patently absurd or comic ('. . . the troops of Midian prowl and prowl around . . .'); but nevertheless, the symbolism surrounding the event can even supervene over inappropriate words, and the joining in aesthetically pleasing music in a church or sacred setting is likely to produce at least some concurrence in the act of group worship that goes on. This is not to say that there is no distinction between the validity of worship during hymns and that during prayers. The spoken group prayers without music seem, from the writings, to have the least validity as worship.

Apart from choirs as a method of involving girls in worship, another way has been to allocate the performance of part of a service (usually readings, sometimes prayers) to one class or age group. In some schools the younger girls can thus share in choosing what is to be read, and (shyly enough) read it themselves. In one school a pupil group even wrote some of the words used in a service, but this was not the common procedure always – it merely happened to occur during the research visit.

A third important and possibly most popular way of involving the girls in religion in the broadest sense is by good works. These activities may well have no relevance whatsoever in improving the quality of corporate worship (in church), though social action can also be seen as a type of (unsung) corporate worship. The types of social action met with have included hospital visiting, being companion to an aged person, collecting money by any of the usual devices (box-shaking, jumble, miles of pennies) and the relatively new idea (at the time the schools were visited) of walking for money. In this latter, the collector persuades people to pay for the number of miles she walks (frequently in some collective youth organization). The idea is rather surprising, as it implies that contributors will not pay unless the girl undergoes some socially approved form of self-sacrifice or discomfort; clearly this is more likely than the idea that people are paying when girls do healthy outdoor exercise. No instances of money collected for a number of tennis sets played were found. On the other hand, it would presumably not be forth-coming if the subjects underwent flagellation. The 'sacrifice' has to be a socially approved form. Often organized by Christian bodies, it may take the form of a (financially) rewarding pilgrimage, walk-ing to some religious site, like a cathedral. As far as boarders are concerned, it means getting out of school, perhaps with other young people, perhaps with boys. The ultimate altruistic purpose is borne in mind, however.

It is worth noting that in several schools there was a norm that determined who the recipients of collections might be. There would be missions among England's poor, or charities for the hungry abroad. Often, also, a substantial amount of argument concerned changing the recipient; in one school it might be: 'we never help any local charities, they've got a "thing" about the starving natives abroad'; elsewhere it would be: 'we usually send our money to people who already have the welfare state – what about the *real* needy, abroad?' Perhaps there is a surfeit of charitable com-passion, which wants to help all problems everywhere.

What I have said about differences between schools has so far been impressionistic. There were no measures devised to gauge religious experience or attitudes, except for those items present in the questionnaire on goals. The figures from these questionnaires were not related by computer to all the other factors measured about schools, as the resources available for computation were allocated for other matters. I have chosen to investigate through calculations 'by hand' one simple question about religious goals. This is, is there any difference between boarders at mainly-day and those at mainly-boarding schools as to the results on religious and moral goals? I have considered the same three goals analysed at the start of this chapter and included for sake of comparison the goal of promoting success in examinations. The schools have been ranked in order from that with the highest score (first) to that with the lowest on any goal. Out of twenty schools ranked in this way, six were 'mainly-day' schools according to the definition given in Chapter One. The average rank for these mainly-day schools was worked out and compared with the average rank for the mainly-boarding and boarding-only schools combined.

Table 10·4. Mean rankings of six mainly-day and fourteen mainly-boarding schools on four different goals

	mean rankings on the issues that schools:					
	do try to achieve		should try to achieve		actually achieve	
goals	day	boarding	day	boarding	day	boarding
moral sense	14·0	9·0	12·33	9·71	12·83	9·50
Christian principles	12·16	9·70	11·33	10·14	13·66	9·14
living together	15·0	8·50	11·16	10·21	14·33	8·85
exam success	12·33	9·71	9·66	10·87	10·16	10·62
mean difference in ranks on first three goals between day and boarding	4·65		1·58		4·44	

The first thing to understand is that a smaller number in this table refers to a higher average rank; that is, more importance is accorded to that item in those schools. Broadly speaking, it is the boarding schools which accord more importance to most of these goals compared with mainly-day schools.

In the case of ideal goals ('should try to achieve') the differences in ranking between boarding and day types of school are relatively small. In fact on the goal of promoting success at exams, the group of mainly-day accords slightly more importance; on the three 're-ligious or moral' goals, however, it is the boarding-type schools which show some priority of importance.

As to what girls think their schools are trying to achieve, efforts towards exam success are ranked higher in boarding than in day-type schools; the difference in ranks here is 2·6. But with moral and religious goals the importance reckoned in boarding schools leads on average to more than four places higher rank than among day-type schools. The difference is particularly clear on the 'moral' goals where it seems that girls in mainly-boarding schools thought that their schools were trying to a much greater extent to teach people how to live together happily, and how to judge for themselves between right and wrong.

Actual success of schools on their judged efforts follows the pattern of what girls see as the pattern of efforts. There is no difference in the average rank from boarding or day-type schools about the success girls think is achieved with exams. This serves as a non-religious topic to establish some kind of base-line on which boarding and day-type schools appear as similar. Against this we see that boarding-type schools are judged on average to be more successful in inculcating Christian principles (4·5 places of rank difference); they are judged more successful on teaching girls to judge between right and wrong (3·3 places of rank difference); and they are thought of as being particularly more successful in teaching people to live happily together (5·4 places of rank difference).

It is most important in all this to remember that we are not comparing boarding with day education. We are comparing the evaluation of boarders in mainly-boarding-type schools with the observations of boarders in mainly-day-type schools. Naturally, the mainly-day-type of schools are not organized primarily for boarders; they do not devote resources towards the facilities that are provided in some boarding-type schools for a thorough communal life in evenings and at week-ends. Nevertheless, it is of interest to note that boarders in such day-type schools do not record differences of evaluation regarding academic goals (success at exams); they do show differences on the goals to which religion is relevant.

We may now summarize some of the points made in this chapter. Most of the schools visited were overtly Christian organizations, and some of them stated their aims of building corporate and individual lives on a foundation of Christianity. The pupils in most schools showed a majority of the same denomination as the school. Those of non-Christian religions were very few in the first place; often marked as apart by different nationality, they reported friendliness and no discrimination; this appeared to go with a situation where the society perceived them formally and informally as 'clearly distinct though very nice of course', rather than having doubts about whether they were distinct or not. There were no tests to verify this, but it seemed that non-Christian girls had greater scope to develop individuality of feeling within the school society. Where the girl was not happy or even maladjusted this might serve to magnify her problems. Where she was internally secure, the religious difference might well promote a greater inner strength.

Religion is manifest in worship, and in human relations. As to human relations in the school, the rest of this book is testimony. Outside the school, especially on the issues of freedom and responsibility, and sexual morality, girls wished for moral guidance. They saw religious lessons as possibly the relevant place wherefrom to derive some moral criteria, but often showed the feeling that religious lessons appeared morally irrelevant to their immediate problems in detail, or even preoccupied with theology and hagiology.

The presentation of religion was, of course, not all abstruse and ritualistic. At one school the head clearly made an effort to make religion seem relevant by explaining a current political crisis (Rhodesia) during morning assembly, and praying for a benevolent outcome. Some girls might become disillusioned about the role of prayer for public benefit when they contemplate the state of the world around them. This potential 'loss of faith' is combated in some cases by an encouragement of good works, though I never heard any attention given by staff to explaining a possible connection between prayer and the propensity for doing good works, even if such a connection exists.

At one school, grace before meals was sung as a three-part round; it may be that when presented popularly religious reference ceases to be perceived as 'religion' by the girls; but then again this may not matter. One incident when religious allusion was made to a topical event was when the Israelis captured Jerusalem in 1967, and during prayers the quotation was read from Micah, Chapter 4:

And many peoples will go and say: come ye and let us go up to the mountain of the Lord to the house of the God of Jacob, and he will teach us of his ways and we will walk in his paths. For out of Zion shall go forth the Law and the word of the Lord from Jerusalem. And he shall judge among many people, and rebuke strong nations afar off, and they shall beat their swords into ploughshares and their spears into pruning hooks: nation shall not lift up a sword against nation, neither shall they learn war any more.

To the best of my knowledge there could not have been more than one or two girls of Jewish origin present: though a Muslim girl was at the school she would not have heard this reading as she was excused from attending prayers. On another occasion a Sunday club was run with a revivalistic flavour, some aura of a select group membership and also a welfare function. The group had books with about thirty songs from which individuals would choose numbers to be sung with enthusiasm; these songs made frequent use of the imagery of Calvary and of Salvation being involved with washing with the blood of the Lamb; one meeting I attended was dedicated to Jesus, and at the end, the members were exhorted to 'go forth into the next four days shining with Jesus's joy'. In formal terms, they did try to spread joy, and with some success, as they sang at a nearby prison and at other schools and were asked to come again.

Religion was used in some cases to determine ways of self-discipline, as in the institution of the Sabbath. In one school this was taken quite seriously; whereas in some places Sabbath was a day when liberty was reduced because facilities were locked or unused because there were fewer staff on duty, in this school Sabbath implied clear rules. Piano practice was forbidden. Piano playing clearly was not forbidden as it could be used to produce religious music, and arguably all pieces could be construed as religious, or as a relaxation. Accordingly, practice was defined as 'repetition of portions' of pieces and disallowed. It is not clear how consistent such a position can be; for example, playing tennis was allowed and included knocking up before the game. Nevertheless, in as much as all these issues get discussed, awareness of religion is increased, even if it is eventually in many cases to its detriment.

Finally, if I am not mistaken, an attempt may have been made in one school to influence my own work. Quoting only from my own notes, which are therefore not verbatim since they were written down some hours after the event, a prayer was included during one service with words such as:

We pray to Thee to bless those who guide our public affairs with discretion and responsibility.   [chaplain]

Aware as I was of the fears in some schools that the research was being done for the Public Schools' Commission to advise the government about taking over independent schools, I took this as possibly a message in my direction. I hope if that was the case that it has had its desired effect. Checking with a senior prefect afterwards I was told that a prayer of this type was often said in this school. This episode illustrates some of the difficulties of interpretation that can arise in sociological fieldwork.

Statistically the chapter has shown that boarders are keen that schools should work towards a moral education; they are less keen about 'Christian principles' (which probably is taken as referring to formalized religion). Boarders feel that schools fall seriously behind expectation in inculcating moral sense and the ability to live together happily. Staff also share this pattern of views, though to a substantially lesser extent. Boarders in chiefly-boarding schools rank their schools as trying harder, and as succeeding more in inculcating all three goals touching on religion, than boarders in chiefly-day schools do.

The chapter has, however, been chiefly concerned with analysing qualitative aspects of religion and in understanding something about worship, particularly communal worship. Several kinds of condition in worship have been recognized here. In one, successful group worship, it is probable that the participants need to have a major historical life-story or myth in common; the worshippers act in expressing themselves together, and achieve in group devotion something greater than the sum of its parts. The group experience is a condition of individual surrender; only perhaps in the conditions of a convent, where all participants are highly dedicated, selected and trained to direct their individual experiences nearly identically in the same way, does group worship offer the individual a lyrical experience. By lyrical, I mean the individual inner adventure, liberated from physical conditions of space, and especially free in time. Virtually none of the girls hinted at having lyrical experience in prayer, unless it be solo; group prayer interfered with this and did not attain for schoolgirls the harmony of which it is capable. It usually fell very short. The difficulties in the way of success in group worship include the fact that the girls are being trained by the school in some respects to develop their individual selves, to increase the articulation of relationships between themselves and the community. For these reasons, girls needed a high degree of compatibility between themselves and what they might choose to be devoted to, which would not necessarily turn out to be formal religion; in aesthetic terms, individual lyric devotion was sometimes responsive to and inspired by poetry. For some, sharing in choral singing provided an approximation to group worship (during hymns or anthems), though this was not apparently sustained during group prayers. It may be that the girls who achieved successful devotion in group prayer never wrote about it; but there is no reason to suppose this was likely.

Older girls were probably more certain in their religious stance; some were devout Christians and contributed to and benefited from school services (though writing exceedingly little about it). Others had rebelled into atheism, or forms of pantheism or even the fashionable narcissism.* These girls may well have developed the skills of reverie, of discovery of inner space; many might take pleasure in poetry, reading it or especially writing it. This latter appears to be one sign of the individual highly detachable from the community and unlikely to give, or get, anything from corporate worship. A very few girls may have developed an appetite of interest in non-Christian religions, while a larger number are likely to have retained some residual belief in God. The forms of corporate worship existing, except for a few cases where innovation or overt study of the forms of worship improve the situation, suggest that they are inappropriate to the diversity of congregants. The congregation is diverse in that there are highly individuated older girls, disillusioned middle girls, and distracted younger ones; only the very youngest may still be sufficiently awed by the forms of ritual worship to give themselves whole-heartedly, and even among them, boredom appears to start early. Among all, there is undoubtedly a body of believing Christians, but these do not clearly constitute a congregation in the sense that such is found in a convent, or even in an African village. Various aids to enhancing the place of religion in the girls' minds have been discussed, including choir participation, girls officiating and social service actions. These are varyingly successful, some very much so in themselves, though there is no reason to suppose that they improve group worship. Private worship, nevertheless, continues in its various forms, as it always will.

* Basically the worship of humanity, rather than of a personal self.

Notes

1. For each goal, one could respond that efforts were exerted 'very much', 'medium' or 'hardly at all'; these were marked 3, 2 and 1: so one extreme of view, if held by all, would yield an average mark of 3·00. The minimum possible average was 1·00, giving a range of 2·00. The formula for converting an average calculated mark of x is: percentage $= \dfrac{x-1}{2} \times 100$. Thus a mark of 3·00 represents 100 per cent, 2·75 represents 87·5 per cent, 2·50 represents 75 per cent and 2·00 is 50 per cent.
2. Success in this case means having a great deal of communal Christian observance, as well as the possibility that girls may take some of it in.
3. This extract is not abbreviated for quotation by . . . marks, but is given exactly as it was written.

Overview

What does this study amount to? What lessons can be drawn from it? Both of these are deceptively simple questions. What I can do here is to point out certain issues that have emerged so far which seem to have relevance for any further educative legislation or reform. I will also have to refer to information from other researches, particularly anthropological ones, to sketch out the context in which I believe the present results should be judged. This process of depicting a context and of highlighting the significance of certain new facts is inevitably a personal one which must be acknowledged at the outset. Another judge might focus differently upon the findings here, and derive from his own context of values and principles that one or another course of action is the only proper consequence to press for.

An example of the multi-faceted nature of this question of context is that of the issue of divisiveness, raised in the preview. To some judges, any aspect of divisiveness is unacceptable if it exists at all, and action must be taken to alter the situation. The Public Schools' Commission started its work by accepting a statement that the public schools are divisive, and set out to discover and suggest corrective policies. It seems to me in the light of questions I have already raised about divisiveness that the problem is more complex than can be dealt with by pronouncing a definition at the outset. In the context of the fee-paying characteristic and the mutual access facilitated to members of the economically dominant sub-culture, public schools are largely divisive. But in the context of nationalism versus regionalism, or that of inter-generational social mobility, there are senses in which public schools (or boarding schools, in my perspective) are cohesive.

The kind of questions I will raise here, in order to set the context in which I shall judge my findings, are these. Is there an existing demand, or an unfulfilled need (which will have to be specified in some agreed way) for boarding education? What is meant by the question 'is boarding natural?', and how might we answer this? How does the pattern of educating children in boarding correlate, if at all, with other elements of structure in societies? What kinds of questions should we ask about where our society is going, in order to assess how boarding (or its abolition) might fit in with social development? I shall also discuss some detailed implications drawn from my evidence which might be worth examining in the light of any intentions for boarding that might be developed following the above considerations.

As to an existing demand, three points must be mentioned. First there is the self-evident demand embodied in the number of parents, and in the few local authorities, who already use boarding. This includes parents with jobs that involve travel, either within Britain or abroad, whose children would otherwise have a highly unstable education. Middle-class parents strongly express the need to instil middle-class attitudes in their children – a demand which they may feel might be overlooked in the local comprehensive. This issue is that which gives rise to the famous accusation of 'snobbery'. Here we must distinguish that intention which is focused merely on fostering a particular way of behaviour (which I do not call snobbery), from that which focuses on presenting and inculcating a pattern of behaviour as being superior to some other pattern, and in underlining the superiority thought to characterize such a difference (snobbery).

Two types of effect resulting from the satisfaction of this middle-class demand can be distinguished. The first is cultural, in which a certain range of tastes and attitudes may come to be acquired. Secondly, friendships, and ultimately marriages, are fostered within the middle class, and this tends to support their economic status. It might be decided that the old-school-tie networks should be cut down because they afford their members unfair economic advantages. However, this would also have the effect of destroying part of the machinery whereby the middle class, for better or worse in this country, transmits its culture. It would be easy to argue that middle-class aesthetic culture is inseparable from its economic concomitants, and that to intervene over the latter must needs involve some sacrifice of the former. This is not the place to offer a verdict on what it would be right to do; the point is to try and present the dilemma involved, and particularly to show its relevance to boarding.

The second aspect of existing demand to discuss is that which may exist but remain largely unfulfilled. A piece of research by Raymond Woolfe* involved asking over 2,000 parents in three parts of the country about their wishes for boarding for their children. He reported that twelve per cent of these parents would want some sort of boarding at some time for their children. This would imply a total requirement for over 160,000 places in secondary schools for girls, which would mean at least four times the existing amount of boarding. Most parents would prefer what was termed 'local boarding', though one-fifth (of the twelve per cent) chose 'public school type' boarding. Woolfe found that nearly sixty per cent of parents of girls would want single-sex schools for their daughters (parents of boys were more inclined to want mixed boarding).

Some observers might view these boarding-requesting parents as 'social climbers' who want to do so through education at the government's expense. In this perspective there would be a good reason for deciding to leave provision of maintained boarding as a low priority project. Curiously, if Conservatives thought it might fortify the middle-class ranks, the provision of boarding might appeal to them as a suitable project despite their usual reluctance to spend public money on the public. It would be worth pointing out that boarding not done well leads to low morale and a degree of disaffection with the responsible authorities, which Conservatives might not want to encourage. There would seem to be considerable problems, therefore, in deciding to spend public funds on expanding boarding places to fulfil a mere 'boarding demand'.

However, Woolfe went on to estimate need for boarding (according to judgements made by teachers) and to 'translate need into demand' by finding how many of those described as needing boarding also had parents who requested it for their children. The result of this was an estimate that about 14,000 secondary boarding places for girls might be needed nationally. This figure comes from families whose children are at present in day schools, and is therefore supplementary to the first kind of demand mentioned, which is already being filled. Such an added demand would involve the creation of about forty schools (of 300 in each) which therefore represents a considerable requirement said to exist on a national basis.

* R. Woolfe, *Demand and Need for Boarding Education*. An interim report (Cambridge, King's College, Research Unit into Boarding Education, 1968).

As well as pointing to two kinds of demand which are relatively easy to discern, there is the question of the susceptibility of each of these types of demand to the prevailing winds of public opinion. To discuss boarding in the national press and among responsible public exponents as an acceptable form of education, with certain advantages and dangers, might be to extend demand; but to treat boarding as a topic for silence, combined with covert suspicions of snobbery and occasional outbursts of derision and public disapproval would doubtless diminish demand. Thus demand will not only be inherent in people's cultural and social needs, but will also be susceptible in some degree to the nature of the currents of controversy which may surround the topic.

We can see now that the answer to the first question is that there certainly is some kind of demand for boarding. Some of it is easily satisfied, as with rich parents who have no trouble in securing places for their children. Part of the demand is an intense one, in which parents accept degrees of financial sacrifice to afford boarding education. Yet another section of demand may be one that is not yet fulfilled, but which expresses an implied desire to 'give the children a better chance', or in other words, to rise in socioeconomic class. I believe it should be distinguished conceptually – and then empirically in some investigation – whether there may be two components to this kind of demand. One part may consist in parents wanting a certain style of 'culture' for their children – preference for a particular range of artistic, sporting or other interests, and certain modes of social behaviour; the other part, which is linked to, but not identical with the first, involves giving children access to a range of better paid and more secure jobs, which help powerfully in establishing a foundation on which the 'cultural' component of needs can be based.

For the government to arrange to satisfy this type of cultural and economic demand might mean that such people were being helped into a position in which the class their offspring attain (in terms of job chances and cultural attitudes) is 'higher' than the class they started from. This would appear to be a process of dividing a proportion of a class from its main body and 'promoting' it socially.

Are there ways of satisfying a demand and need for boarding which would not involve divisiveness? This again is a false question, though one that is sometimes asked in this field. For if we posit a school full of 'social mix' which produces a socio-economically homogeneous body of people who 'start' at school-leaving age with similar chances in life – though they may diverge in their fortunes later – then in terms of their relation to each other the school has not been divisive. But in terms of the relations between the pupils and their home backgrounds (because 'social mix' implies that pupils have been drawn from a range of backgrounds), a homogenizing school will have been divisive. For in the case of many pupils the life style which they acquire will be systematically different from that of their parents, and perhaps from that of brothers and sisters who go to other kinds of school. The decisions required from policy-makers involve specifying and choosing what kind of divisiveness will be most acceptable.

Having dealt with the question of demand, we come to that implied in the suggestion, sometimes heard about boarding, that it is 'not natural'. The implication of this is that it is 'natural' for families to bring up their children at home, while it is only those in 'unnatural' circumstances (of travel or parental disruption) who would need to send their children to board. The implication is sometimes further made that it is inhumane for parents to send their children away to board, either at primary or secondary school age.

There is plenty of evidence, however, that boarding occurs in other cultures – in America, Russia, and on the European continent – for a variety of reasons. More interestingly perhaps, if we define boarding as the 'extrusion' of adolescents for education in groups away from their families, there are numerous examples of the practice from among tribal cultures in Africa and elsewhere. There are so many examples in fact that anthropologists have been able to make statistical comparisons of social patterns which are likely to accompany different styles of boarding education. One anthropologist* starts by defining a ceremonial ritual by three characteristics: 1. the rite must be overseen by elders; 2. the rite involves a process of indoctrination into adult roles; 3. the rite involves physical ordeals such as scarification or circumcision (clitoridectomy). By this definition, English boarding is not a ceremonial ritual since it lacks the third criterion. However, it shares the first

* Y. A. Cohen, *The Transition from Childhood to Adolescence* (Chicago, 1964).

two criteria with cultures Cohen has studied, and we may consider to what extent his findings might have implications which could be instructive for the English situation.*

In over fifty societies where socialization is done by non-members of a child's descent group (i.e. roughly where the teachers are unrelated to the children) initiation ceremonies are virtually absent. The English boarding system fits with this finding. The teachers at boarding schools are not pupils' relatives, and physical insults are not built into the process. We learn next that tribal societies often used nakedness or bizarre body painting to reduce the child's previous identity in the transitory state before appearing in society again with new identity as an adult; in English boarding, uniform is often used for similar purposes. In one school there was even a quasi-medical inspection in which girls had to strip completely, and this possibly served unwittingly as a de-identifying step before joining the relatively homogeneous society of the junior girls. In the one school where I found any semblance of an aspect of physical threat to the girls (thus coming close to the definition of the initiatory rite) there was a common social bond which united the girls not with all the staff, but with the governors. So on this point the English material also resembles the statistical trends discovered in other cultures.

The import of this is two-fold. First, it indicates that English boarding is not 'unnatural'; secondly, it suggests that boarding is a certain pattern of social machinery which may fit in with other aspects of a sub-culture's overall purpose and design. Cohen also finds that in societies where 'extrusion' exists, where children receive part of their education away from their families, and the teachers are unrelated, that the practice of joint legal liability for misdemeanours is not likely to occur. Where children are educated at home, joint legal liability is more likely to exist. This suggests on a cross-cultural basis that extrusion, or boarding, works in some way to develop individual responsibility for one's personal behaviour – and not for behaviour enacted by others in one's group. Extrusion is not essential for this, but it seems to work in this direction.

* There are grounds for thinking that, for reasons domestic to the profession of anthropology, it has somewhat overemphasized the more sensational third criterion at the expense of the first two.

K

Further, in tribes where initiation ceremonies are practised there seems to be equal likelihood that pre-marital sex relations will, as will not, be allowed; whereas in cultures where no initiation ceremonies occur, pre-marital sex relations are somewhat more likely to be permitted than not. Now English boarding would seem to approximate more to the first case, with English day education more like the second type where no initiation ceremonies occur. The latter is slightly more likely to be associated with pre-marital sexual permissiveness in the culture. So boarding may not just incidentally be a quixotic corner of the educational system where a semblance of 'Victorian' sexual principles is maintained; but it may be both an expression of and a means for reinforcing the values of a sector of society which avows less permissive sexual attitudes among other things.

It would be tempting to link this reticent aspect of the boarding-supporting sub-culture, via the Freudian idea of arrest at an anal stage of sexuality, with the promotion of a capitalist outlook. This anal stage of development is supposed to imply traits of methodicalness, obsessive tidiness, collection or hoarding of assets, and ultimately avarice. Thus it could be represented that the money-accumulating classes are involved in supporting boarding, which works as a means for negating the free flow of personal assets of any kind, of money across class boundaries, and in particular of permissive sexuality either within or across class lines. It could also be said that boarding works as a relatively closed circuit for ensuring personal contacts so that marriages will tend to occur within rather than across socio-economic strata, and that this helps to conserve attitudes as well as material assets within the sub-culture.

We may now see that boarding is not 'unnatural' in that versions of it occur in various cultures the world over. It is a social device that apparently serves to fit those who experience it into certain kinds of adult roles within society. Empirically, it is more natural for girls to go to secondary boarding in England than at a primary age, and in this sense it is relatively unnatural for girls to board aged between 8 and 11.

Aside from the anthropological evidence, much of the foregoing material suggests that boarding schools are associated with parental and staff attitudes that would much prefer pre-marital sex not to occur. This attitude is set, however, against a context of very different trends of development in society. Focusing first on women's roles in work, and as voters, pressure built up for the general proposition that 'women's equality' was desirable. Recent developments in which Britain is to an extent influenced by foreign cultures include pressures encouraging tolerance and even flaunting of pre-marital sex. These pressures are facilitated by research developments which (at the time of writing) promise early access to drugs whose 'use' will blur the existing distinctions between abortion and birth control. These drugs will enable any girl to experiment heterosexually without incurring parental knowledge, let alone disapproval. The development of inter-sex equality in occupational, political and sexual behaviour (both in initiating contacts, and having them) will constitute a tremendous cultural change which will probably swamp the salience of differences between subcultures which previously (and now) evoked so much attention.

The tide towards women's equality, however, will encounter some obstacles. One of these is cited by Roy D'Andrade* in a survey of cross-cultural research on sexual roles. He points out that in all known human populations males differ from females in primary as well as secondary sex characteristics. The chief of these (which he manages somehow not to mention) is the division of roles in the task of procreation. Until research eliminates this difference, by enabling foeti to be nurtured outside their 'mothers', the implication is quite clear that sexual roles in any culture will continue to differ. In as much as control over research goals and finance is largely in the hands of men, they will covertly (or overtly) be motivated to avoid such a research achievement that would upset their social position.

An intuitive realization of all this will certainly occur to many people. They are recipients of an inherited tradition embodied and transmitted in the great corpus of English literature, which steadily reflects to a greater or lesser degree the position (as described by D'Andrade) that 'males are sexually active, more dominant, more deferred to, more aggressive, less responsible, less nurturant and less emotionally expressive than females'. In order to empathize with the dramatic experiences of Rosalind, Juliet, Jane

* Roy D'Andrade, 'Sex Differences and Cultural Institutions', in *The Ecology of Human Intelligence*, ed. Liam Hudson (Harmondsworth, 1970), pp. 15–49.

Eyre, or almost any other heroine, readers become involved in accepting to some extent that sex roles are radically founded in almost immutable differences. The alternative is to deal with literature with critical detachment; but this is unlikely to be able to occur until a mature state of education is reached. By this time, in order for critical abilities to have been developed, pupils will either have to have been nurtured on a completely new literature constructed on assumptions of thorough sex-role equality, or they will have acquired the conventions against which they may rebel but which they almost certainly will not be able to eradicate.

Now the anthropological literature does not firmly suggest that boarding is incompatible with a trend towards sex-role equality. In fact, co-educational schools might well promote this, with or without the practice of pre-marital sex – already being broached in Sweden as a likely, perhaps necessary school subject. However, with their existing staffs, tradition, facilities and momentum, it seems more likely that single-sex girls' boarding schools will be increasingly supported by those who value an older model of the ideal woman. This demand may even increase in proportion to indices of greater sexual permissiveness in society; these include films which set examples of uninhibited behaviour to be copied, pop music and musicians setting apparent norms for teenage behaviour, politicians and the press soliciting for markets and votes among as young a public as possible, and 'medical aids' which enable unrestrained sexual behaviour to occur without pregnancy.

If the dominant culture does move towards permissiveness over the coming decades, one may foresee a continuing demand for single-sex boarding, with the expectation among the clients that it should promote traditional attitudes. This will be increasingly difficult for schools to accomplish, as commerce in ideas, objects and relationships becomes more efficient. There will be a mounting shortage of good female staff and it will require alert and flexible staffing policies for schools to survive, let alone thrive. Signs are that the presence of more married staff, including masters, will more likely convey to the pupils that the ideals of sexual careful-ness (if not exactly chastity) are directed towards a later ideal – that of a stable family life – that the girls may more readily accept.

The problems that girls' boarding schools will encounter if they are to continue to cater for their existing type of demand will be considerable. But they will be compounded by the trend – which a Conservative government might only have the effect of slowing down – towards non-divisiveness with regard to the social class distribution of school populations. In general, I will refer to situations where schools will probably be brought, by subsidies or other means, to cater for 'integrant' pupils.

Among boys, schools have been described which include a high proportion of 'integrant' pupils or of 'need cases'. These are, broadly speaking, children from families which could not have afforded boarding, but who wanted it or agreed to it and who for reasons of family fracture or maladjustment also needed it. There are also girls who can similarly be seen as being 'integrant' pupils. A large proportion of these come from families which have not previously experienced boarding. In fact, among the girls in this book, about forty-five per cent were first generation boarders. Some of them had newly rich parents who paid their way. School staff sometimes mentioned these as newcomers to the culture, whom they snobbishly resented if their means had arrived before their manners. Other girls came from families which had not previously used boarding and who therefore had attitudes and ways of behaviour not necessarily in line with the 'traditional' boarders. Where girls come from families who have been selected primarily for their explicit needs, they may not start off from a happy home base line, and this has implications for the effect of schools on them, and almost certainly also for the effect they have on their schools.

I have shown that, where schools contained a large proportion of pupils whose parents had themselves been boarders, the girls also tended to say that boarding was having a good effect on their family relationships. These schools also tended to be the happier schools – even though happier schools did not necessarily contain more girls from happy or from unhappy families. These findings have considerable implications for any large-scale plans to place 'need-cases' (girls from difficult homes) into boarding schools as they are. These girls are less likely to be happy in school; if they are in schools which have social structural characteristics associated with less happiness (stricter, larger schools), and if they are present in such numbers as to affect the general level of happiness, this is likely to rebound unfavourably on their perception of their predicament and of their home situations. There will then have been no point (other than perhaps a doctrinaire political one) in catering for 'need' by using boarding.

Several conditions would have to be satisfied to enable 'need-cases' to benefit from boarding. They should be very carefully prepared, psychologically, for their departure to school;* it would certainly be useful for schools to be particularly aware of the delicacy of this transition, but it would be making it more difficult for even the most sympathetic and understanding welcome if girls were to arrive with negative feelings towards the school and anything it is or does. It seems then that the chances of happiness in school are also better in more lenient, smaller schools. The smaller schools seem, however, to have been more likely to foster interests in domestic science than the larger schools and to contain less able (on two tests) pupil populations. These facets are likely to be involved with the financial difficulties for smaller schools in providing the staff, the expensive laboratories, other equipment, and up-to-date text books on which high academic standards could be based. Therefore, if 'need cases' are to be educated happily and at a high academic standard it would probably need relatively small and expensively well-staffed and equipped schools to do this. An alternative may be to depend on the good works of convents and nuns, who are sometimes able to provide tolerance and charisma at low staff cost to the public. This, of course, involves a religious commitment which will affect which pupils can be sent to which school.

I also found that prior experience in preparatory schooling was linked with happiness in school. In particular, in the four schools at which there was nearest to a 50–50 proportion of girls with and without experience of private prep schooling, there were relatively higher proportions of rebellious pupils. Here again are facts with serious implications for any scheme designed to integrate independent boarding facilities with the state-maintained pupil population. It seems that 'boarding-trained' parents may know what kind of culture they want their daughters to acquire, and can pre-train their daughters and manoeuvre them into appropriate schools where what is being inculcated at home matches what happens in school. Parents without this expertise will leave their daughters at

* Regardless of the school, it is the departure itself which must be accepted by the child.

a disadvantage, and this would have to be made up for, either by expert social work presence at the introduction to school, or probably with that and continuous social work mediation as well. The point is that young girls will be undergoing a two-cultural experience, and this will need to be interpreted successfully both to them and their parents. It is assumed also that the schools will sympathetically understand the cultures of the integrant families.*

Schools' perception of and relations with integrant families will pose considerable problems. If the families are defined as being in 'need', then it is difficult to avoid perceiving them as families-as-families-shouldn't-be. If, furthermore, the social work mediation is done by specially trained teachers or by social workers attached to the schools, then the structure of the situation defines the families being perceived as at a disadvantage, in need of 'improvement'; it becomes difficult then for a school culture to avoid a covert implication that it is somehow superior to that of the family – especially if the latter is broken and seen as a source of distress for the 'integrant' girl. This analysis of the problem argues for the use of non-school-based social workers whose first loyalty should be to the family and the pupil, and who would deal with the school as a body serving the family. Fee-paying parents have as one of their reasons for doing so that they are in the position of customer, requiring a service from the school. This they are often aware is different from the position of parents who have to accept what the school does to or for their children. If a sizeable proportion of parents are subsidized clients, then there would seem good reason, if they were not to find themselves at a considerable disadvantage vis-à-vis the fee-paying families, for them to be supported by an agency other than one emanating from or linked with the school.

The fact that a large measure of pastoral care is accomplished between the girls is yet another situation which poses questions regarding possible integration plans. Providing a girl finds a friend,

* Some social thinkers have supported the idea that schools will be able to manifest an ethos and culture similar to those of the emotionally and financially needy families whose children will attend. I believe this will ultimately give rise to a 'secondary modern' ethos which will be rejected as unworthy. The 'culture of education' will ultimately be seen by the more expressive and articulate thinkers on the subject, as the goal to which schools should strive. This 'culture of education' is less dissimilar from middle-class than from working-class ethos and culture.

she may have a confidante. But there is evidence that friendship is relatively evanescent among the younger girls, which means that it would be best if girls could find like spirits easily. On one hand it may be less likely that a socially mixed body of girls would readily enable kindred types to make close friendships than a more socially uniform school would. On the other hand, it could be that, in sharing their troubles, girls of different backgrounds might discover a mutual sympathy that could help cohesion to develop in an integrant situation.

In one school with a very large proportion of subsidized boarders who would not have been there but for certain family problems, the pastoral readiness level placed it twelfth out of nineteen schools. In another school with a high proportion of subsidized boarders, pastoral readiness was good enough to place it at the top of the list (though the sample of girls answering the question there was unfortunately small). It seems, therefore, on slight evidence that a heterogeneous group can lead to a healthy pastoral care response among the girls; whether the staff and formal structure will meet and satisfy this responsiveness among the girls will depend on the quality of the former, and it is fortunate if they do because good pastoral care is one of the conditions associated with the happier schools. The pastoral element I am discussing here is the NPF, or the willingness to discuss personal problems with somebody. In fact, most of this care devolves upon other girls and this need can in some schools increase if the formal organization seems more distant and severe. This is therefore an area to approach with care, but also with confidence if integration is to be promoted happily. Either boarding could be so nasty that rich and poor alike would be companions in distress; or the staff could so win the confidence of the pupils that they could trust each other and enjoy membership in the same sustaining group. I have seen examples of both types of school.

A most important goal in the girls' view is that schools should teach people to live together happily; another is that schools should develop an inner morality that will sustain any girl. There seems promising ground here, therefore, on which to build schemes of integration. However, again things are not so simple. We asked people if they want a moral code to be inculcated, and they agreed in principle; but we have not specified what this moral code is to be. As far as present evidence is concerned, one of the main shapes the moral argument has taken has been over the place and proportion of ceremonial and formal worship wanted in school life. Any new intake of girls who were bored with formal worship would not differ much in this respect from those whom I met already in most schools. However, some girls might decide to go along with the religious forms if their parents wanted them to; whereas integrants' parents might be less keen on preserving formal religion, in which case these girls might oppose religion more strongly than girls from boarding-accustomed families. Also, if middle-class morals, which girls support to some extent in harmony with their parents, include the preservation of virginity at least until school-leaving age, then if newcomers agree with this view of sexual morality there would be no consequent stress on this issue – and the question of sex relations and of family harmony is clearly of great importance to most girls. However, if newcomers brought a different attitude to teenage chastity, then there would very likely be dissension. This might develop along two directions: one, that early sexuality might be seen as 'common', connoting yielding to immediate instead of delayed (more 'romantic') gratification; the other direction would involve difficulties with what families are thought to expect of their daughters and their friends.

Finally, I may offer some of my own judgements about English girls' boarding as I have observed it. Out of the twenty-three schools I visited, I would only be happy to see a daughter of mine, depending on her nature, sent to any one of six of them. I would be definitely averse to the thought of patronizing seven of the others. For all I know, if one took a sample of twenty-three maintained day schools, my judgements might be made in the same proportion. It seems, however, that though girls are happy and getting a good education in the good schools, they may have something more to get from co-education. This may depend in part on the interaction of staff with pupils of both sexes, as well as the possible interaction of the pupils with each other. However, a family which is not isolated could manage a reasonably mixed background of friendships for their daughters during the holidays, which occupy a third of the year.

A disadvantage of boarding is the interruption of friendships; but an asset is the use of distance which can add perspective. The pain of partings can be balanced by the poignancy of valuing friendships which can last well enough to bridge time. The difference being dramatized here is between an approach which favours a mild hedonism in which gratification and frustration work themselves out on a more immediate and day-to-day basis of little delay; and the romantically accented articulation of individual satisfactions and emotions which infuses delayed gratifications with dramatic value. Some children simply want and need a direct short-span articulation of their experience: they will tend not to find value in boarding, however well their families and teachers may interpret it to them. Others may find that their outlook, which is suitable to the experience patterns linked with boarding, does not develop well in this direction because families or teachers do not support these trends. Yet some will find that the experience of boarding has built in them a certain romanticism; this may often be tactfully hidden from the public, and even from the individual's own explicit awareness. Yet boarding schooling is a mechanism for producing a romantic structure in the individual, however well it may often be hidden.

I have just said that I consider some schools good, others not. How do I make this judgement? After having studied other people's attempts to describe and administer good schools, how would I myself specify what I would call good and bad? I would say that a good school is a place led by people who are socially sensitive and aware; they work for a structure which is flexible though secure. They enable individuals to develop in ways best suited to each of them (which implies a wide range of academic and cultural facilities and encouragement), yet inculcate a sense of the individual's obligations to society. A good school is a place also where provisions are made that even a good home cannot offer. One of these provisions is that of a group life, a community of friendship that need not supplant but can supplement a happy home life. Another provision in many a good school is its siting in a gracious building in beautiful surroundings, constituting an aesthetic training and experience which is rarely available. One is not denying that beauty is in the eye of the beholder; that one may find beauty in the organic life of a grimy neighbourhood in industrial back streets. Yet our culture in its literature and art carries a tide of aesthetic content such that beauty is more often found in the beholder's eye when he is put in some surroundings rather than others.

Beautiful surroundings can be in scarce supply, and it may be an élitist privilege to enjoy them. Beauty may even be squandered by a school which devises an array of regulations about going out, or leaving free time for people to enjoy the environment. But beautiful surroundings can be used well, and when this happens it is unquestionably something special which boarding can offer. Good surroundings do not make the school, but poor ones can help to minimize its other values. In one school, the closeness of a busy thoroughfare brought many graffiti on the walls, and broken windows; school staff became annoyed with the townspeople and with girls who played up to local youngsters by appearing provocatively in windows; other staff were sympathetically aware of some resentment among townspeople of the school's desire to keep to itself. Some girls thought that the school was unnecessarily isolationist, while others agreed with it in finding the graffiti distasteful. Thus an environmental circumstance detracted from the harmony of life in the school. It will be said that any school which denies full social contact with its neighbourhood is incapable of achieving inner harmony; but this is less true for schools which are sited on their own. There they may develop a blind social isolationism; or an awareness and willingness to interact with all levels of outside society though in ways which do not swamp the cultural entity of the school.

Good schools are also places where pupils can meet a wide range of other young people, though (in my view) with sufficient space and time to get past acquaintance to knowledge. In this respect, boarding involves girls in living together with each other in much deeper ways than would be possible in day school where pupils can see school as a place principally for learning, and if strangers are disliked then they can be retreated from back to a safe home in the evenings. By these tokens of what is a good school, a bad one has an unaware staff, or one that is socially withdrawn; with an inflexible structure leaving neither much room nor encouragement for individual development; there may be ugly surroundings and a socially restricted and restricting pupil group. A bad school may have all these unfavourable characteristics, or one or two of them in sufficient measure to negate any other virtues.

Some of the schools I visited (and probably many of those outside my sampling framework) were in a double sense special schools. For while depending on fee-paying, some took only very able girls, others chiefly the less able ones. Schools for the latter seemed to serve a middle-class sector of society who feel that their daughters would not 'hold their own' in local schools. They would be socialized with manners, attitudes and tastes that are not middle class. Therefore they are sent to schools which may not aspire to high academic results, but which concentrate on cultural training.

The morality of this position is easy to assail; but it is also easy to defend. On the one hand the privilege of money is used to secure something 'better in life' (remaining in the middle class, marrying a similar class person); yet it is a sub-culture's means of staying alive. And in an era when societies are formed to defend the existence of species of insects, or animals, or the right of South American tribes to exist according to their chosen mores, or the right for one part or another of Vietnam to determine its own cultural destiny without interference from outside, it becomes difficult to know why English middle-class culture should not also seek to maintain itself. If the argument is that this class maintains itself at the expense of others, is it necessarily impossible that it could maintain its cultural values and attitudes without involving the oppression of others? And if these cultural aspects cannot be separated from the economic ones, and for economic reasons the culture has to be altered by outside force, then is this not an oppressive correction of oppression? The situation appears fraught with political and moral dilemma, and one might argue powerfully for choosing a social response which guides changes along the path of least pain, instead of choosing what appears to be the course of greatest gain – to one side. On the other hand, it may be said that one should not confuse class with culture; so it should be possible to maintain the attitudes and aesthetics of a sub-culture while altering its economic and power relations to the rest of society. If this kind of change is mooted, and credible means for effecting it are proposed, then the socio-economic bastions of the middle class and its culture would not be quite so stoutly defended.

It is not the purpose of this book to preach legislation, either for protection or for change. I think that a measure of both is desirable. In a free society which admires tolerance in itself, it should be permissible for middle-class people to try to educate their children along certain cultural and aesthetic lines. If they have to pay for this to be done in boarding schools then they should be free to do so. At the same time the independent schools should not effectively sap the strength of the state system, and in the case of girls' boarding schools the relative sizes of the two sectors (just over five per cent of the girls' secondary school population in 1965 was in the independent sector) are such that the state part is not being bled. The inspection of schools and their recognition as efficient should, I believe, be done so that if a school falls below a recognized standard for more than, say, two years, it would have to close. In fact economic factors and shortage of staff are together closing many of the less viable independent schools. This will provide a small but sound number of independent schools which will be élitist; on the other hand, the proportion of their relevance, in their present form, in the national culture will reduce unless the state decides to maintain sizeable numbers of pupils therein. More middle-class parents will patronize the maintained sector, which will change somewhat under their influence. With the rise of the average school-leaving age, and the greater contact this will imply between parents and school, which will probably be expressed also in the growth of parent–teacher associations, the culture-of-education, which corresponds somewhat with middle-class culture, will increasingly affect the state-maintained system.

It is quite possible that the state will see fit to set up separate boarding schools to accommodate 'cases of need'. The culture of these, the attitudes and values fostered therein may be different from the cultures of many independent schools. Nevertheless, the state boarding sector could benefit by drawing on the expertise and experience of the independent sector. This will probably happen in informal ways with interchange of staff and in realizing that certain kinds of experience are shared in both types of school. With the advent of state-run boarding, even for children from problem families, and with the increasing patronage of the state day system by middle-class parents, the parent–school pattern of relationships in the state system is likely to change towards embodying more equal terms. This will reduce one of the springs of the need for independent boarding.

Some of the better and more suitably sited boarding schools

could run courses in the holidays for children at state day schools, in the same way as American families like to send their children to summer camps. With opportunities of this sort, seen as excursions into the ecological and cultural history of this country much in the same way as schools now support excursions to visit other countries, middle-class parents would increasingly choose to patronize the maintained system of day schools, and try to arrange the experience of group life in beautiful surroundings for their children as a holiday-time activity.

But with all this, independent boarding should survive. Perhaps one function of this book may be to strengthen the remnant, even though it may reduce its size. For if there is anything valid in this book, it should increase awareness among school staffs, governors, inspectors, legislators and parents concerning the schools' natures; this awareness should help to improve quality, as well as making it more difficult for schools of marginal quality to survive. And even if this book contains nothing valid, it may provoke valid criticism and further insight, and have the same effect as I have just described. Either way, we have considered a phenomenon and sought after an understanding of its nature in some depth; this search is in itself of merit, and out of it should also come some good.

Appendix: Research Methods

In most human communication the opening of acquaintance proceeds according to some sort of rules. These may work to define the relationships between the two parties and to clarify the status of each. Strangely enough, many sociological books start without such a clarification, but I think such a step is necessary.

A convention in sociological literature has it that authors refer to themselves in the third person. 'The present author thinks' that this is out of a desire to appear as objective, somehow detached from the situation being described. I am sure that this is misguided, and a misleading mannerism. I did not think of myself as 'him' or 'the author' when doing the fieldwork, but of 'me' or 'I'. The process of entering the third person when reporting seems to me to be a false precaution; if such objectivity were to be attempted it would be necessary to become emotionally and psychologically detached from one's body while somehow pushing it through the fieldwork by remote control. I have never heard of this being done, and consider that to pretend that the mind behind 'the author' somehow is separate from the hand of the author when he writes, is a tawdry piece of self-deception. If it hides the personal realities of the fieldwork situation from the reader, this is delusive, and also duller to read than an honest first person.

On the other hand, it is not the usual aim in sociology to provide personal memoirs. The accent is not on the personal experience of the author, but on what outside him he has to report. With these limitations on either side, I tried to be as objective as possible in collecting and recording the views and experience of others, and also in reporting them.

Though I have not tried to tie the present data and results in with the large body of specialized academic literature on similar topics, there is one body of work which must be considered. This research is described by Rosenthal* and concerns the relationship between a scientist and his material. Briefly, Rosenthal shows that

* R. Rosenthal, *Experimenter Effects in Behavioural Research* (New York, 1966).

investigators in social or psychological research often find what they expect to find. This is not necessarily because, in their wisdom, they have unerringly known what to look for and where. Rosenthal, and several others, showed that investigators actually unwittingly influence their subjects. Even if this research has not always been confirmed, it simply cannot be ignored by an honest and aware investigator or reporter.

What precautions could I take to avoid the danger that I may have partly modelled the response I collected on my own attitudes and expectations? First, very few well defined hypotheses were started with. I did not set out to prove (for example) that schools with more liberty achieved certain kinds of success, while schools with less liberty produced other results. I held that several factors about schools (e.g. liberty, size, etc.) would each bear upon each other; similarly, that several factors among the girls would be interconnected (e.g. age, intelligence, satisfaction, etc.). I did not set out to prove that more intelligent girls are less satisfied, or the reverse. This illustrates the first precaution, that an open mind should be kept as to how one factor may influence another.

A second precaution is met by keeping a complex net of hypotheses in play. If one is collecting girls' writings about how happy they are (or not), then if one hypothesizes that younger girls are happier, one might unwittingly put questions to them with infectious enthusiasm, and to older girls more dourly; thus one's own attitudes could affect the results. But if there was also a hypothesis that smaller schools were happier, that academic stream was also reflected in the level of happiness and so on, one would not know what to expect of the results from any one class.

Pupils might still feel that their investigator was biased, and respond accordingly. In some schools I visited, pupils had clearly formed the impression before my arrival that I was hostile to their school. I therefore had to do my best, admittedly with an unknown degree of success, to tell every class, or person interviewed, that I stood as an impartial observer.

A fourth difficulty is that though I might try to refrain from developing and communicating expectancies about what I would find had been written by the girls, I was at the same time trying as a 'participant observer' to develop insights about the social situation. This inevitably meant that initial impressions and hypotheses, even crystallized nightly in the form of fieldwork notes and questions to be looked into for the next day, would possibly operate in later testing and questionnaire sessions. There is not much an investigator can do about this, but try to forestall any 'influence of expectancy' by being aware of the process and trying to avoid influencing others. At any rate, this whole approach is different from one which is politically committed, and determined to drag out every last available piece of evidence to illustrate some partisan point. This latter makes a virtue of such diligence, and sometimes goes as far as saying that anyone who is not similarly committed implicitly supports the opposition. I do not accept such a 'bimodal' model of the social possibilities of the commitment situation; rather, I think a 'triangular' (or more-sided) structure is possible. But this must be left for the reader to judge.

Two further notes on general methodology concern selectivity and the use of statistics. I would prefer to show all the figures collected and tabulated, so the reader can judge whether he would make the same interpretations as I offer. This would be so impossibly lengthy that I must edit out inconclusive or less useful statistics. The fact that I draw attention to this process I hope illustrates my concern that selectivity in the use of statistics will not bias the picture presented. Secondly, I believe that interpretation should follow an examination of statistical results; the alternative, where a case is made first, and suitable figures used as illustrations magically to support the thesis, I think is the wrong way.

The reader will not find the book condensed into a series of pithy conclusions in summaries after each chapter. Nor will a glance at chapter headings tell the story, as a procession of slogans might do in a street. If you do not want to understand the book, or have not the time, put it down. Some of the chapters are complex. Nevertheless, I have tried to leaven the work by quoting from the girls' own writings, and I have had three intentions to fulfil. First is accurately and fairly to present the data; second is to make it all intelligible to anybody as inquiring as an intelligent sixth-former; third is to include at least a minimum to laugh, or smile, at. There is no reason why people reading sociology books, difficult as it may be to arrange, should not laugh occasionally.

Girls' own writings, while vivifying, can be used either to strengthen veracity, or to distort it. I have tried to follow the principle that the burden of quotations should illustrate the major trends revealed in the statistics. The most vivid writers may not represent the views of the majority. Further, different parts of what one girl writes may be quoted to suggest very different judgements. For example, one girl wrote:

> . . . you have to sign a promise to obey [rules]. . . . Honestly, it's all very stupid . . . the water facilities are terrible . . . [the] evening service [is] usually dead boring . . . a couple of weeks ago . . . it left several of us feeling depressed and fed up.   (17)

This could be quoted to contribute to a picture of frustration and dissatisfaction; indeed, it cannot be escaped from that these are elements in this girl's experience. Yet she herself went on to write:

> Boarding school . . . broadens the mind . . . you love your parents more. I hope Boarding Schools are still around when its time for my children to go to school.   (17)

So it is possible to pick quotations to build up different kinds of pictures. For this reason, quotations should mirror the gist of majority opinions found in the statistics. However, minority views must not be excluded. Often it is the exceptional people who have valuable perceptions to offer. The views of articulate minorities must be presented carefully, without mistaking these ideas for the general rule. Every effort should also be made to elicit the views of inarticulate minorities, with one exception.

The exception concerns those who disapprove of the methods, or what they have understood to be the goals of the research. I held it to be their right, taking the United Nations Charter item on free speech to imply the right to silence, to be left alone and not forced to give views or information. I made this point as often as I could; in practice very few claimed their right to privacy. One governor pointed out that this right had been opposed as early as the last century, when the Factory Acts made it obligatory for workers to answer questions from inspectors, and the Census also requires information from private individuals. In a sense, though it would have made the research more difficult, and less valid in its conclusions, I am sorry not to have met more insistence on privacy.

The Research Setting

The research took place during a Labour government; although the finance had been provided (through King's College) by the Department of Education and Science at the request of the Public Schools' Commission (which had a clear brief to deal with the independent schools because of their divisive nature), this research was not directed by the Commission. I myself never saw a Commissioner, except one, eating his breakfast at the Copper Kettle in Cambridge, and he did not speak to me.

Some people in the schools saw me as a Commission investigator, and feared the idea. One teacher, however, welcomed me as a Commission member, believing that at last they would get the true story about the public schools! To him, as to all others, I explained my detachment; none of my findings was disclosed to the Commission; in fact there had been no pressure on me to publish any results at all; rather the reverse. However, I have taken it as a duty to the task undertaken, to the Department which financed it, to my College which accommodated it, to the schools who tolerated and sometimes welcomed it, to publish the work.

Most of the work was my own. However, my colleagues who had started studies in boys' schools showed me the theoretical schema to use, methods to follow, and pitfalls to avoid. For a few visits, I had the help of my colleagues, Penny Fitzgerald and Roger Bullock. I thus gained some idea as to how information I collected as a man might differ from that gathered by a woman; and also saw how situations at girls' schools compared with those at boys', judged by one who had visited many of the latter.

The Research Centre provided efficient clerical and administrative support, and data were also promptly coded. The production of this research is thus an independent enterprise within a co-ordinated setting organized by Dr Royston Lambert.

Research Methods and Fieldwork

School lists were prepared, as described in Chapter One. A letter was then sent to each school by Royston Lambert outlining the research aims, and asking permission for a visit. I handled the subsequent correspondence.

Most schools agreed to be visited. Some tried Fabian tactics of delay: 'write to us again next term'. At one school, the head even told me in the presence of senior staff that she had tried to head off the visit. I quite understood that a research visit, from an un-evaluated stranger, could be thought of as a risk and a nuisance; but other schools showed me that where the visit was treated as an interesting event to be entered into with frankness and security, it became of value to the school and pleasant for myself. Only one such school withdrew from an agreement it had made to be visited, and this was not a public school.

Following the practice in visiting boys' schools, I tried to arrange to stay in, or as near as possible to each school. The point was to be immersed as far as possible within the school community. At some schools I was lodged in the headmistress's house, with staff, even in sick- or spare-rooms alongside girls' dormitories. At some I got the impression that the closer I was, the more an eye could be kept on me; at most I felt it expressed an ability and desire to be welcom-ing and homely, for which I was very grateful. Several schools were not able to accommodate a visitor, however, and I stayed in nearby hotels.

I judged that the schools would expect a research visitor from King's College to be older than myself (31), probably a person of high staff status, who would relate to pupils from this position of power and authority, and would be able 'by virtue of' his status, to talk on level terms with the head. Such a person should pre-sumably arrive in a well-groomed car, of medium price range; highly unlikely to arrive chauffeur-driven, or in a leather jacket, or on a motor bike. Even a red sports car could suggest a provoking stimulus to the girls and a threat to the staff. Actually, I used a shabby van more suggestive of a down-at-heel market gardener. For arrival and introductions, I wore a dark suit of sober cut, calculated to please more conservative older staff, as well as my-self.

Entry to a school community was always an emotional experience in which I was conscious of being admitted into a living body. A piece of roughage eaten by a person passes through and out of the body without being incorporated into it. To enter a school for a few days is to hope to be wholesome, that the community will nourish itself with a newcomer, that one will be assimilated and become part of the body. This question of approach is particularly significant for a man visiting a girls' school, and it registers, more or less subconsciously, with all concerned. At one school, I was put in an ante-room to wait to see the head, and left there for over an hour. Most schools welcomed me with tea, a wise English ritual which enables parties in an incipient social relationship to assess each other while occupied with some neutral, mildly pleasant activity.

Schools presented deep and different first impressions, probably much affected by season. Some were imposing buildings surrounded by lawns and parks with crunchy drives isolating them from the worldly traffic outside. Others were set in towns. In most cases, no matter at what time one arrived, the schools appeared quiet; girls, if seen, were scurrying about, uniformed, book-laden, whispering. At one school the quiet contrasted with the energetic din arising from a nearby maintained school at 'break'; the boarders were also at break, but separated out into house rooms, studies and other places.

On arrival, the first thing to do was to talk to the head. Only in two schools did this not happen; once I arrived late and was delegated to see an assistant master; I judged this to be a sign of internal confidence in this school where a possibly important visitor did not mechanically have to see the head first. In another school the head was busy and I met a housemistress first. I was once shown straight into a staff meeting being chaired by the head; they were discussing girls' reports and, though I had no chance properly to explain my presence to all, I was well received and the episode provided a most helpful introduction to the school.

I had to explain the research to each head, try to establish confidence, and work out a routine that would enable me to do the work. Heads showed many different attitudes; one described the research as an asset to independent schools, and likely to help them to stay independent; one was uneasy about leaving me in the school at the week-end ('as I won't be there to take the responsibility'). One head was sure the questionnaires would not be understood by the girls, and the results would have no true bearing on their real views – before I had even shown her the papers. Some heads seemed at pains to show that their schools already manifested reforms which they appeared to take the research as advocating.

In face of these varied responses – and most were straightfor-
wardly helpful – I tried to establish that I wanted information dis-
interestedly. This could have scientific and administrative value, to
schools or parents surveying the situation and making their own
educational decisions, and political value for anyone who wanted
to try and influence policy. I was, and am sure that supporters of
opposite political views will find material they like and dislike in
evidence here. In a good relationship there should be give as well as
take, and as I was extracting information about the schools' nature
and identity, so I told something of myself – of my own happy
experience as a pupil at a boarding school, and of my previous
research work in Africa.

In some schools I did not discuss the girls' questionnaire forms
beforehand with staff; this was not very satisfactory, but in one
school the (unfilled) papers were pinned up in the staff-room. This
seemed to be still less satisfactory, and I settled for explaining their
purpose briefly at a staff meeting. It was clear that staff members
were less forthcoming than those in boys' schools, except for senior
mistresses, who were in central staff positions and often formally
delegated by heads to guide me through my stay. Staff started by
being reluctant to part with their classes for questionnaire sessions,
but after a day or two usually became quite willing and I often had
more classes to meet than I really wanted.

It was a major point to make, that all the information I would get
was to be confidential. Girls would tell me things that I would not
pass on. In schools where staff were accustomed to being close
guardians of the girls' lives, this could create a formal gap in their
knowledge and control. A few members of staff showed signs of
opposition. One stated clearly that it was wrong to orient research
towards, and ultimately influence policy on, information got from
girls; this view seemed to imply that information should flow
downwards to, and not so much upwards from, the girls. Other
staff were less explicit, and seemed to fear the consequences of
authority being momentarily breached.

After informing the head and senior staff, I had also to bring
senior girls into the picture as soon as possible. These people in
authority planned how I should meet all the others, and use my
time economically. I was particularly impressed by the devotion
and hard work of senior mistresses, and by the help they gave me,

for which I want to thank them. I noticed few attempts to steer me away from certain people, and such attempts would not be likely to work, as they would probably be betrayed by pointers from mischievous juniors; more often I found attempts to 'prepare' me to understand the rebels.

There were others who had pivotal positions in some schools, of experience, authority or involvement; sometimes it was a secretary, or a bursar, or a confidante. It was important to tell these people about the research and spend time with them. Some of them seemed to talk motivated by a sense of incompleteness that it was not 'their' school (as heads), though they felt it was theirs in many ways. Such people gave many little details which, even if they do not appear in the book, have contributed to my being able to write about the schools at all.

I made clear to staff that I was not present to inspect teaching. A few nevertheless invited me to their classes, usually in arts subjects. I had also to explain that I should take no part in the apparent assumption that 'adults support school rules'. If I saw criminal behaviour I should act as a citizen, but I would not report infringement of the school's private code (I witnessed smoking, meetings with young men and an experiment in levitation). I made the same clear to the girls, who obviously would have been less frank without this assurance.

My first appearance to the whole school was often at a morning assembly. I often felt awkward being placed with the staff on their usual dais; sometimes I could stay at the back, but once (towards the end of a visit) I played the piano while the girls marched in and out. Next, I met classes of girls in their respective form rooms. I introduced myself to each group anew, and tried to insulate the proceedings from leaks and gossip. Often I said: 'Well, you all know what this is all about, so shall we get started . . . ?' After a mystified pause, I would say, 'Don't you know . . . ? Didn't the others tell you? Didn't you ask?' The reactions to this showed me how many leaks had occurred from previous sessions. Some girls said, 'We asked them, but they wouldn't tell'. This was the opportunity to remind them, in turn, not to discuss the questions. Sometimes I said I knew that girls could not keep secrets, and would be assured that they could. I also told girls what they might say to their friends who might press them to reveal the secrets of the questionnaires:

that I would come round eventually to most classes, and they would find out soon enough; also, that in a climate of rumour, confidences might be wrung from those unwilling to disclose them. So in several ways, I spent much time explaining my questions, and trying to ensure that there was little gossip.

These methods certainly contributed to security. There were leaks, however, which were deducible from the remarks made by staff, who sometimes seemed to need to show how close their ears were to the ground. These instances of 'feedback' seemed to come from staff who had a one-to-one teaching or other functional relationship (such as music teachers, coaches) with girls, rather than from those who were formally supposed to cater for the personal problems of school life (such as housemistresses).

I asked several classes to say how far my information given on questionnaires would fall short of giving a true and vivid picture of life in school. There was much agreement (sometimes scorn) that my information thus gathered was inadequate, so I appealed then for people to write further material in any form – diary, essay, letter or verse, to be given in confidentially towards the end of my visit. Thus a few, though generally very valuable, writings were collected. There was frequent need ('You're not going to show this to the staff . . . ?') to reassure girls that the whole proceedings were confidential. I said that I would quote from writings, but attribute neither name nor school. I am very aware of the responsibilities to people's privacy; for quotation offers less risk of embarrassment by exposure to the public than to one's friends; and even unattributed writings can be recognized by friends of girls who have written them. Most of the problems depicted, however, have occurred in more than one school; so by leaving out the particular clues, readers who were pupils in schools I visited cannot be certain that they can truly recognize any remarks and reports apart from their own.

As far as possible, I tried to join informally in accessible parts of the school life. Once, my suggestion to join in music-making was derided ('You've brought your piccolo in your pocket have you, then?'); elsewhere, I played the piano, guitar or sang in a choir. These expressive occasions allowed one to be a person among the girls, to reveal feelings in an acceptable context; this allowed relationships to begin, in which girls could and did also discuss their feelings in ways which left the questionnaires far behind. This was by no means a trick to extract confidences. Where such opportunity occurred, I valued it intrinsically for getting to know people. The art room and, in the summer, the tennis courts were similar places of acquaintance. In every school, with one exception in playing duets with an accomplished pianist, there were always two or more girls in these informal groups. As far as I know, there have been no offensive rumours; though some of the more 'normal-minded' schools ridiculed all these precautions as excessive, I think they contributed to the visits having gone by without major trouble.

Joining in worship presented a particular problem to a person who is not a Christian. There were two important things to say to the head early in my visits; first, that I am not confirmed, and thus ineligible to take communion; second, that I respect worship, whatever my views as to the means and methods. This would explain my absence from communion services, or from the communicants if I went to a service, which in more than one school might strike some strict staff as odd in a person who had said he wanted to take part in all facets of a school's life. In talks with girls, I early on discovered the depth and importance of the issue of religion, and saw that I should not disclose my own views, as these could be used to support the position of partisan groups.

At some schools, real and informal contact was simply not allowed to develop. At others, over a few days, occasions had occurred for discussion with small groups, making friends and establishing some sort of confidence. At this stage the time for departure was usually close at hand; one girl said, 'It's a pity you're not staying longer; you're just getting to know us properly and we are beginning to tell you things'. She seemed to realize the difficulty that when there was a real possibility that the flood gates of confidences might be opened, this would involve too much risk for others. At one or two schools indeed, clear hints were provided that the visit should end sooner rather than later. Most other schools either courteously waited until the agreed time elapsed, or a few showed they were comfortable and let me feel I could stay on or come again if I wished. Departure from a school was as significant as arrival, involving a complete break (often at some personal cost) of relationships which I had been trying hard to establish. Subsequent contact was minimized in that a very few letters were exchanged with heads, or with girls. Several schools supervised girls' letters, if not opening them, at least seeing where they came from; this could cause difficulties, even imagined ones, so keeping up with the development of events by letter was not possible.

Index